AN ISLAMIC VISION OF INTELLECTUAL PROPERTY

For over a century, intellectual property (IP) regimes have been justified using Western philosophical theories rooted in the idea that IP must reward talent and maximize global stocks of knowledge and cultural products. Reframing IP in a context of legal pluralism, Ezieddin Elmahjub brings an Islamic and comparative narrative to the appropriate design and scope of IP rights, and in doing so criticizes the dominance of Western influence on a global regime that impacts the ability of people to access medicine, to read, to imagine, and to reshape popular culture. The Islamic vision of IP, which is based on a broad theory of social justice, maintains that IP cannot simply be seen as a reward for effort or a tool to maximize economic efficiency but as one legal right within a complicated distributive scheme affecting fundamental human rights, equal opportunities, and human capabilities.

Ezieddin Elmahjub is a Lecturer in the Law School at Swinburne University of Technology in Australia and Visiting Research Fellow at both the Asian Law Institute and the Center for Asian Legal Studies, National University of Singapore. His research interests include Islamic studies, comparative legal philosophy, and IP.

An Islamic Vision of Intellectual Property

THEORY AND PRACTICE

EZIEDDIN ELMAHJUB
Swinburne University of Technology, Victoria

CAMBRIDGE
UNIVERSITY PRESS

CAMBRIDGE
UNIVERSITY PRESS

University Printing House, Cambridge CB2 8BS, United Kingdom

One Liberty Plaza, 20th Floor, New York, NY 10006, USA

477 Williamstown Road, Port Melbourne, VIC 3207, Australia

314–321, 3rd Floor, Plot 3, Splendor Forum, Jasola District Centre, New Delhi – 110025, India

79 Anson Road, #06–04/06, Singapore 079906

Cambridge University Press is part of the University of Cambridge.

It furthers the University's mission by disseminating knowledge in the pursuit of education, learning, and research at the highest international levels of excellence.

www.cambridge.org
Information on this title: www.cambridge.org/9781107182837
DOI: 10.1017/9781316863398

First published 2018

Printed and bound in Great Britain by Clays Ltd, Elcograf S.p.A.

A catalogue record for this publication is available from the British Library.

ISBN 978-1-107-18283-7 Hardback
ISBN 978-1-316-63269-7 Paperback

For Manal, Isaac, and Jacob

Contents

Preface

Since intellectual property became a global construct in the late nineteenth century, its normative design and theoretical justifications have been exclusively dominated by an Anglo-European influence. I wrote this book to introduce a novel theoretical and normative vision of intellectual property. It proposes an Islamic philosophical account to justify and regulate access to, and reuse of, knowledge and culture through intellectual property rights. The overarching framework of this account is an Islamic theory of social justice that views intellectual property as a social institution that affects the distribution of rights and obligations to access, use, and reshape knowledge and culture and make a living through that.

Modern intellectual property systems emerged and developed in the West. Western philosophical thought, particularly on natural rights and utilitarian ethics, influenced and continues to influence global intellectual property regulation and policymaking. In the nineteenth century, intellectual property standard setting was exclusively initiated and shaped by the major European colonial powers. After World War II, the United States enhanced its position as the strongest economy and the largest exporter of knowledge and cultural products. While the European influence over global intellectual property standard setting was mainly oriented towards providing protection for creators as a matter of natural rights, the US approach viewed intellectual property as a utilitarian bargain. In utilitarian terms, intellectual property is seen as a tool to incentivize individuals to invest in the production of intellectual products, such as software, movies, and drugs, thereby increasing wealth in society. The overwhelming majority of intellectual property commentaries explain the societal need to protect intellectual property, citing Western philosophical scholarship including John Locke, Immanuel Kant, Jeremy Bentham, and John Stuart Mill, among others.

A vision of intellectual property as a reward for creators and a tool to maximize social utility has – for very long – favored more property rights in knowledge and culture as the norm. Eventually, intellectual property protection exponentially expanded to cover not only genuine intellectual creations but also facts, discoveries, and information. More property rights in knowledge and culture did not leave everyone better off. A large body of research, both quantitative and qualitative, indicates that the current doctrinal structures and the operational features of the dominant global intellectual property regimes are securing substantial benefits for large producers and distributors of intellectual content in rich, developed countries. The same research also indicates that the way in which those regimes operate effectively marginalizes fundamental human development concerns, including access to medicine, educational materials, protection of traditional knowledge, and economic growth in developing countries.

An alternative vision of the global intellectual property systems is long overdue – not only for the sake of theoretical indulgence, but because of the significant gaps in the oft-cited policy rationales for global intellectual property policymaking and their impact on human development, particularly in developing countries. First, the proposition that depicts property rights in knowledge and culture as a fair reward for intellectual labor is fundamentally flawed. It does not tell us why property rights are the most appropriate reward for intellectual creativity. It also overestimates the relative creative powers of authors and inventors. It does not account for the fact that innovation and creativity are accumulative processes where one rarely, if ever, creates standalone creative content. William Shakespeare himself turned out to be a frequent borrower from the creative works of his contemporaries.[1] Second, justifying intellectual property as a tool to maximize social utility for the majority is both unpersuasive and narrow. It is unpersuasive because, in fact, we do not know for sure that property rights in knowledge would maximize social utility. It is also narrow because it is intrinsically blind to distributive concerns. Even if we accept that intellectual property is necessary to maximize social utility for the majority, why would we assume that the benefits generated for the majority would somehow compensate for ignoring the minority? This proposition is particularly worrying if the minority includes large groups of people lacking access to medicine and educational material.

[1] Michael Blanding, "Plagiarism Software Unveils a New Source for 11 of Shakespeare's Plays," www.nytimes.com/2018/02/07/books/plagiarism-software-unveils-a-new-source-for-11-of-shakespeares-plays.html

I found that Islamic sources approach intellectual property in a very different way. They propose a broad theory of social justice to inform the global debate over, and design of, intellectual property policies. The theory starts from a human flourishing perspective. Intellectual property is seen as one of the many tools to coordinate social cooperation to achieve collective social good. While the Islamic theory of social justice does not entirely reject intellectual property as a reward or tool to maximize economic efficiency, it reframes the analytical importance of these views. Reward and utility-based arguments can form one benchmark in a much larger analytical framework of fair distribution of rights and obligations to access and reuse knowledge and culture. This framework has two overarching features:

First, it starts by emphasizing the overarching priority of a bundle of deontological values before even considering justifying intellectual property rights. Every member of society is to have equal access to basic human needs to permit autonomy and enable life to flourish. This includes a broad right to life, health, education, cultural participation, and decent living standards. These basic needs must be distributed equally to everyone, regardless of their ability to work and pay, or the potential impact on economic efficiency. Interestingly, there is considerable overlap between this aspect of the Islamic theory of justice and the so-called Global South's vision of reorienting intellectual property to serve human development concerns, including access to medicine, food, educational materials, and economic growth.

Second, after securing the priority of these basic human needs, the Islamic theory of justice turns to assess the need to grant exclusive property rights in ideas and expressions. In this context, the starting point is that property rights should not enjoy regulatory priority in coordinating access to, and reuse of, intellectual content. The norm is to keep knowledge and culture in the commons, open for everyone to access, use, and reshape for their particular ends. In a sense, intellectual property rights should be considered an exceptional departure from this norm. The theory is open to considering situations where granting intellectual property rights in knowledge and culture is needed to fairly reward hardworking authors and inventors. It is also open to the possibility of using intellectual property as a tool to maximize intellectual production. However, the intrinsic powers of these property rights must be proportionate to the labor exerted to create the intellectual product. On top of that, intellectual property rights need to be framed in such a way as to take account of their potential impact on fair equality of opportunity. They must not become a tool to enable a few powerful producers and distributors of intellectual content to excessively concentrate powers to control knowledge and culture. There should be well-defined mechanisms to redistribute the power to reshape knowledge and culture and to earn a living doing that. In this context, the Islamic vision overlaps with a loose coalition of intellectual property scholars critical of modern intellectual property regimes' perceived tendencies to concentrate powers within the hands of rich and resourceful producers and distributors of content. In particular, those scholars' proposals to expand the public domain of free content and the rights of users of protected intellectual content have considerable merit in the Islamic vision of a fair and efficient intellectual property regime.

The ideas discussed in this book come from research I have been doing in the last eight years as a PhD student and academic in different universities both inside and outside Australia.[2] During this time, a long list of people – some of whom I have never met – taught me so many things about intellectual property, philosophy, human development, and social justice. I can only include a partial list of those people. I apologize to those I learned a lot from, but unintentionally omitted.

Most of the writing of this book happened while working at the Law School in the Swinburne University of Technology in Melbourne, where I teach real and intellectual property units. I owe the greatest debt to my mentor and friend Dan Hunter, the Founding Dean of Swinburne Law School. Dan's leadership and brilliant research ideas opened the door for me to write this book and develop its content in its current form. First of all, he inspired me to write the book. Then he helped me refine my ideas while writing the proposal and commented on its final draft. My Swinburne colleague, Benjamen Gussen, reviewed the first draft of this book. He provided thorough and detailed feedback – though I did not always listen.

Most of the ideas concerning the Islamic notions of the social good and public interests included in Chapter 2 were formed and refined while working as a joint research fellow for the Asian Law Institute and the Centre for Asian Legal Studies at the National University of Singapore. Thanks to the directors of both the Institute and the Centre, Garry Bill and Dan Puchniak respectively, for commenting on my research while working there. Special thanks to my colleague Arif Jamal from the Law School at the National University of Singapore for chairing the research seminar organized around my research on the role of law in Islamic legal philosophy.

I have been very lucky to work in three different Australian universities in the last several years, where kind, bright, and capable academics influenced

[2] Portions of Chapters 4 and 7 of this book appeared in my PhD thesis completed in 2014 at the Queensland University of Technology.

the way I think about intellectual property and its theoretical and practical design. Mark Perry of the Law School at the University of New England provided extensive comments on the ideas I developed in my PhD thesis and helped me transform those ideas into a book proposal. Kylie Pappalardo of the Queensland University of Technology commented on my arguments about transforming abstract notions of social justice into debates concerning the public domain and users' rights. I am also grateful to Ismail Albayrak of the Australian Catholic University for making me think very carefully about making my arguments about Islamic jurisprudence accessible to Western audiences. This work developed in part from my PhD research at the Queensland University of Technology completed in 2014. Thanks are due to Nic Suzor, Brian Fitzgerald, and Anne Fitzgerald for supervising my research and helping me to successfully complete the degree. Thanks also to Peter Drahos for encouraging me to write this book when we met during the Australian Intellectual Property Conference held in Brisbane in February 2014.

This book will show you how a broad Islamic theory of social justice can reframe global intellectual property regimes both in theory and practice. However, not every argument made in it is exclusively derived from the Islamic worldview of social justice. My vision of the Islamic theory of justice was profoundly influenced by the work of some of the most brilliant minds of our time. I must acknowledge that John Rawls's *Theory of Justice* made me think differently about the basic structure of a fair society. I learned from his work that the fair distribution of the societal benefits and burdens of social cooperation requires us to take into consideration complicated propositions that include, but go beyond, the narrow visions of merit and aggregate utility. Elinor Ostrom's *Governance of the Commons* taught me that property systems are not the only, nor the most ideal, mechanisms to govern resources of different sorts, from jungles to codes. Openness and cooperation can also be fair and beneficial. Amartya Sen's and Martha Nussbaum's work on human development theories made me realize that a fair society is not necessarily a rich society that is mainly concerned with maximizing production. It is one that actively enables people to create and expand a set of fundamental human capabilities, including living healthy and productive lives, nourishing one's intellectual capabilities, and enjoying an extensive list of rights and freedoms. Interestingly, these works opened new horizons for me to read, understand, and analyze Islamic sources in a fundamentally different way compared to mainstream Islamic jurisprudence.

Finally, I am deeply grateful to my wife Manal and our two boys Isaac and Jacob. They provided me with the courage and motivation to undertake the complicated task of writing about intellectual property, religion, and comparative philosophy. They patiently tolerated my increased absences during family times and on weekends – not to mention taking the laptop with me to public parks and shopping malls to finish my work. No words of gratitude could possibly do justice to their sacrifices.

Note on the Text

1 The romanization of Arabic letters follows the Oxford system.
2 Arabic terms are italicized.

1

An Islamic Vision of Intellectual Property

I ISLAMIC VISION AND THE GLOBAL INTELLECTUAL PROPERTY LANDSCAPE

Intellectual Property (IP) is a product of the Western normative environment. From the Venetian patent statute of 1474 and the Statute of Anne in 1710 to the Berne Convention and the TRIPS Agreement, IP developed to reflect the legislative agendas of a few European countries, and later the United States. The vision that animated the doctrinal development of comparative IP laws is one centered on creating property rights in ideas and expressions to reward creators for their investments, or in an attempt to maximize the aggregate sum of knowledge and cultural products. In this book, I try to locate the Islamic vision on governing intellectual production and inquire whether this vision is different from the mainstream doctrinal structures of IP. In particular, I answer why and how Islamic legal philosophy allocates property rights in the products of the human intellect.

The Islamic vision of IP developed in this book locates IP in a multi-dimensional framework of a broader theory on social justice. The primary feature of this vision is that IP is not seen as a well-deserved reward for the genius/lone creator, or a tool to maximize innovation to benefit the greatest number of people. Rather, IP in the Islamic vision is located within a complex web of deontological and consequentialist considerations that do not necessarily impose a blanket rejection of merit and utility-based justifications of IP, but contextualizes their normative importance in overarching principles of fairness. These principles assign rights and obligations in governing knowledge and culture to serve basic human needs so that people can live healthy and productive lives, nurture a set of intellectual capabilities, and enhance their moral powers to influence their world. The need to reward investors who create knowledge to increase its production must abide by the principle of fair equality of opportunity. The exclusive right to control intellectual content must not transform into the ability to concentrate power to control such content at all times. Individuals interacting with protected intellectual content must not be deprived of equal opportunities to reshape their knowledge and cultural mediums simply because they cannot pay or obtain permissions from gatekeepers.

IP is everywhere. It intervenes to regulate the distribution of rights and obligations to access a diverse array of knowledge and cultural contents. Patents regulate access to essential knowledge underpinning inventions in medicine, food, and technologies that make our lives easier and more productive. Copyright governs access and use of educational materials of all levels and cultural artifacts including literature, art, and digital materials distributed on internet platforms. In this sense, IP has a visible impact on individuals' ability to live healthy lives and exercise their intellectual capabilities to recast texts, images, and inventions around them into new forms.

The global architecture of IP was largely designed through two essential milestones. First, an agreement among major European colonial powers including Belgium, France, Italy, Portugal, and the United Kingdom in the late nineteenth century CE led to the Berne and Paris conventions on the protection of copyright and patents. The rhetoric that dominated the discussion then was one centered on creators. The global IP regime sought to reward authors and inventors with property rights in knowledge and culture in the hope that this would create flourishing global markets. In relation to the 1886 Berne Convention for the Protection of Literary and Artistic Works, Sam Ricketson and Jane Ginsburg note that the drafters of the convention were essentially "concerned with the private interests of authors and with raising the level of protection that is accorded to them."[1] The second milestone came with the negotiation and conclusion of the Agreement on Trade-Related Aspects of Intellectual Property (TRIPS Agreement) in 1994. At that stage, the United States joined the old colonial club, as a powerful new player in the global IP landscape, for the purpose of defining the scope and strength of property rights in knowledge and culture. This time, the forum and the content of the negotiation agenda were fundamentally trade and commerce-oriented. IP issues were brought to a trade forum to be part of negotiating the framework of the World Trade Organization. Research on the Uruguay Round, which led up to the adoption of the TRIPS Agreement, shows that the distribution of rights and obligations in knowledge and culture was largely

[1] Sam Ricketson and Jane Ginsburg, *International Copyright and Neighbouring Rights: The Berne Convention and Beyond* (Oxford University Press, 2006) vol. 2, 881.

discussed in economic terms. More and stronger property rights in inventions and various forms of cultural expressions were seen as the best way to induce more innovation and creativity to benefit the greatest number of citizens in the contracting states. Behind the scenes, large stakeholders in IP-intensive industries such as pharmaceuticals, computer software, entertainment, and biotechnology pushed exporting IP countries – mainly the United States – to create more rights, make them stronger, and ensure strong enforcement mechanisms to expand their markets in the developing world.[2] The TRIPS Agreement ended up setting minimum standards of IP protection that would favor right holders and make access to knowledge an exceptional departure from what should be the norm. In other words, the agreement reinforced a state of affairs where the right to exclude people from knowledge and culture is the norm and access is the exception.

By and large, the rest of the world in Asia, Africa, and South America came to live within the preformed global architecture of IP. In the pre-TRIPS era, IP rules were transplanted into the legal systems of developing countries via colonization.[3] In fact, four major countries that had signed the Berne Convention in 1886 (France, Germany, Spain, and the United Kingdom) took advantage of Article 19 of the Berne Act relating to the Berne Convention, which gave them the right to accede to the convention at any time on behalf of their colonies.[4] These included colonies around the world, with the consequence that most developing countries had their copyright laws tailored for them.[5] The TRIPS Agreement came to consolidate and expand the strength and scope of the IP rights created under the old regimes. Despite the fact that the developing countries of Asia, Africa, and South America were independent when the negotiations started in 1986, their influence in the norm-setting process for the agreement was extremely limited. Peter Drahos and John Braithwaite traced the negotiation history leading up to the TRIPS Agreement and noted that there was a significant imbalance in bargaining power between developed countries, led by the United States, and developing countries. Major developed countries knew exactly what they wanted. They came prepared with draft provisions tailored to protect the interests of their

2 Gana Ruth, "Prospects for Developing Countries under the TRIPS Agreement" (1996) 29(4) *Vanderbilt Journal of Transnational Law* 735, 737.

3 Peter K Yu, "International Enclosure, the Regime Complex, and Intellectual Property Schizophrenia" (2007) *Michigan State Law Review* 5.

4 Sam Ricketson, *The Berne Convention for the Protection of Literary and Artistic Works: 1886–1986* (Kluwer, 1987) 791.

5 Peter Drahos, "Developing Countries and International Intellectual Property Standard-Setting" (2002) 5 *The Journal of World Intellectual Property* 765, 767.

large taxpayers. Developing countries lacked adequate information and expertise on the likely effects of the TRIPS provisions in relation to access to medicine, educational materials, and indigenous innovation capabilities. Furthermore, the United States exerted a great deal of pressure on developing countries to accept the minimum standards for IP protection. In 1989, the US Trade Act section 301 entered into operation against the developing countries that resisted US views on what should and should not be included on the TRIPS Agreement. Brazil and India found themselves on the Priority Watch List, which indicates the countries that are most worthy of trade sanctions, while Argentina, Egypt, and Yugoslavia were placed on the Watch List. Developing countries were in no position to negotiate; either they accepted the minimum standards promoted by the United States and its partners, or faced sanctions that would certainly harm their economies in the short term.[6]

Here is a rough vision of what the life of a product of the intellect would look like under the dominant doctrinal constructs of the global IP architecture: If you compose a song, you can sing and distribute it for free, or sell it to others. But your best chance of making real money out of it would probably come if a large distributor, such as Universal Music Group (UMG), decided to purchase your copyright for a lump-sum payment. In this instance, copyright law not only gives UMG the right to resell copies of the song to the public, but also the right to control how, when, and where others can use the song. In principle, if someone else decided to use the song, or even part of it, to create a documentary or family video to post on the Internet, they would need to obtain permission from, and possibly pay fees to, UMG. UMG can also choose not to respond on time when permission is needed. When the song is sung in the public sphere, it becomes part of culture. Copyright law does not treat it that way, but merely as an intellectual product protected by various rules of legal liability.

It is true that there are several circumstances where the law would allow reuse for specific purposes related to education, free speech, and so on. It is also true that some countries provide a broad "fair use" right that would allow transformative uses of copyrighted content. However, as I will show in several places throughout this book, permissions to reuse are introduced as exceptions that must be interpreted narrowly. They are not seen as legal rights for the public that could be used to redistribute the power to challenge and remake

6 Drahos and Braithwaite, *Information Feudalism*, 190 et seq.; Bello H. Judith, "Section 301: The United States' Response to Latin American Trade Barriers Involving Intellectual Property" (1989–1990) 21 *University of Miami Inter-American Law Review* 495, 502.

culture. Even in countries where a broad "fair use" exception exists, it is largely discussed in economic terms. It does not take into account who reuses copyright, whether they are rich, poor, or disadvantaged. "Fair use" essentially operates to permit use when there is no threat to *potential* licensing markets for the right holder, rather than as a mechanism to widely redistribute opportunities to express and earn by working through culture.

II IP THROUGH AN ISLAMIC LENS

IP in its modern forms, as manifested both in its global rules and in the laws of major developed countries, attracted widespread criticism. Developing countries and large bodies of comparative critical assessments of IP are skeptical of IP's ability to serve broader concerns related to the social good of the wider global population. At a foundational level, critics of modern IP systems question the soundness of justifying IP as reward for labor or as a utilitarian bargain to make the majority better off. First, labor justifications for IP assume that authors and inventors create out of the thin air. This vision fails to view innovation and creativity as an accumulative process where creative individuals recast existing knowledge and culture into new ideas and expressions. Also, these justifications do not account for situations where an IP holder enjoys substantial market leverage for something that did not require equivalent labor. Second, utilitarian justifications fail to establish that without property rights over ideas and expressions, innovation and creativity would decline. We simply do not know whether, for instance, if authors are not rewarded – or are rewarded with fewer exclusive rights – fewer books and songs would be produced. Furthermore, utilitarian justifications of IP are inherently blind to distributive concerns. They direct IP to maximize the aggregate welfare for the majority and assume that the happiness of the majority will somehow compensate for the mischief of the minority. At an operational level, critics of modern IP rules hotly debate the appropriate strength and scope of IP rights. Developing countries and a great number of IP scholars are concerned that expansive exclusive rights and limited permissions to reuse knowledge and cultural resources are in effect benefiting a few well-established corporations in rich countries while harming the economies of developing countries and cash-strapped users of knowledge and culture in developed countries.

My task is to bring the Islamic vision of the social good to the global debate surrounding the appropriate justifications, scope, and limits of property rights in knowledge and culture. While Islamic civilization did not develop an indigenous counterpart to IP as we think of it today, Islamic sources contain diverse and rich notions of the social good. I locate these notions in the normative language of the Quran, the teaching of the Prophet Muhammad, and the large body of classic and modern Islamic jurisprudence. I will show that these notions can inform discussions on the appropriate institutional framework to govern knowledge and culture in a fair society. At their core, Islamic notions of the social good share the main concerns of developing countries and comparative scholarship critical of modern IP doctrines. In the Islamic vision, IP cannot only be seen as mere reward for creative individuals or a tool to maximize creative outputs. These singular visions could turn IP into a tool with which to lock up knowledge and culture for the benefit of minorities of well-established stakeholders.

The Islamic vision on the social good starts from a human flourishing perspective. At an abstract level, the rules on distributing the benefits and burdens of social cooperation must be designed to make everyone better off. To achieve this, the social good must have an overarching deontological framework to ensure a continuing normative duty to fulfill basic social needs, including promoting life, health, intellectual capabilities, autonomy, and opportunities to pursue one's life plans. These basic needs must be distributed fairly to everyone regardless of the ability to pay, work, or potential impact on aggregate utility. Once these basic social needs have been met, distribution of sources of happiness such as income, wealth, and power can be based on merit or promotion of economic efficiency through maximizing goods and resources. However, since distribution based on merit and promotion of economic efficiency can lead to economic and social inequalities, the public system of rules must ensure that inequalities are not transformed into an ability to concentrate power in the hands of a few in society, in turn undermining equal opportunities for others.

It is important to keep in mind that the task of encapsulating an Islamic theory of justice in a formula accessible to comparative moral philosophy is a challenging one. Even more challenging is trying to talk about an Islamic vision of IP based on such a theory. By and large, Islamic jurisprudence has deeply rooted positivist conceptions of the social good. Right and wrong, good and evil, fair and unfair are determined through various interpretations of the Quran and the traditions of the Prophet of Islam. As I discuss below, a unified theory of social justice – at least in a sense comparable to major social contract theories – is not a visible feature of Islamic jurisprudence. Hence, I offer a preliminary foray into various textual sources and a large body of Islamic jurisprudence to assemble scattered notions of fairness and the social good into one normative framework to inform the justification and design of IP laws. Within this framework, the governance and the distribution of rights, obligations, privileges, and burdens regarding knowledge and cultural resources are informed by two overarching considerations:

First, in an Islamic vision of a fair society, governing knowledge and cultural resources through private property rights will not enjoy normative priority. The original position on governing resources is common ownership. In the Islamic worldview, tangible and intangible resources are presented as part of trusteeship arrangements between the Creator and humankind. I will call these trusteeship arrangements "the Pact of *Istikhlaf*." *Istikhlaf* (trusteeship/stewardship), according to Islamic belief, means that God created the earth and all resources and entrusted them to humans as His most intelligent creations. In their original position, all resources remain equally open for everyone to benefit from. God's ownership of resources is manifested in common ownership for people, dedicated to making everyone better off. There is no general assumption in Islamic theology that keeping resources open to everyone would lead to depletion. A generalized fear of a tragedy of the commons in the form that Garrett Hardin warned against is not part of the Islamic vision on governing resources.[7] However, there is no blanket rejection of notions of private ownership of tangible and intangible resources. Humankind will not be denied fair individual rights of ownership to reward labor, satisfy their intrinsic personal needs for possession, or to maximize resources to efficient levels. A good case must be made to show that property rights are needed to reward labor, satisfy personal needs, or maximize efficiency. This initial normative view towards property rights could prove useful when debating the need to protect various forms of ideas and expressions such as business methods, methods of medical treatment, or databases.

Second, if we decide to create IP rights, they must operate within a broad framework of distributive justice. Society must create mechanisms capable of constantly adjusting individual IP rights so that a proportionate response to concerns of fair reward and economic efficiency can be found. This means that when an IP right transforms into a substantial ability to concentrate power over large markets or restrict potential opportunities to recast knowledge and culture into novel forms, it must be rearranged to restore a balance. For instance, if a corporation created an essential drug to cure a terrible illness by investing hundreds of millions of dollars and relying on publicly funded research, we should be cautious about accepting arguments that such a corporation can rely on patent law to exercise broad control powers. We should question the extent to which it can exercise its monopoly to set

7 Garrett Hardin, "The Tragedy of the Commons" (December 13, 1968) 162(3859) *Science, New Series* 1243–48.

prices, prevent others from reverse-engineering the drug, or prevent others from producing generic versions of the drug for deprived populations in poor countries. Furthermore, an IP right must recognize that its existence can affect the fair distribution of a broad set of intellectual freedoms and capabilities. While the right to exclude under IP may empower rights holders to sell, reproduce, and distribute intellectual content, it must not prevent others from reading, imitating, transforming, contextualizing, and challenging IP-protected culture and knowledge. Distribution of these capabilities should not depend on the ability to pay.

III WHY AN ISLAMIC VISION OF IP MATTERS

We have a global IP system that influences people across the ideological and ethical spectrum around the world. This system defines rights and obligations in relation to knowledge and culture. As such, the system is important to people's life plans, just as knowledge and culture themselves are important. IP can affect the accessibility of medicine or food, the ability to protect traditional knowledge and cultural expressions, and participation in the processes of innovation and creativity. We want this system to be fair, efficient, and to leave everyone better off. No particular normative environment should dominate shaping the metes and bounds of such an important global regime where there are wide varieties of worldviews with different ideas about justice and the social good. Accordingly, the global normative analysis of IP should be mindful of pluralism and the rich platforms of comparative views on justice and the social good.

An Islamic vision of justice and the social good is part of this pluralistic reality. Muslims represent a significant element in the fabric of pluralism throughout the world. One in five individuals in the world is Muslim, and they live almost everywhere. There are more than 50 countries with majority Muslim populations and Muslims are minorities in many other countries across Asia, Africa, Europe and North America. There is good reason to believe that introducing the Islamic vision on social justice and the social good as a benchmark for assessing and developing IP would be a good addition to the global efforts to make IP regimes more just for everyone. In this context, John Rawls theorized that a fair and stable society must be mindful of the fact that societies are complex entities. Different people will have different views on social justice and social good. If we are to create a just and stable society, our moral standards and normative rules for social cooperation must converge on a focal point of justice. The diverse and sometimes conflicting doctrines of peoples sharing time and space must engage in dialogues to find common grounds so that they can achieve what Rawls calls an "overlapping consensus" on the social good despite being different.[8] In a sense, this book engages in the search for an overlapping consensus on shared commitments to social justice that could influence the remaking of a fairer global IP regimes. This could happen along two lines.

At a broad philosophical level, the Islamic vision on social justice and the social good coincides with global comparative efforts to define justice beyond merit and economic efficiency. I will show that the vision introduced in this book significantly overlaps with comparative and influential theoretical frameworks on justice and human flourishing within the liberal philosophical sphere. In several places I show that the Islamic vision subscribes to a pluralist conception of the social good with striking similarities to dominant comparative theories on social justice. For instance, John Rawls's theory of *Justice as Fairness*, Amartya Sen's *Human Development Paradigm*, and Martha Nussbaum's *Central Capabilities Approach* all share with the Islamic vision broad and fundamental views on justice. As in the Islamic vision, they theorize that justice can be achieved when the public system of rules promotes a set of essential social needs and recognizes the intrinsic worth of human life, intellect, dignity, and freedom. They also agree with the Islamic vision in emphasizing that justice is not necessarily achieved by pursuing choices that maximize the good consequences for the majority. Justice must also be concerned with minorities when they are dropped out of aggregate calculations – particularly when the systems that are supposed to serve the majority end up skewing power and wealth under the control of a few while marginalizing large segments of society, including those who are least well off.[9] This comparative, broad vision on social justice would likely affect IP in a variety of ways. It could significantly contribute to the debates on IP and its development. The Islamic conception of social justice would support the developing world's agendas on IP, which seek to achieve more access to knowledge and culture not only to promote economic growth but also to serve fundamental human needs such as access to essential drugs, food, and educational material. Such an agenda has long been in conflict with that of powerful stakeholders in the developed world, which seeks to lock up content to achieve more economic gains.

At a doctrinal level, this book will end up locating various normative signals that would contribute to holding IP doctrines accountable to the Islamic

8 John Rawls, *Political Liberalism* (Columbia University Press, 1993).

9 John Rawls, *Justice as Fairness: A Restatement* (Harvard University Press, 2001); Amartya Sen, *Development as Freedom* (Anchor Books, 2000); Martha Nussbaum, *Creating Capabilities: The Human Development Approach* (Harvard University Press, 2011).

vision of justice. In different chapters of this book, I outline the basic features of these principles. First, a fair system of governing knowledge and culture does not necessarily presuppose that property rights have priority over common ownership. It is open to the possibility that, in many situations, keeping knowledge and culture outside property systems is conducive to the collective social good. Second, fair property rights in knowledge and culture must not create an enabling environment for a few rights holders in society to concentrate power to control access to knowledge and culture, while leaving large groups of users without access to essential goods or unable to fully participate in the knowledge and cultural mediums to which they aspire. Large bodies of comparative IP scholarship offer a wealth of proposals that would contribute to fairer distribution of rights and obligations in knowledge and culture. As far as the Islamic vision on social justice and IP is concerned, this body of scholarship is extremely critical of IP's expansion and its focus on construing efficiency-based concerns to the benefit of a small set of well-established rights holders. I will show that discourses around recognizing the public domain and expanding the rights and capabilities of users of knowledge and culture could go a long way in realizing the Islamic vision of fair and efficient systems to govern knowledge and culture. Here as well, the Islamic normative vision on IP overlaps with critical IP studies.

IV TOWARDS AN ISLAMIC VISION OF A FAIR IP LANDSCAPE

Chapter 2 offers a quick and informative tour of the main sources of Islamic law and standards of morality – namely, the Quran, the recorded traditions of the Prophet, and various versions of Islamic jurisprudence. Particular focus will be given to explaining how notions of social good and social justice as understood in mainstream Islamic legal theory. Muslims do not disagree that their comprehensive doctrine of life (known as *Islamic Sharia)* is fundamentally oriented towards promoting justice and the public interest. Islamic scholar Ibn Qayyim al-Jawziyya (d. 1350 CE) famously wrote: "Sharia is founded on wisdom and social good of the people ... all of its rules are dedicated to justice and welfare ... matters in which justice is replaced with oppression ... [or] in which good is replaced with evil are not part of Sharia."[10] But how do Muslims define justice and social good? A clear answer to this challenging question is significant. Once something is proclaimed as good or fair, Islamic law must promote it. I show that Muslims start from the Quran, and the recorded traditions of the Prophet known as the Sunnah, to make

10 Ibn Qayyim al-Jawziyya, *I'lām al-Muwaqqi'īn* (Dar al-Kutub al-'Ilmiyah, 1991) vol. 3, 12.

a decision on what is good and right. Islamic jurisprudence largely operates with a positivist mindset. The first point of reference on justice and the social good is the textual authorities and their various interpretations. However, the positivist sphere of Islamic doctrine is extremely limited. It would be unrealistic to assume that textual authorities are capable of capturing matters that were not known in the seventh century CE (which is when Muslims believe the texts were revealed).

The limitations of the positivist sphere prompted Muslim jurists to construct a normative sphere for Islamic notions of justice and the social good. As early as the seventh century CE, Muslims developed various analytical tools to extend the application of textual authorities beyond explicit textual stipulations. The mainstream views of the majority of jurists agreed that rational analysis of Islamic scripture could expand Islamic notions of the social good beyond textual constraints. I explain how Islamic jurisprudence engaged in a process of identifying underlying design principles for Islamic lawmaking through what is famously known as *maqasid al-Sharia* (the jurisprudence of the purposes of *Sharia*). Scholars here hypothesize that within the positivist structure of Islamic doctrine there are various signals showing that the Lawgiver is acting with a normative vision centered around fairness and the social good. In the concluding parts of Chapter 2, I explore the nature of social good under Islamic doctrine. Should we explain it in consequentialist or deontological terms? I end up explaining how Islamic sources generally promote deontological values as a first order principle while placing the utilitarian promotion of a good state of affairs as a secondary objective for lawmaking. I show that this conceptualization largely fits with comparative theories on human development and human capabilities.

Chapter 3 frames the discussion on IP and Islamic doctrine. I start this discussion by first explaining how scholars interpreted and applied Islamic doctrine to understand and justify IP. Generally, research on IP and Islamic notions of the social good is scarce. However, the available commentary approached IP with the understanding that it is a novel regime for which there is no comprehensive set of rules in Islamic law. The existing accounts on IP and Islamic doctrine can be traced back to two conflicting views. A minority view started from a positivist interpretation of the Islamic sources. According to this view, notions of private property rights in knowledge and culture are not supported by the textual authorities of Islamic doctrine. Textual sources promote ideals of wide dissemination of knowledge to benefit society at large. Locking up the flow of knowledge through patent and copyright was interpreted as Western innovation, not supported by Islamic law. By contrast, the majority of scholars agree that IP has a place in a fair society according to the Islamic worldview. They interpret textual sources and Islamic values on labor and social utility to make a rough case to justify IP as fair reward for labor or as a necessary means to encourage innovation and creativity. In this chapter, I show that both views failed to produce a broad theoretical framework to justify or reject IP from an Islamic perspective. IP cannot be explained by merely identifying conceptual similarities or differences between isolated notions in patent and copyright regimes and isolated authorities from Islamic doctrine. There is room for a much broader theoretical framework to justify and limit IP rights from an Islamic perspective. To make the point accessible to comparative scholarship on IP theories, I construct a comparative framework in which I compare labor and utilitarian justifications of IP with their counterparts in Islamic doctrine. I show that there are broad similarities between Western theories justifying concepts of ownership of intangible content and Islamic doctrine. However, Islamic notions of the social good and the priority of the deontological duty to widely distribute basic social needs reframe the normative importance of labor and utility-based justifications into a broader vision of social justice.

Chapter 4 turns from theory to practice, examining the relationship between notions of the social good as introduced in Chapters 2 and 3 and various doctrinal features of global IP regimes. In general, Islamic doctrine defines morally required choices through an overarching deontological framework. Utility-based considerations are not the primary guiding principle of policymaking in the Islamic worldview. Classic Islamic jurisprudence since Abu Hamid al-Ghazali (d. 1111 CE) has captured this blend between deontological and utility-based considerations in a set of objectives that the law must promote. These objectives include the promotion of human life, intellectual capabilities, and wealth.[11] I analyze the global IP regime to determine to what extent its major operational features fit within Islamic definitions of the social good. Taking the TRIPS Agreement as a case study, I argue that the discourse that prevailed in the TRIPS norm-setting process was largely concerned with promoting economic efficiency. Major IP-intensive industries, such as pharmaceutical, entertainment, biotechnology, and computer firms, successfully pushed influential, developed countries such as the United States, Japan, and several European countries to present IP rights as tools to promote economic growth and welfare. The system was not designed with a deliberate awareness of IP's potential impact on basic human needs. This is why the system ended up causing legal and public opinion battles around access to medicine, educational material, and economic growth in developing countries.

11 Abu Hamid al-Ghazali, al-Mustasfa (al-Jami'a al-Islamiyya) vol. 2.

I conclude by showing that the global IP regime lacks a broad theory of justice. It perceives knowledge and culture as potential property for investors, overlooking its potential impact on satisfying essential needs in relation to health, education, and economic growth in developing countries.

The next two chapters take a different path in explaining the relationship between IP and Islamic notions of justice and the social good. Instead of analyzing IP in light of *maqasid al-Sharia* alone, as the mainstream modern Islamic jurisprudence would suggest, I propose integrating *maqasid al-Sharia* into a broader Islamic theory of social justice. Here IP will be discussed as a social institution that is central to the distribution of basic needs and opportunities to create content and earn from working through knowledge and culture. Notions of efficiency and merit will form part of a much larger analytical benchmark rather than being the dominant normative tools in IP policymaking. The shift towards a broad Islamic theory of justice is an important move in recognizing Islamic moral perceptions as part of the pluralist global sphere. I would expect that many will find the way in which Islamic jurisprudence presents Islamic normativity through *maqasid al-Sharia* to be challenging. Apart from the 1.5 billion Muslims who believe in the metaphysical and moral authorities of Islamic doctrine, the rest of the world adheres to different and sometimes conflicting worldviews. I draw on Jürgen Habermas's work "Religion in the Public Sphere" to situate the Islamic theory of justice as possible input to IP policymaking. Habermas opines that if religious notions on the social good are to have a productive presence in the pluralist public sphere, they must be presented in a language that nonreligious citizens and citizens following other religions can understand. In other words, the metaphysical and moral intuitions that originate from a religious doctrine must be translated into language everyone can understand and relate to.[12]

Chapter 5 reconstructs an Islamic theory of justice by identifying three principles of justice supported by various textual authorities from the Quran, the Sunnah, and both classic and modern Islamic jurisprudence. Combined, these sources propose that a fair society must leave everyone better off. According to the Quran, God created the earth for the settlement and betterment of humankind. Humans were collectively entrusted with all of its resources and instructed to cooperate to achieve common good. The original position of humankind is one of equality, with limited organizational exceptions along the way. Law and various social institutions must operate collectively to advance three broad principles in organizing social

[12] Jürgen Habermas, "Religion in the Public Sphere" (2006) 14(1) *European Journal of Philosophy*.

cooperation and leave everyone better off: First, believers are required to abide by a categorical moral duty ensuring that everyone enjoys equal access to essential needs to enable them to live a stable, autonomous, and productive human life. These needs include life, health, intellectual capabilities, and comfortable living standards. Classic Islamic jurisprudence identifies these needs as *had al-kifayah* (self-sufficiency baseline). Second, society must operate within an overarching principle of fair equality of opportunity in circumstances where power, wealth, and control over resources are to be distributed based on merit or to increase production of more wealth and resources. Third, whenever unequal talents and luck enable some to possess unequal amounts of wealth and power, inequalities must be continually addressed to benefit everyone in society, particularly marginalized and poor groups.

I apply these three principles to modern forms of IP both globally and in certain influential developed countries around the world. I share empirical and theoretical observations showing that various aspects of IP's main doctrines – such as the scope of exclusive rights, the duration of protection, and rights of access without permission – are not compatible with the Islamic principles of justice. First, IP can unnecessarily obstruct sustainable access to basic needs such as medicine, educational materials, and economic growth in poor countries. IP holders' exclusive rights are designed to enable well-established market actors to concentrate wealth and power to the exclusion of large segments of the society. Finally, IP can have a negative impact on equal opportunities to remake knowledge and culture and earn a living through it. I conclude that a fair IP system must reverse these perceived inequalities.

Chapter 6 moves on to assess the normative importance of ownership as a modality for governing intangible resources. In the bulk of Islamic sources, including the Quran and the Sunnah, God is believed to be the creator of the universe and the ultimate owner of all resources that the earth yields. I show that the broad language of these sources extends to encompass intangible resources, including knowledge and culture in the broadest sense. Islamic jurisprudence maintains that God's ownership – as is the case with any divine right in Islamic theology – is dedicated to promoting the collective interests of humankind. Accordingly, the original position of all resources is, by default, common ownership accessible to all members of society to use and transform to their benefit. Exclusive possession under property regimes has no presupposed priority as a modality for governing rights and obligations relating to all resources, including intangible resources. Accordingly, private control cannot be sanctioned unless justified as fair reward for productive labor and/or needed to increase the sum of available resources. Reflecting on current debates on IP and the public domain, I show that the Islamic vision supports institutional arrangements where knowledge and cultural resources are widely available and accessible to everyone. Those who argue that IP protection is a fair reward for their investment or the only mechanism to promote the production of more creative content must bear the burden of proving their claims. Empirical research and observations from internet platforms show that, although IP rights might encourage investment in creating more knowledge and culture, openness, sharing, and cooperation can promote social good as well.

The final Chapter explores how a fair IP landscape might emerge through the Islamic vision of justice and the social good introduced in this book. To be clear, in this chapter, I do not argue that Islamic doctrine will invent a new system to govern knowledge and culture in modern societies. Rather, I show that Islamic normative principles overlap with a large body of comparative IP scholarship critical of global IP regimes. Many world-renowned scholars, including Lawrence Lessig, Yochai Benkler, Jessica Litman, James Boyle, and Peter Drahos, are extremely critical of various established doctrines and operational details of the IP systems. They argue that major rich and resourceful stakeholders are increasingly shaping the content of IP laws around the world. IP has collectively become a protective doctrine for the well-established distributors of, and large investors in, knowledge and culture. The system constantly expands to lock up knowledge and culture under private control with more legal rights for longer periods. In many cases, we do not even know that property rights are the appropriate modality for governing a particular intangible asset in a given context. Modern IP systems are marked by substantial control and concentration of power to make and remake knowledge and culture. A few well-established patentees and copyright holders can prevent people from reading, listening, transforming, researching, and reinventing without convincing reason. Even more troubling, patentees and copyright holders can use their "property rights" to bargain with representatives of disadvantaged groups and delay or deny access to medicine and educational materials, or make access unnecessarily difficult.

Large bodies of comparative scholarship critical of current IP regimes propose a wide range of legislative and policy measures to make IP fair. These measures are designed to disable the concentration of power and control over knowledge and culture while ensuring that IP is not used to deny access to essential goods and capabilities to participate in reshaping knowledge and culture. I locate these measures in two major discourses in comparative IP scholarship. First, a great number of IP scholars argue that knowledge and culture should be protected against undue privatization through IP rights. To do that, they introduce the public domain as a legal and rhetorical construct to counter arguments for private property. The public domain is the realm of the commons, where knowledge and culture are widely available and freely accessible. Everyone can learn, invent, transform, and reimagine themselves and their world without the need for permission or the threat of legal action. This view of an open zone of knowledge and culture is particularly important in light of modern advancements in technology and communications where people are not only passive consumers but also future authors and inventors. Second, IP must continually adjust its baseline rules to empower users of knowledge and culture. Their entitlements should not be treated as marginal exceptions that need to be interpreted narrowly; the system needs to shift the power from rich and resourceful investors to a diffuse group of users. This is needed not only to fix market failures as an economic analysis of IP would suggest but also – and more importantly – to redistribute wealth and power to make new meanings or to challenge existing cultural norms.

2

The Structure of Islamic Doctrine and the Search for the Social Good

The worldview of the social good under which IP will be assessed in this book must start with an understanding of the basic structure of this very worldview. For Muslims, notions such as right and wrong or good and evil are generally defined by the dictates and the various interpretations of the Islamic doctrine. In this chapter, I provide an introductory account for understanding the main features of Islamic doctrine. This account is not a summary of literature on Islamic legal theory but a customized preface to understanding Islamic legal philosophy as it relates to IP, with a particular focus on its notions of the social good, which the law must promote. The language used here will be accessible to those interested in comparative legal philosophy, without neglecting the metaphysical dimension that animates Islamic doctrine.

I will start by describing the widely held conviction in Islamic jurisprudence concerning the positivist pedigree of Islamic doctrine. The scriptures are the ultimate authority on the social good. The first point of reference on what good *is* must be whatever the scripture commanded believers to do. The revelation halted in the seventh century CE, yet societies kept changing. Muslims, throughout their history, have faced unlimited emerging social and legal challenges for which there is no textual authority from the scriptures. IP is but one of the relatively recent examples of those challenges.

After I have identified the sphere of the positivist structure of Islamic doctrine, I move on to lay the ground for its normative sphere. Since the eleventh century CE, a number of Islamic jurists have suggested that the structure of the positivist texts shows that the Lawgiver is acting with a normative vision centered around the promotion of the good life on the earth. A recurring theme throughout the textual sources indicates that promoting life, fairness, wealth, and dignity is the essential objective of Islamic law. This line of scholarship generally suggests that Muslims need to deploy reason to develop a normative sphere of influence for Islamic doctrine in order to protect and promote the social good in dynamic societies.

Muslim jurists disagree on the appropriate scope of rational analysis of justice and the social good in light of the textual origins of the Islamic worldview. Despite the fact that the arguments around an active role for reason in determining the social good generally prevailed, its exact nature remains unclear. Should the social good be understood in consequentialist or deontological terms? In this chapter, I show that social good under Islamic doctrine has close links to deontological ethics but does not entirely banish consequentialism. Many Islamic sources show that deontological values such as the right to life, fairness, and dignity form a first order principle, while the utilitarian promotion of wealth is deemed secondary. In other words, under Islamic doctrine, the overarching purpose of the Lawgiver's order is the people themselves.

In the concluding part of this chapter, I explore possibilities to contextualize Islamic normative thought within modern comparative theories on human flourishing. I believe this will help in two ways. First, it will consolidate the understanding of the scope of social good in Islamic doctrine. Second, it will open promising possibilities to construct a conceptual framework for modern Islamic lawmaking. Some of the existing measures on human development, as well as theories of leading philosophers including Amartya Sen and Martha Nussbaum on human capabilities, share common ground with Islamic doctrine: They promote the interests of people as the ultimate purpose of the social order by emphasizing that the morally required choices are not necessarily those which maximize the good consequences for the majority. Rather, the goal is to establish a society that promotes life, good health, knowledge, and opportunities.

I am aware that it is a significant challenge to introduce a comprehensive doctrine with an enormous textual structure and different internal visions of the social good. I run the risk of oversimplifying a complex system that took centuries to develop, containing a wide variety of approaches, and theories whose positions may overlap in many instances but can sharply diverge on a particular issue. Advanced readers interested in understanding more about the history and the making of Islamic doctrine and its philosophy of law and social good may learn more from the sources I cite in this chapter. My purpose is to introduce the main features of Islamic doctrine in accessible language to help start the discussion on IP from an Islamic perspective.

I THE TEXTUAL ORIGINS OF ISLAMIC DOCTRINE

Islamic doctrine is based essentially on the Quran and the teaching of the Prophet, known as the Sunnah. Both of these sources represent a medium of positive law and broad normative values on matters of religion, such as prayers and fasting, as well as transactions, torts, and criminal conduct. The positivist pedigree of Islamic doctrine means that the scriptures are the ultimate authority on good and evil. Whatever is explicitly regulated in the Quran and the Sunnah forms the supreme source of the law.

A widely accepted definition in Islamic scholarship describes the Quran as the text that God revealed to the Prophet Muhammad, which was transmitted by collective testimony (*tawathur*).[1] The Quran comprises more than 6,200 verses. Large parts of these verses consist of historical narrations about ancient nations in religious, social, and economic contexts. In particular, the Quran contains extensive accounts on several earlier prophets and their missions to inform their nations of the existence of one all-knowing and omnipotent deity and their calls to obey a divine system of rules to achieve social good and eternal salvation. By and large, these parts of the Quran do not provide positive law in the form of specific behavioral instructions. Nevertheless, they could provide a versatile source from which to derive moral values and broad normative signals as discussed below.

In general, Islamic jurisprudence contends that the positivist dominion of Islamic doctrine is very limited in comparison to the entire body of Islamic scriptures. This observation essentially relates to the Quran. There is wide agreement among Muslim scholars that the Quran contains approximately 500 verses with legal instructions on prayers, alms tax (*zakat*), and fasting, as well as practical legal rules on the family, inheritance, property, transactions, criminal law, and public affairs.[2] Some scholars suggest that the portion of verses with specific legislative content is even smaller. Fazlur Raḥmān asserts that there are around 80 verses, among the 500 verses, that directly address specific legal matters.[3] Examples of these include instructions on regulating marriage, inheritance, and corporal punishments (*hudud*). In the mainstream Islamic jurisprudence, assessing the merit or demerit of these verses is not open to discussion. They are the ultimate source for the social good and for regulating the legal matters which they address.

The Quran assumes the highest position in the hierarchy of sources in Islamic doctrine. Other sources, textual or otherwise, must refer to the Quran for authority and legitimacy.[4] They include the Sunnah. The Sunnah refers to the exemplary behavior of the Prophet in acting according to the divine

1 Al-Amidi, *al-Ihkām fi Usūl al-Ahkām* (Dār al-Sumai'ī 2003) 215 et seq.
2 Wahba al-Zuhili, *Usūl al-Fiqh al-Islami* (Dār al-Fikr,1986).
3 Fazlur Raḥmān, *Islamic Methodology in History* (Central Institute of Islamic Research, 1965) 17.
4 Abd al-karim Zedan *al-Wajīz fi Usūl al-Fiqh* (Mu'assasat Qurtaba, 1976) 148.

commands in his sayings, actions, or whatever sayings or actions of his companions he tacitly approved as acceptable behavior under Islam.[5]

The Sunnah has a significant role in explaining and applying the Quran. It is also an independent source for Islamic law.[6] Several verses in the Quran confirm the Sunnah to be a source of Islamic law in addition to the Quran,[7] and scholars are in agreement that the Sunnah takes the second position after the Quran in the hierarchy of the sources of Islamic law. Its second place among the sources of Islamic law is not only attributed to the fact that it derives its legitimacy from the Quran, but also to the debates around the certainty of its content. Unlike the Quran, the Sunnah was not recorded during the lifetime of the Prophet[8] and therefore was not transmitted to subsequent generations of Muslims by collective testimony. Most of the available texts of the Sunnah were recorded several generations after the Prophet's death. This made large parts of its content of uncertain authenticity.[9] Despite the fact that there are several textual sources of the Sunnah with extensive texts addressing legal matters, sometimes in greater detail than the Quran, the authority (*hujiyya*) of these texts as positive law is debated in Islamic jurisprudence. For instance, in the Maliki school of Islamic jurisprudence, narrations that are not transmitted by collective testimony (*khabr al-wahid*) can be set aside if it is possible to find another source or methodology which allows an existing textual authority to be extended to provide a solution for the matter before the jurist.

The scriptures stopped developing after the seventh century CE, even though societies continued to change. A fundamental belief that permeates Islamic doctrine is that the teachings of Islam are universal. They were revealed to apply beyond the specific environment of tribal Arabia to Muslims anywhere and at any time. In Islamic jurisprudence, there is a widely held, conventional belief that the positivist texts of the scriptures are finite, while developments through time and space are not (*al-nusus mutanahiyya wa al-waqaei ' ghaiyru muntanahiyya*). Accordingly, Muslims as early as the seventh century CE started to introduce nontextual instruments to inject flexibility into the positivist structure of Islamic law.

5 Muhammed Abu Zahra, *Usūl al-Fiqh* (Dār al-Fikr al-Arabi, 2006) 105.
6 Muhammed Kamali, *Principles of Islamic Jurisprudence* (Pelanduk Publications, 1989), 79.
7 Quran, trans. Sahih International, 4:59, 4:80, 33:36, 53:5.
8 The Sunnah started to be recorded in various collections approximately 200 years after the death of the Prophet. The most reliable sources of the Sunnah are *al-sihah al-sitah* (the Six Authentic), namely, al-Bukhari, Muslim, al-Termidi, Ibn majjah, al-Nasā'i, abu Dawūd, and Musnad Ahmad B. Hanbil.
9 Wahba al-Zuhili, *Usūl al-Fiqh al-islami* (Dār al-Fikr,1986) 460 et seq.

II POST-SCRIPTURAL NORMATIVITY

After the Prophet's death in 632 CE, early Muslims faced incidents that required responses from Islamic texts. However, neither the texts of the Quran nor precedents from the Prophet's traditions provided specific solutions for these emerging incidents. The immediate successors of the Prophet, particularly his close companions, initiated a process of legal reasoning (*ijtihad*) to provide textually inspired solutions for textually unqualified issues. This development, roughly speaking, marked the start of post-scriptural normativity in the history of Islamic legal theory. It is important to note that jurists and lawmakers in the premodern Islamic era were not only concerned with providing solutions that primarily satisfy the needs and aspirations of Muslims. From the very beginning, the dominant trend in Islamic jurisprudence sought to develop a process of lawmaking where the realities and needs of Muslims did not constitute the sole formative source of the law. The modus operandi was to ensure that the lawmaking process was not arbitrary but fundamentally anchored in the scriptures. In this sense, lawmaking for new, emerging realities is not extrascriptural or completely detached from the norms and bounds contained in the Quran and the Sunnah.

There are several examples of post-scriptural normativity in the history of the development of Islamic law. One important example is *ijma'*, which literally means consensus. *Ijma'* was developed shortly after the Prophet's death to operate as a nontextual source for adapting Islamic law to the textually unregulated, emerging realities of Muslims.[10] The immediate successors of the Prophet needed to deal with cases for which there was no specific injunction in the Quran or in the Sunnah. The process of reaching an *ijma'* is described in Islamic jurisprudence as a process of deliberation among Muslims with knowledge of the Islamic scriptures for the purpose of reaching an agreement on a textually unqualified matter. If an agreement is reached stating that Islamic law on a particular matter will take a certain form, that agreement will be deemed *ijma'*, which will become a binding precedent when addressing similar issues in the future. A frequently used example of *ijma'* in Islamic jurisprudence is the rule on assigning to grandchildren shares in the estates of their grandparents. The companions of the Prophet faced a situation where a person died before his parents and left children of his own. There was no textual authority to address this situation. The Quran only prescribes that shares in the estate pass to the living sons and daughters of the deceased but says nothing about when a person dies before his or her father

10 Al-Amidi, *al-Ihkām fi Usūl al-Ahkām* (Dār al-Sumai'ī 2003) 262.

while leaving children of his or her own. The companions applied *ijma'* in this case to make it obligatory for the grandparents to allocate a share of their wealth to their grandchildren.[11]

Another example of post-scriptural normativity is *qiyas*, which literally means analogical deduction. *Qiyas* is a methodology that is used to extend textual authorities to new cases.[12] It operates by extending the injunction from a textually qualified case to a new case due to their sharing the same rationale.[13] In other words, under *qiyas*, a jurist would identify *a ratio legis* for a particular legal rule stated in the textual sources and extend the application of that rule to cases with similar features. The most cited example of *qiyas* in Islamic jurisprudence is the extension of the textual prohibition on drinking alcohol in the Quran to other intoxicating substances.[14] The *ratio legis* underlying the Quran's description of the intoxication that results from drinking alcohol as a cause of further *haram* (illegal behavior) is seen to extend to any substance of an intoxicating nature.[15]

Scholarship relating to *usul al-fiqh* (principles of Islamic jurisprudence) is replete with additional examples of non-textual sources for Islamic normativity, including *istihsan* (juristic preference), *istishab* (presumption of continuity), and *urf* (customary traditions). However, I discuss in greater detail what I think of as the most significant development in post-scriptural normativity: the introduction of *maslaha* (consideration of public interest) as a guiding principle for Islamic lawmaking in the pursuit of the social good. The introduction of *maslaha* marked a fundamental shift in Islamic legal theory. The focus extended beyond mere attempts to extend the application of the texts through *ijma* or *qiyas* to a search for a more flexible and overarching legal philosophy for Islamic doctrine.

As from the eleventh century CE, particularly in the scholarship of Abû al-Ma'âlî al-Juwaynî (d. 1085 CE) and Abu Hamid al-Ghazali (d. 1111 CE), ideas around notions of public interest as the overarching objective of the Islamic texts started to crystalize and gain momentum. From that time, a branch of Islamic jurisprudence began to analyze scripture to articulate a philosophy for lawmaking that draws legitimacy from scripture and addresses challenges for which there was no specific textual authority. This branch is widely known as the objectives of Islamic law (*maqasid al-Sharia*).

11 Mustafa al-Zarqa, *al-Madkhal al-Fiqhi al-'ām* (Dār al-Qalam, 1998) 78.
12 Kamali, *Principles of Islamic Jurisprudence*, 248.
13 Muhammed al-Shawakani, *Irshad al-Fuhul* (Dār al-Fazila, 2000) 840 et seq.
14 Abd al-karim Zedan, *al-Wajīz fi Usūl al-Fiqh* (Mu'assasat Qurtaba, 1976) 196.
15 Quran, trans. Sahih International, 5:90.

Maqasid al-Sharia starts from the proposition that only small portions of the Quran are strictly positivist. Muslims must realize that the Quran was not intended to be a legislative instrument with detailed instructions on every situation that might occur in society. Societies are by definition dynamic. It would be wrong to assume that there should be a textual solution for every possible novel scenario. Accordingly, it is necessary to search for underlying design principles in the entire scriptures to identify *masalih* (interests) and then use the law as an instrument to promote them. This should not be impossible. For instance, we know that the texts of the Quran come in the form of general principles, and in many cases with underlying purposes (*hikam*). The underlying purposes of the texts reveal that the Lawgiver consistently seeks to promote and nurture people's interests. In the words of Al-'izz Ibn Abd-al-Salam (d. 1261 CE), the purpose of Islamic texts "is the social good of people either through averting potential harm or bringing about benefits."[16] This objective of the Lawgiver could be gleaned from examining underlying design principles of the scriptures, which demonstrate that the Lawgiver systemically aims to bring about good and prevent evil. The task of the jurist is to extend Islamic law to novel situations through understanding the inner reason (*hikmah*) of a particular verse. The *hikmah* represents a *maslaha* (interest) that the Lawgiver intended to promote through textual instructions.

The underlying purposes of the texts are to be discovered through a process of inductive survey (*istiqra*). *Istiqra* involves scanning the scripture to infer *maqsad* (plural *maqasid*). If we take the texts of the Quran and the Sunnah which address the protection of life and property or the promotion of justice and leniency, we should be able to proclaim that protecting life and property and promoting justice and leniency are principles of general applicability in Islamic law. Thus, these principles should be used as benchmarks to guide the normative analysis of emerging issues for which there is no specific textual authority.

The purpose of inferring *maqasid* objectives from the Quran and the Sunnah is to transform them into foundational principles to guide lawmaking. The idea here is to extend the spirit of the sources (promotion of public interests) to address potential, novel interests (*masalih mursala*) and adopt them into Islamic law, through normative analysis, whenever doing so could bring about a social good. The process of deducing *maqasid* is not identical to natural law, particularly in one of its historical manifestations, as a process of pure rational analysis of human nature to construct universal rules of moral

16 Al-'izz Ibn Abd al-Salam, *Qaw'aid al-Ahkām fi Islāh al-Anām* (Dār ibn Hazm, 2003) 14.

behavior. This is not to say that reason has no place in identifying *maqasid al-Sharia*. In fact, a theory of *maqasid* would not be possible without the use of reason to analyze the scriptures with a view to deducing objectives and then to proclaim those objectives as *masalih* (public interest/social good). Furthermore, human nature (e.g., society's needs and circumstances) is also taken into consideration to guide the scripturally based analysis and applications of *maqasid*. However, it is the use of pure reason to attribute normative instructions to the divine will that is highly contested in Islamic jurisprudence. Muslim jurists of Ash'arite and Mu'tazilite convictions disagreed on the exact role of human reason in engaging in normative analysis outside the scriptural environment. A detailed analysis of their disagreements is well beyond the scope of this chapter.

Be that as it may, the majority of leading figures in modern Islamic jurisprudence held the view that using the intellect is crucial to understanding the underlying interests from the texts and extending them to address progress in a way that secures the social good.[17] A movement led by one of the most renowned reformers in modern Islamic legal history, Mohamed Abduh (d. 1905 CE), advanced the view that there is no conflict between reason and the scripture. God, in His commands, promotes the good and forbids the evil. The human intellect is capable, through careful rational analysis, of determining good and evil and extending them, through normative analysis, to emerging issues.[18] Ibn Ashur defends the proposition that it is permissible to apply the intellect to derive the underlying purposes of lawmaking from the scriptures. He argues that rejecting the use of reason to derive *masalih* from the texts and extending them to unqualified emerging issues runs the risk of undermining the entire validity of Islamic doctrine as a universal and eternal system of rules oriented to achieving the social good.[19] He constantly advocates the idea that the people's *masalih* articulated in the texts are grounded in natural reason (*fitrah*). Therefore, it is important to use reason to derive interests from the texts and protect them at all times. For instance, the group of interests protected by various textual authorities such as the sanctity of life, promotion of the intellect, and wealth are simultaneously self-evident to human reason and grounded in the empirical nature of the world. There is no conflict between reason and the texts. We intrinsically know that killing is wrong, the intellect is a means to progress, and wealth is important for

17 Wael Hallaq, *An Introduction to Islamic Law* (Cambridge University Press) 15.

18 Malcolm Kerr, *Islamic Reform: The Political and Legal Theories of Muhammad 'Abduh and Rashid Rida* (University of California Press, 1966), 107 et seq.

19 Muhammed al-Taher Ibn Ashour, *Treatise on Maqasid al-Sharia*, trans. Mohamed El-Tahir El-Mesawi (The International Institute of Islamic Thought, 2006), 63.

a comfortable life.[20] Ibn Ashur draws heavily from Al-'izz Ibn Abd al-Salam, who devoted parts of his treatise, *al-Qawa'id*, to stressing the proposition that the entire texts of the scripture came to promote all that is socially good (*manfa'a*) and prevent what is socially evil (*mafsada*). Good and evil are attributes subject to rational analysis.[21]

However, it should be noted that the position in modern mainstream Islamic jurisprudence is that the use of reason is not an arbitrary intellectual exercise that aims to question divine prescriptions. Reason has a somewhat limited sphere of analysis and influence. The majority of reformers concede that reason should not circumvent detailed commands in the scriptures, particularly those that could be classified under the 80 to 500 verses of the Quran which imposed specific instructions in areas of the law including inheritance or some aspects of family law. Rather, reason could work hand in hand with revelation to promote public interests where revelation omits details. For example, reason could rely on the scripture to decide on the system of governance that should be promoted under Islamic law in modern societies. Here, the scripture simply praises government through consultation (*shura*) without any further details. Arguably, reason could be used to conduct an inductive survey (*istiqra*) to determine the interests God aims to promote from the Quran and then use them as a benchmark to set standards for the ideal procedural and substantive structures of Islamic government. For instance, can we derive a conception of the rule of law in Islam? If yes, does that include human rights and freedoms? Does it place limits on a government's power? What is the nature and scope of those limits? The possibilities are endless.[22]

III THE PHILOSOPHY OF *MASLAHA*

The proposition that there exists a philosophy on the social good that derives content and authority from scripture is now widely accepted in Islamic scholarship. Those who write in the discipline of *maqasid al-Sharia* submit that the normative vision underpinning the textual structure of Islamic doctrine on the social good must be mobilized to address continuing cultural, social, and economic changes. The potential so far is limitless. Working through *maqasid al-Sharia*, jurists scan the texts of the Quran and the Sunnah to determine the *masalih*/social good that the Lawgiver aims to achieve through commands and instructions prescribed in Islamic textual

[20] Ibn Ashour, *Maqasid*, 81–85.
[21] Abd al-Salam, *Qaw'aid al-Ahkām fi Islāh al-Anām*, 9.
[22] Yusuf Al-Qaradawi, *al-Siyāsa al-Shar'iyya* (Maktabat Wahba, 2011) 103.

authorities. The theory here is that the texts of the Quran and the Sunnah provide indicants on the Lawgiver's objectives/*maqasid* in addressing a particular state of affairs. The prevailing hypothesis in *maqasid* is that the Lawgiver, through scripture, acts with a normative vision centered around the promotion of a good life on the earth.[23] In every relevant text in the Quran or divinely guided practice from the Sunnah, the Lawgiver systematically aims to promote people's *masalih*.

Even premodern Islamic jurists who adopted views on the limited capacity of human reason to make normative statements on the social good subscribed – albeit with certain stipulations – to this hypothesis. The leading Ash'arite jurist al-Juwaynī (d. 1085 CE) started the discussion when he noted that "*maṣlaḥa* [is] an expression of people's well-being that results from the implementation of God's laws in this world whereby people's lives are well-ordered."[24] His disciple al-Ghazālī (d. 1111 CE) was the first to initiate a systematic and comprehensive analysis of social good as the purpose (*maqsad*) of textual authorities in Islamic doctrine. For al-Ghazālī, the purpose of Islamic scriptures (*maqṣūd al-shar'*) is to preserve people's interests. He is also widely known as the first scholar to construct a taxonomy of manifestations of the social goods/*masalih* emphasized by the scriptures. In al-Ghazālī's understanding of the social good, he maintains that Islamic scripture is revealed to secure basic purposes that are crucial to the functioning of society. In his survey of the scripture, al-Ghazālī quantifies these purposes into five essentials, namely the preservation of religion, life, intellect, honor, and wealth.[25] For those who would come after al-Ghazālī, these five manifestations of the social good are to be used as benchmarks for conducting a normative analysis to address new, textually unqualified challenges that face Muslims through changing times, places, and traditions.[26]

According to Ibn Ashur, it is essential for Muslim scholars, policymakers, and advisers today to familiarize themselves with the philosophy of *maslaha* through the discipline of *maqasid al-Sharia* and to understand the manifestations of the social good that the Lawgiver aims to promote through divine law. In his opinion, this would be an effective way to extend the finite Islamic texts to the infinite social, cultural, and technological changes. The way to do that is to conduct an inductive survey of the textual sources (*istiqra*) and use them as

23 Allal al-Fassi, *Maqasid al-Sharia al-Islamiyya wa-Makarimuha* (Maktabat al-Wahda al-Arabiyya, 1963) 3–7, 41.
24 Felicitas Opwis, *Maṣlaḥa and the Purpose of the Law* (Brill, 2010).
25 Al-Ghazālī, *al-Mustaṣfa*, 2: 481–82.
26 Wael Halaq, *A History of Islamic Law and Legal Theories* (Cambridge University Press, 1997) 67.

benchmarks to determine the categories of public interest/*masalih* that should be considered in formulating Islamic law's responses to novel situations. Ibn Ashur maintains that the commands, instructions, and statements of the scriptures are associated with underlying wisdoms (*hikam*). Through *istiqra*, jurists can infer the *ratio legis* that represents the objective intended by the Lawgiver.[27] For instance, al-Ghazali inferred his classification of the five manifestations of social good in Islamic doctrine from various textual authorities. Texts that promise rewards or warn against punishment to incentivize people to abide by religion or prevent them from killing, drinking alcohol, stealing, or committing adultery illustrate that the intended purposes of law-making in Islamic doctrine is to promote religion (*din*), life (*nafs*), reason (*'aql*), lineage (*nasl*), and property (*mal*).[28]

By and large, premodern Islamic scholarship on *maqasid al-Sharia* kept on working with al-Ghazali's taxonomy of the five manifestations of social good in Islamic doctrine. For instance, both Fakhr al-Din al-Razi (d. 1210 CE) and Abu Ishaq al-Shatibi (d. 1388 CE) discuss *maqasid al-Sharia as* comprising five categories. However, modern scholarship on *maqasid al-Sharia* argues that many more could be added to the list. This scholarship emphasizes the need to have an open mind when reading scripture to derive more examples for the social good and set the law to protect and promote them. The process of deducing and inducing purposes for the social order from the Quran and the Sunnah does not necessarily require an exhaustive examination of textual authorities. The process could be simpler than that. For instance, Ibn Ashur argues that facilitation (*taysir*) is the definitive purpose of Sharia, based on a direct verse from the Quran (2:185) that states "God wills that you shall have ease, and does not want you to *suffer hardship*."[29] There is a prevailing trend in Islamic scholarship that seeks to significantly expand on al-Ghazali's initial classification in terms of both the scope of, and the various manifestations of, the social good.

Mohamed Abu Zahra maintains that preserving life (*nafs*) goes beyond mere protection against murder or the infliction of bodily harm on human beings to include broad categories of interest attached to human life, such as promoting personal freedoms, freedom of movement, and freedom of expression.[30] Ahmad al-Raysuni, in his analysis of various textual authorities, does not accept a limited understanding of promoting the intellect (*aql*) as an

27 Ibn Ashur, *Maqasid*, 14 et seq.

28 Al-Ghazali, *al-Mustasfa*, 481.

29 Ibn Ashur, *Maqasid*, 56.

30 Muhammad Abu Zahrah, *Tanzim al-Islam li al-Mujtama* (Dār alFikr al-'Arabi, n.d.) 57.

objective of Islamic doctrine. He maintains that promoting the intellect should not only be discussed in the context of the need to prohibit alcohol and intoxicants with similar effects. The Lawgiver's purpose behind promoting the intellect should be understood broadly to encompass whatever nourishes the mind, including education, knowledge of logic, and the dissemination of knowledge.[31] Similarly, other scholars question the soundness of restricting the scope of preserving honor as social good to matters related to progeny. They propose to replace this narrow view with a broader understanding of honor that includes the objectives of Islamic doctrine protecting human dignity and human rights.[32] In the context of expanding the scope of al-Ghazali's five objectives, some argue for more developed notions around the preservation and promotion of wealth. This objective should not only be understood in the context of protecting property as a way to achieve social good. The understanding of this objective must evolve to include economic growth and social justice.[33]

The modern view in Islamic scholarship also maintains that the number of objectives of lawmaking in Islam goes well beyond the list of five objectives as introduced by al-Ghazali and subsequently adopted by classical scholarship. Rashid Rida added reform and the promotion of women's human rights to the *maqasid*.[34] Ibn Ashur also added freedom of faith to the list of *maqasid al-Sharia* based on a direct textual authority from the Quran. "Let there be no compulsion in religion."[35] Muhamed al-Ghazali (d. 1996 CE) and Yusuf al-Qaradwi call for the construction of a theory of *maqasid al Sharia* that relies on the scriptures to enhance and enforce modern universal values and institutions such as justice, freedom, and social collaboration (*takaful*). In introducing universal freedom, justice, and fairness as part of an overarching social good in Islamic doctrine, Muhamed al-Ghazali highlights the need to expand on the five objectives. He maintains that freedom and justice are additional manifestations of the social good. The Quran is clear on these matters: "We have already sent Our messengers with clear evidences and sent down with them the Scripture and the balance that the people may maintain [their affairs] in justice."[36] An interpretation of this verse is that

31 Ahmed Al-Raysuni, *Nazariyyat al-Maqasid 'ind al-Imam al-Shatibi* (The International Institute of Islamic Thought, 1995) 229–40.

32 Jasser Auda, *Maqasid al-Sharia as Philosophy of Islamic Law A Systems Approach* (The International Institute of Islamic Thought, 1995) 90.

33 Auda, *Maqasid al-Sharia*, 52.

34 Ibid., 6.

35 Quran, trans. Sahih International, 2:256.

36 Ibid., 57:27.

justice is an overarching principle of Islamic doctrine. It is the entire purpose behind revelation. In the context of preserving freedoms and human rights, justice would require the rule of law to be established to control state powers by preventing the government from encroaching on the liberties and freedoms of individuals. Accordingly, promoting justice and freedom is *maqsad Shar'i* (objective of Islamic law), which must be upheld as a form of social good and the law must be mobilized in pursuit of it.[37]

IV DEVELOPING ISLAMIC LAW THROUGH NORMATIVE ANALYSIS: *AL-MASLIH AL-MURSALA*

The concept of *maslaha* as a normative tool within Islamic doctrine is used to pursue a socially good state of affairs whenever scripture is silent on a particular novel situation. It is a two-step process. First, a jurist would conduct an inductive survey of the texts of scripture in order to locate scriptural indicants to the effect of promoting a particular manifestation of social good. This would include interests that could be deduced from a literal understanding of scripture, such as the promotion of life or *taysir* as per ibn Ashur, or some interests that require a consolidated inductive survey (*istiqra*), such as freedom and the rule of law. The next step for a jurist is to set those manifestations of social good as standards and apply them to emerging issues that are not directly addressed in the textual sources. In other words, after locating *masalih*, those *masalih* are to be used as a point of reference to guide scripturally justified normative analysis to incorporate novel situations into Islamic doctrine. The entire notion of integrating new emerging issues that correspond to the interests derived from the scriptures is known as *al-masalih al-mursala*, meaning emerging issues of interest to the community that are not sanctioned or prohibited in the Quran or the Sunnah.

Textually unqualified, novel situations faced Muslims immediately after the death of the Prophet. Consistent reports in Islamic jurisprudence indicated that the immediate successors of the Prophet (known as the Righteous Successors) – Abu Bakr, Umar, Othman, and Ali – applied rational analysis in deciding on social good in situations where there were no explicit textual authorities. Some of the frequently used examples in this context include the second Caliph Umar's order to establish public registers (*dawawin*) and build prisons, and Utman's decision to develop the sacred mosque in Mecca.

37 Jamalu al-Din Attiyya, *Nahwa Taf'il Maqasid al-Sharia* (The International Institute of Islamic Thought, 1995) 98.

Islamic jurisprudence on *maqasid* represents these examples as situations where the social good was considered as a guiding principle under Islamic doctrine. Here, no textual authority was used to justify these decisions. They were taken on the basis of a potential social good that could be secured for the relevant Muslim community.[38]

Very early in the formative phase of developing *maslaha* as a philosophy for lawmaking in Islamic doctrine, Abu Hamid al-Ghazali sought to infuse a level of formality in dealing with emerging issues on the basis of *maslaha*. In line with his Ashi'rite understanding of the social good, al-Ghazali was concerned that relying on *maslaha* would undermine the authority of textual sources through the creation of arbitrary rules disconnected from the divine revelation.[39] So he classified textually unqualified *masalih* into three levels – necessities (*ḍarūrāt*), needs (*ḥājāt*), and improvements (*taḥsīnāt*) – and stipulated three conditions for adopting an emerging issue into Islamic law.

Firstly, it is not enough for an emerging issue to be an interest safeguarded by the texts. It must be a necessity without which the legal system would not function properly and the existence of the community could be jeopardized. In other words, not every social good that could be derived from scripture can guide the normative analysis towards making law for novel situations. The social good must be crucial to the existence of the community. A potential social good that is simply needed to alleviate hardship (*ḥājāt*) or improve the quality of life (*taḥsīnāt*) is not a salient *maslaha* worthy of consideration and, according to al-Ghazali, should not be adapted under Islamic law. Second, it must also be certain (*qatiyya*). We must know, or at least have strong reasons to believe, that the emerging issue will bring about an interest or avert harm from the community. Thirdly, it must be universal (*kullyia*), so as to benefit the entire Muslim community and not just part of it.

Al-Ghazali gives an example where a novel situation could represent necessary, certain, and universal social good that corresponds to the objectives of scripture in safeguarding human life. It involves a hypothetical scenario where an army of non-Muslims invades Muslim land and captures innocent Muslims to use them as human shields. Here, no textual authority could be invoked to aid on what is the right thing to do. Al-Ghazali argues that if we strike at the shield, we certainly would kill innocent Muslims. If we do not strike, the enemy will conquer the Muslim land and kill everyone, including the innocent Muslims used as shields. Al-Ghazali states that:

38 Opwis, *Maṣlaḥa and the Purpose of the Law*, 136.

39 Al-Ghazali, *al-Mustasfa*, 477 et seq.

It is possible to say that the innocent captives will be killed anyway. Therefore, we need to protect the lives of the entire Muslim community being invaded by non-Muslims. Preserving the lives of Muslims in this scenario corresponds with the intention of the Lawgiver as stated not in one but many textual authorities.[40]

Although both classical and modern scholars frequently discuss al-Ghazali's classification of the social good into necessities (*ḍarūrāt*), needs (*ḥājāt*), and improvements (*taḥsīnāt*), many do not subscribe to his opinion that the emerging social good must be a necessity. From the classical camp of Muslim scholars, Shihab al-Din al-Qarafi (d. 1285 CE) does not restrict emerging interests to the level of necessities. In *al-Dhakhira*, he maintains that unattested *maslaha* (textually unqualified social good) could be integrated without requiring any of the conditions mentioned by al-Ghazali to be met.[41] In another work, *Sharh Tanqih al-Fusul*, he refers to examples where the companions of the Prophet integrated novel situations into Islamic law without laying down any conditions other than that they should benefit the Muslim community (*mutlaq al-maslaha*). Examples of this include writing the Quran in a single book, building prisons, and introducing coins as a medium of exchange.[42] Al-Shatibi, in *al-'itesam*, also cites another example to the same effect, where the companions of the Prophet ruled, without textual authority, that craftsmen should bear civil liability for objects under their care given the social good that could follow from such rule.[43]

The majority of modern jurists hold the view that using the interests articulated within the Quran to address change does not require any level of necessity in the emerging new issues.[44] In other words, the philosophy of lawmaking in Islam aims to promote the interests of people. Those interests do not have to be necessary to the existence of the community. It is sufficient for an emerging new interest to have the potential of making life easier or more productive to be integrated within Islamic law. Accordingly, when facing new issues for which there is no positivist text, scholars will need to conduct a normative analysis based on the textual authority to determine whether the emerging issue brings about a social good that corresponds to an objective (*maqsad*) safeguarded by the texts of the Quran and the Sunnah. For example, scholars of *maqasid al-Sharia* agree on the proposition that protecting and

40 Al-Ghazali, *al-Mustasfa*, 477 et seq.
41 Shihāb al-Dīn al-Qarāfī, *al-Dhakhira* (Dar al-Gharb al-Islami, 1994) 151.
42 Shihāb al-Dīn al-Qarāfī, *Sharh Tanqih al-Fusul* (Dar al-fikr, 2004) 351.
43 Al-Shatibi, *al-I'tisam* (Maktabat al-Tawhīd) vol. 3, 319.
44 Al-Qaradawi, *al-Siyāsa al-Shar'iyya*, 103 et seq.

promoting life, intellect, and wealth are manifestations of the social good that correspond to the objectives of the texts. Accordingly, novel situations involving potential interests for the community need to be assessed from the perspective of these broad considerations to determine whether they respond to emerging issues in health care, education, and economic development, regardless of the level of necessity.[45]

V THE NATURE OF SOCIAL GOOD IN ISLAMIC DOCTRINE

So far, I have been vague about the nature of social good in Islamic doctrine. Where does it fit in with the dominant normative theories, namely deontology and consequentialism? Does the Islamic conception of the social good entail a consequentialist or deontological view on what is morally required? I mentioned above that the promotion of life and wealth are widely accepted as manifestations of the social good in Islamic doctrine. However, how should these be understood? Should they be analyzed through utilitarian lenses? In this line of thinking, the social good when deciding on promoting life and wealth would revolve around saving the lives of the majority and achieving the greatest wealth for the greatest number. Or, alternatively, should social good be analyzed through a deontological lens? Here, the social good would lie in adhering to a duty to protect life at all cost and pursue distributive fairness regardless of the consequences.

The issue at hand is open to debate in Islamic jurisprudence. If we take a look at part of premodern Islamic jurisprudence, we notice that some of the terminology used may indicate a strong connection between textually unqualified interest in Islamic doctrine and utilitarianism. For instance, according to Fakhr al-Din al-Razi (d. 1210 CE), *maslaha*/social good is the purpose of God's law. It means utility (*manfa'a*).[46] *Manfa'a* means pleasure (*ladha*) and the means of achieving pleasure.[47] Jeremy Bentham, one of the founders of modern utilitarianism, defined utility as pleasure, or happiness.[48] Leading modern reformers such as Muḥammad Rashīd Riḍa (1865–1935) introduced *maslaha* as a means of promoting the social good in society. His theory of *maslaha* is a pragmatic one: Rida proposed resorting to a rational analysis of mundane matters that face Muslims and integrating them into Islamic law

45 Al-Zarqa, *al-Madkhal al-Fiqhi al-ʿam*, 114 et seq.
46 Opwis, *Maṣlaḥa and the Purpose of the Law*, 90.
47 Al-Razi, *al-Mahsul*, 194.
48 Jeremy Bentham, *An Introduction to the Principles of Morals and Legislation* (Batoche Books, 2000).

when they secure social good for the community. He did not elaborate further on the nature of the social good that should be pursued.[49]

Mohamed Abu Zahra (1898–1974) explicitly linked social good in *maqasid al-Sharia* to utilitarianism as developed by Jeremy Bentham and John Stuart Mill. He argues that *madhab al-manfa'a* (utilitarianism) guides lawmaking in modern society in order to achieve the greatest good for the greatest number of people. He further elaborates that "*istiqra* (inductive survey) from the Quranic principles proves that social systems are promoted through achieving as much material and spiritual happiness as possible for the greatest number of people."[50] He also understands the five objectives of Islamic law as articulated in classical Islamic scholarship in utilitarian terms, as means to promote the good for the overwhelming majority.[51]

This understanding of *maslaha*/social good has drawn criticism in Islamic scholarship that aims to distance the Islamic conception of *maslaha*/social good from the concept of social good as understood in utilitarian ethics.[52] Mohamed Saed al-Buti heavily criticized the drawing of links between the Islamic conception of social good and utilitarianism. He argues that Western utilitarian philosophy as introduced by Mill and Bentham has completely different characteristics to the concept of *maslaha*/social good in the Islamic worldview. For al-Buti, utilitarianism uses different measures to determine good and evil. It relies on calculating the increase and decrease in worldly pleasures. This is not the case in Islamic doctrine, where observing the duties and commands of the revealed texts is the highest good humankind can achieve, even if this leads to sacrificing worldly pleasures such as property and wealth.[53]

My hypothesis is that an Islamic conception of social good is not consequentialist. In the paragraphs that follow, I include, in very broad and rough terms, insights from textual sources, practical applications by the companions of the Prophet, and positions taken in Islamic scholarship to the effect that the nature of social good in Islamic doctrine is predominantly deontological. These insights provide a preliminary understanding that shows Islamic doctrine does not promote a bleak, utilitarian analysis of what is morally

49 Malcolm Kerr, *Islamic Reform: The Political and Legal Theories of Muhammad 'Abduh and Rashid Rida* (University of California Press, 1966) 187–208.

50 Abu Zahrah, *Tanzim*, 54–55.

51 Ibid., 55–56.

52 Albert Hourani, *Arabic Thought in the Liberal Age* (Oxford University Press, 1962) 65; Abd al-Wahhāb Khallāf, *Maṣādir al-tashrī' al-islāmī fīmā lā naṣṣ fīh* (6th ed., Dār al-Qalam, 1993) 92.

53 Muhammed Sa'īd al-Būti, *dawābit al-maslaha fi al-shari'a al-islamiyya* (PhD thesis, Faculty of Shari'a al-Azhar University, 1965) 23–60.

required. There are situations where efficiency could be considered, but efficiency-based considerations can only serve as a second order principle. In other words, maximizing happiness in a particular state of affairs is acceptable only when it does not contradict a deontological duty. I understand that this hypothesis is a bold one. It would most certainly require additional research and discussion in Islamic jurisprudence. However, as a start, I would propose four premises to support it.

First, the entire concept of *masalih*/social good is grounded in the texts of the Quran and the Sunnah. What makes a particular choice or emerging issue a *maslaha* or *mafsada* (evil) does not rest on calculating the consequences of the said choice or emerging issue in light of other options. For an emerging *maslaha* to be considered valid under Islamic doctrine, it must correspond to an interest safeguarded by the scriptures. In other words, the reference to what is morally required as "the good thing to do" is what is promoted by the texts as "the right thing to do." For instance, according to the texts, the protection of human life is a fundamental objective/interest in Islamic law. Accordingly, human life must be protected at all times, regardless of the consequences. The life of a poor and sick person suffering from an incurable disease must be protected, according to the texts, for the sake of preserving human life regardless of any consequences related to the financial cost to society or the potential pain for that sick person.[54]

Second, an inductive survey (*istiqra*) of several textual authorities shows that scripture generally promotes deontological values. If we take freedom from slavery as an example, one would find that scripture systematically sought to promote freedom as a fundamental deontological value, as opposed to the possible utilitarian benefits of slavery in the primitive economies of Arabia in the seventh century CE. To appreciate the deontological emphasis of the textual authority, one must travel back in time. In the seventh century CE, the institution of slavery was common sense and was a well-established social construct. It was important to regional trade and a means to economic growth in the region. While scripture did not prohibit it, unlike alcohol and other forms of behavior, scripture placed the elimination of slavery as a significant objective on its agenda for social reform. Arguably, the deontological approach of the texts towards slavery cannot be mistaken. Many examples demonstrate that scripture sought to promote freedom as a basic human value, as opposed to the growth that could be generated through slavery. For instance, Islamic law abolished several causes of slavery, including voluntary enslavement, slavery as punishment for committing a crime, and enslavement

[54] Compare Ibn Ashour, *Maqasid*, 98.

in payment of a debt.[55] On the other hand, many textual sources sought to incentivize Muslims to emancipate slaves. For instance, one of the methods of paying annual obligatory charity (*zakat*) is to emancipate slaves. Additionally, textual sources made emancipation a fundamental door for atonement in many cases.[56]

Third, Umar ibn al-Khatab, one of the most important figures and authorities on interpreting positivist law in Islamic history, leaned towards a deontological understanding of the social good. After Muslim armies entered Iraq and Egypt, Umar rejected distribution of the newly seized lands among fighters, despite prevailing interpretations of the Quran that require Muslim commanders to distribute the bounties of war among the participating fighters. The verse aims to encourage fighters in Muslim armies to engage in battles with the promise that the valuables taken will be divided among them. After fighters in Umar's army secured victory in both Egypt and Iraq, they seized large pieces of agricultural land in Iraq known as *al-sawad*. They asked Umar – as per the customary interpretations of the Quran at the time – to divide those lands amongst the army. Umar declared that the general purpose of God's law is to ensure that wealth is distributed fairly among Muslims, not circulated among the rich Muslims (Quran, 59:7). Distributing those large pieces of land would benefit a few Muslims at the expense of the larger populations and future generations. Thus, Umar understood the social good as promoting a duty to uphold distributive fairness rather than incentivizing fighters to conquer land and expand the Islamic empire.[57] If we assess Umar's actions in today's terms, we would find that he sought the social good in the duty to promote distributive fairness rather than worrying about the potential consequences that may result from discouraging fighters from engaging in battles.

Finally, Abu Hamid al-Ghazali, the first jurist to define *maslaha* and discuss its use to provide flexibility in the positivist scriptures, was not interested in the utilitarian calculus of achieving the greatest good for the greatest number. Al-Ghazali's captives scenario suggests that his vision of Islamic doctrine promotes consequentialism. However, al-Ghazali was keen, as shown in the following examples, to affirm that he was not adopting a consequentialist perspective on the nature of social good. The first example al-Ghazali introduced was about a sinking boat, where he imagines that a boat filled with

55 Ibid., 157.

56 Abu Zahra, *Tanzim*, 28.

57 Compare Auda, Maqasid al-Sharia, 10, citing Ya'qub Abu Yusuf, *al-Kharaj* (al-Maktaba al-Amiriyyah) 14, 81.

passengers is about to sink in the sea and the passengers all agree that if they could throw overboard one passenger, chosen by lottery, the boat could be saved, along with the rest of the passengers. Al-Ghazali suggests that the life of that one person is sacred and cannot be sacrificed for the good of the rest of the passengers.[58] In another example, al-Ghazali also promotes a deontological perspective on social good. The example relates to the torturing of a suspected thief to obtain information. Despite the potential social good that could be generated for society in this case through obtaining information, al-Ghazali rejected the use of torture. In his view, the social good rests in protecting the safety and dignity of the alleged thief. Al-Ghazali stated that "refraining from inflicting physical pain on a guilty person is insignificant compared to torturing an innocent person."[59]

Al-Ghazali's captives scenario must be interpreted in light of the third condition he stipulated for integrating textually unqualified *maslaha* into Islamic doctrine, that is, the condition of scope. Al-Ghazali requires that the novel situation must represent a universal interest (*maslaha kullyia*) that benefits the entire community and is not confined to a segment of it. Nowhere in the captives example does al-Ghazali mention saving the majority as a basis for accepting the sacrifice of innocent captives. Rather, he speaks, on a more holistic level, of "saving the entire Muslim community from destruction." It seems that al-Ghazali's condition of *maslaha kuliyya* is not akin to the greatest good, but is about securing the existence of the entire society and not simply the greatest number of its members.[60]

The overarching deontological framework on social good in Islamic doctrine does not necessarily suggest that considerations of economic efficiency are entirely excluded. As mentioned above, one of the manifestations of social good derived from the scriptures is the promotion of wealth in society. Under this manifestation of social good, efficiency could be considered as a benchmark to guide the normative analysis so as to achieve a socially good state of affairs under Islamic doctrine. There are situations where achieving efficiency will not necessarily entail an attack on deontological values. Life, after all, is not necessarily a zero-sum game where every increase of wealth in society would lead to the undermining of life, freedom, or dignity. On the contrary, increased wealth has potentially instrumental value in promoting life, freedom, and human dignity. However, economic efficiency is not a first

58 Al-Ghazali, *al-Mustasfa*, 489.
59 Ibid., 490.
60 Compare Anver M. Emon, "Natural Law and Natural Rights in Islamic Law" (2004–2005) 20(2) *Journal of Law and Religion* 374.

order principle in Islamic doctrine. The priority is always for a set of duties to promote life, rights, and freedom. Economic efficiency can operate to supplement the deontological framework of the Islamic doctrine but cannot override it.

VI *MAQASID* AS A FRAMEWORK FOR HUMAN FLOURISHING

The existing scholarship on *maqasid* does not provide sufficient guidance on how to translate *maqasid* into a more concrete principle to respond to policy challenges. We do not know how we should go about transferring the objectives of promoting life, intellect, justice, and wealth into implementable normative standards to guide modern-day policymaking. I think the time has come to start searching for a new understanding of notions of the social good that *maqasid al-Sharia* aims to achieve – an understanding that would take *maqasid* into a totally new level of development. I believe it is not enough to understand *maqasid* through an isolated search for *ratio legis* and the purposes of the divine will, and aim to apply them to new challenges. There is room to understand the idea of *maqasid* as a standalone framework for human flourishing in the Islamic worldview. In Chapter 5, I develop the idea of *maqasid al-Sharia* into a broad theory of social justice in Islamic doctrine and analyze the fairness of different social institutions, including IP, within its constraints. Here, I will focus on a more modest task, that is, identifying the main features of *maqasid al-Sharia* as a framework for human flourishing.

First, the social good in *maqasid* is not defined by notions of average income or average happiness. Part of understanding the primary feature of the social good within *maqasid* as predominantly deontological in nature is that pursuit of the social good should not mean maximizing the aggregate good. The focus is not on average income or average happiness, as a simple, consequentialist approach would lead us to accept. *Maqasid* as a framework for human flourishing would focus on the essential needs to empower people to flourish. In this vision, people are treated as the ultimate purpose of the social good. This should not be difficult to accept. The system of *maqasid*, as constantly stressed since the eleventh century CE, seemed to depict the overarching purpose of the Lawgiver's order as the people themselves. Their flourishing is intended by the letters and spirit of the scriptures. Since the very beginning of the idea of *maqasid*, the focus seemed to go beyond promoting choices that maximize good consequences for the majority to considering, inter alia, choices that promote life, intellect, dignity, and freedom. Arguably, these choices are intrinsically valuable for people as individuals. This understanding of *maqasid* is not entirely novel. It is evident from both the classical version of *maqasid*, as introduced by al-Ghazali, and modern versions.

Second, we need to reemphasize that the list of *maqasid* should not be considered a closed one. We should approach the textual authorities from which *maqasid* is to be derived with an open mind. This means that benchmarks for identifying the social good can be developed in number and scope. Most scholars would agree that the Quran and the Sunnah are full of normative visions of the protection of human life, growth, justice, knowledge, cooperation, capabilities, rights, freedoms, political participation, the environment, and so forth. We should take note of these and expand upon them. For instance, we should ask why the Lawgiver emphasizes that establishing justice on the earth is an objective of the entire revelation. Why did there exist constant incentives for Muslims to emancipate slaves in conservative seventh-century Arabia? Why did the Lawgiver command that "There is no compulsion in religion"?[61] Why does the Lawgiver instruct people to cooperate to achieve progress?[62] Why do the texts encourage distribution of wealth through prohibiting monopoly and encouraging *zakat* (alms giving)? Do all these commands and instructions mean that the Lawgiver intends to establish a just, free, and cooperative society? How can we proceed to reflect these conceptions within our lawmaking process and institutional arrangements? In Chapters 5 and 6, I will come back with some illustrative applications of these notions as part of my understanding of the theory of justice in Islamic doctrine.

Finally, a solid understanding of *maqasid* and its associated notions of the social good should be open to learning from comparative research on human flourishing. Islamic jurisprudence would potentially find a rich informational horizon in modern theories on human flourishing. Indeed, there are several theories in modern sociolegal scholarship that broadly intersect with the notions of *maqasid* as a general framework for human flourishing. For instance, the human development paradigm and the capabilities approach, largely associated with the research of Nobel laureate Amartya Sen, Martha Nussbaum, and Mahbub ul-Haq (1995), stress objectives of law and policy-making that are largely compatible with the nature and scope of *maqasid*. As is the case with *maqasid*, which promote the interests of people as the ultimate purpose of the social order, the human development paradigm and the capabilities approach are both centred on enhancing people's lives, freedoms,

61 Quran, trans. Pickthall, 2:256.
62 Ibid., 5:2.

and opportunities. Similar to *maqasid*, these frameworks of human flourishing constantly emphasize that the morally required choices in well-ordered societies are not necessarily those which maximize good consequences for the majority. Rather, the goal is to establish a society that promotes life, good health, knowledge, freedom, and opportunities.[63] In this sense, both *maqasid* and these theories on human flourishing subscribe to a pluralist vision of human flourishing. There is no single merit-based or efficiency-based justification for justice and social good.

While it is not my purpose to embark on a thorough comparative analysis, I would suggest that more research should be done towards that end. I believe that this is important, not only for Muslims in majority Muslim countries, but also in countries where Muslims are small minorities. There is a very good normative reason to bring an Islamic vision of the social good to the public sphere and search for common ground with other visions to foster mutual understanding and a stable social order. Below are two examples.

A *First Example: Maqasid as Human Development Measures*

Sen and ul-Haq proposed a vision of social good and human flourishing that focused on people as both the means and the purpose of the good life. Throughout their influential accounts on human development, they argued that a good life in society is not defined by increased economic growth or any of the income-related measures. A good life is achieved by empowering people through the creation of an enabling environment where people can live healthy lives, obtain access to educational opportunities, and secure a decent standard of living. Some of the objectives of a well-ordered society as introduced by Sen and ul-Haq are reflected in the *Human Development Report* and measured by the Human Development Index (HDI). According to the Report and the HDI, in order for people to flourish, the system must enable them "to lead a long and healthy life, to acquire knowledge and to have access to resources needed for a decent standard of living."[64] The report goes on to mention additional objectives ranging from "political, economic and social freedom to opportunities for ... enjoying personal self-respect and guaranteed human rights."[65] There is an obvious link between the objectives listed in the report and HDI and those of *maqasid*, particularly those related to

63 Amartya Sen, *Development as Freedom* (Anchor Books, 2000) 5, 63; Mahbub ul Haq, *Reflections on Human Development* (Oxford University Press, 1995) 4, 15.

64 United Nations Development Program, *Human Development Report* 1990, 10, http://hdr.undp.org/en/reports/global/hdr1990/chapters

65 Ibid.

the promotion of *nafs* (life), *'aql* (intellect), freedoms, and *mal* (wealth). For instance, the *maqsad* (objective) of preserving *nafs* includes promoting good health, as stated in the report. Similarly, preserving *'aql* and *mal* are tantamount to acquiring knowledge and achieving a decent standard of living.[66] There is an opportunity here to study these measures to broaden our understanding of *maqasid al-sharia* and search for ways to reflect this understanding in more concrete policy measures.

B *Second Example:* Maqasid *as Central Capabilities*

Martha Nussbaum's capabilities approach is another good example with broad similarities to *maqasid*. Nussbaum's central thesis is that in order to establish human flourishing, the constitutional order of a society must mobilize laws and institutions to achieve a threshold level of central capabilities. Broadly speaking, these central capabilities strongly intersect with the notions of *maqasid*. First, in common with *maqasid*'s emphasis on the intrinsic value of human life as an end in itself, the capabilities list includes objectives to preserve and promote (1) "life," (2) "bodily health," and (3) "bodily integrity." Second, the list also includes objectives that reflect the preservation and promotion of *aql* (intellect): (4) "senses, imagination, and thought" and (5) "practical reason." Third, capabilities list includes (6) "being able to hold property and having property rights," which broadly fits into one of the essential *maqasid*, the promotion of wealth (*mal*).

A final interesting parallel between the central capabilities and *maqasid* relates to the concept of *takaful* (social cooperation) as one of the objectives of Islamic law and (7) "affiliation" and (8) "emotion" as part of the central capabilities. Modern Islamic scholarship on *maqasid* introduces *takaful* as a central objective among *maqasid al-Sharia*. For instance, Yusuf al-Qaradawi deduces from several textual authorities a strong emphasis on values such as belonging, brotherhood, sisterhood, interaction, and collaboration.[67] Similarly, Nussbaum argues that human flourishing requires the establishment of an enabling environment where people can interact, care for each other, cooperate, and work together.[68]

Make no mistake, I am not suggesting that *maqasid* is identical to the human development paradigm and the capabilities approach. The scope of

66 Ibn Ashur, *Maqasid*, 65, 302.

67 Yūsuf al-Qaradawi, *al-Takaful al-Ijtima'i fi daw' al-Shari'a al-Islamiyya* (Maktabat Wahba, 2009) 7–40.

68 Martha Nussbaum, *Creating Capabilities: The Human Development Approach* (Harvard University Press, 2011) 33, 34.

maqasid is not necessarily compatible with every detail in these frameworks. There will certainly be room for disagreements, particularly on the scope of malleable concepts such as freedoms and rights. The secular perspective of the human development paradigm and the capabilities approach does not necessarily subscribe to the Islamic worldview on the scope of gender equality, as one example among others. Islamic doctrine would not change any of its positivist stipulations in its textual sphere in order to be compatible with comparative theories on human flourishing. Equally, proponents of comparative theories also have the freedom to reject notions they disagree with. Disagreements over certain issues do not necessarily undermine the common values among these normative frameworks. Similarities, such as treating people as the ultimate purpose of the good and supporting the intrinsic value of life, intellect, justice, freedom, and rights would be a very good place to start.

There are strong reasons to believe that linking *maqasid* to the aforementioned normative frameworks on human flourishing would be a positive addition to the concept of *maqasid* as a vehicle for reform in pluralist societies in and outside the Muslim world. Firstly, the link shows that *maqasid*, as a representation of Islamic legal philosophy, shares with other visions of human flourishing several common values and some common, essential commitments. This represents an opportunity for those who view Islamic doctrine as a source of violence to rethink their assumptions. Second, the link sends a clear message to Muslims, particularly those who view any global normative movement with great skepticism, that many of the values preached by comparative legal philosophies and international organizations are not necessarily tools with which to dominate the Muslim world and undermine its Islamic legal heritage. There is more room for harmony than there is for disagreement over the basic values of human flourishing. Finally, and most importantly, the link provides very rich platforms to inform the scope and application of *maqasid* in modern society. The qualitative and quantitative research conducted to explore ways to promote objectives such as health, education, growth, and justice could also be used to put *maqasid* into action. We know that the promotion of the intellect is central to *maqsad* in Islamic legal philosophy, and modern studies on human flourishing through knowledge and education could enhance our vision on what we need to do within Muslim communities to better realize this central *maqsad*. In fact, this study is largely about exploring the best way to reflect the objectives of Islamic legal philosophy in IP policymaking. In doing so, I rely on modern IP scholarship to craft a vision of how to design an IP system that best reflects the notions of social good in Islamic doctrine.

3

Justifying IP under Islamic Doctrine

The purpose of this chapter is to initiate the discussion on explaining IP within Islamic doctrine. In part, this chapter introduces a descriptive account of the ways in which notions of IP are discussed in Islamic jurisprudence. In the process of doing so, it embarks on a critical analysis of IP theory to provide deeper and broader theoretical coverage of IP under Islamic doctrine.

While very little research has been carried out to justify IP under Islamic doctrine, in reality all countries with predominantly Islamic populations formally recognize and protect IP. Influential Islamic bodies, including the leading Sunni Islam authority al-Azhar[1] and the Council of Islamic *Fiqh* (Jurisprudence) Academy,[2] have issued legal opinions (*fatwas*) legitimizing IP protection under the textual sources of Islamic law.

At a theoretical level, jurists and scholars of Islamic doctrine engage with IP from different perspectives. A minority view within Islamic jurisprudence held, to different degrees, that notions of IP are not compatible with Islamic doctrine. It pointed to the fact that textual sources of Islamic doctrine do not directly address intangible assets and interpreted this lack of direct textual support to mean that IP protection is rejected or should be highly restricted in any legislative environment informed by Islamic doctrine. However, a majority view held the position that IP can find support in the positivist and normative sources of Islamic doctrine. This view sought to make a rough case on IP as being a fair reward for labor and an important means of generating wealth.

I take issue with the way in which existing scholarship has addressed IP theory. Most scholarship consulted while writing this book does a good job in

1 Al-Azhar *Fatwa* Committee in a number of opinions issued on April 20, 2000 and August 16, 2001 (cited in Heba Raslan, "Shari'a and the Protection of Intellectual Property, the Example of Egypt" (2007) Intellectual Property Law Review, 503.

2 International Islamic *Fiqh* Academy, Resolution No. 43 (5/5) 1988 regarding incorporeal rights, http://zulkiflihasan.files.wordpress.com/2009/12/majma-fiqh.pdf

identifying conceptual similarities between notions of IP and a few Islamic principles. However, so much more could be done. The overwhelming majority of jurists contend that Islamic doctrine treats intellectual creations as property and grants protection for owners and creators. I explain that their analysis is fragmented and incomplete.

In this chapter, I explore additional theoretical frameworks in which to canvass Islamic sources and Islamic jurisprudence with a view to providing a more solid theoretical justification for IP. I start this work by consulting comparative scholarship on IP theories. In particular, I enquire into possibilities to access comparative justifications, as introduced in important works in the field including Justin Hughes's, William Fisher's, and Robert Merges's accounts on IP theories. I discuss whether it is possible to broadly talk about labor, efficiency, and personality-based justifications for IP under Islamic doctrine. Then I move on to discuss to what extent IP protection can be justified under Islamic doctrine. Here, I heavily rely on Islamic doctrine's vision of the social good. In particular, I deploy *maqasid* to determine the extent to which an IP holder can control his or her intellectual product under Islamic doctrine.

I IP IN ISLAMIC SCHOLARSHIP: THE MINORITY VIEWS

Scholars of Islamic doctrine have not unanimously agreed that IP protection could be justified under Islamic textual sources. A few objections were raised suggesting the existence of underlying inconsistencies between various injunctions within the Quran and the Sunnah and notions of IP. Those objections, however, do not enjoy wide currency in Islamic studies on IP, so I will not discuss them in any detail.

An extreme view within Islamic legal scholarship holds that IP is a concept alien to Islamic teachings, which has been imposed by the West to dominate and control the developing world.[3] This view relies on an unpopular opinion in Islamic jurisprudence, according to which the sources of Islamic law do not treat intangibles as a proper object of property rights. A reflection of this view can be seen in a *fatwa* issued by the late Mufti of Pakistan Muhammed Shafi'e rejecting copyright protection for authorial works on the basis that they represent an abstract construct unsupported by Islamic sources.[4] I will show

3 Qais Mahafzah, Basem Melhem, and Hitham A. Haloosh, "The Perspective of Moral and Financial Rights of Intellectual Property in Islam" (2009) 23 *Arab Law Quarterly* 464.

4 Abu Zied A. Bakre, "Mulkiyyat al-Ta'if Tarikhan wa Hukman" (1986) 2(2) *Journal of International Islamic Fiqh Academy* 220.

below that, although Islamic law did not develop an indigenous counterpart for IP, it certainly supports notions of ownership over intellectual products.

Another view in Islamic scholarship suggests that some forms of IP, particularly copyright, are inconsistent with fundamental textual principles regarding the management of knowledge in Islam. These are the prohibition on the concealment of knowledge and the encouragement of its dissemination. For instance, the Prophet is reported to have said that "the one who conceals knowledge would appear on the day of resurrection as reined in a bridle of fire."[5] Some scholars read this textual authority broadly and suggested that it categorically prohibits the concealment of useful knowledge in any shape or form, including exclusive rights to control literary works.[6]

I do not agree with this proposition. First, it fails to define "knowledge" in the context of the *hadith* cited. Does it include all forms of knowledge? Could it be that the Prophet only intended to instruct against withholding religious knowledge rather than all forms of ideas and expressions? Second, the proposition does not show whether the prohibition includes situations where the creator or owner puts time, effort, and money into the creation of an intellectual product. In this case, would it be fair, under Islamic law, to deprive the creator of the opportunity to recoup some of the investment made in creating the intellectual product? Finally, the proposition focuses on one aspect of the IP regime, that is, the exclusive rights of the IP owner. It neglects fundamental doctrines within the IP system which require the dissemination of knowledge. These include limited protection terms, the requirement to disclose the specifications of the invention in patent law, and the doctrine of limitations and exceptions where knowledge sharing could take place without the consent of the rights holder.

A third opinion suggests that IP leads to easy gain (*maisir*), while the Quran and the Sunnah prohibit *maisir* and encourage Muslims to earn their *rizq* (income) through work. In many cases, intellectual content protected by IP could yield enormous revenues for the creator, who might have spent little effort and time in making the relevant intellectual product. A novel about a young wizard fighting evil could be written in a few months and end up generating hundreds of millions of dollars in revenue through the sale of books or from derivative works. Similarly, a programmer might spend very little time creating valuable software and earn millions of dollars in revenue. Some

5 Muhammed Amanullah, "Author's Copyright: An Islamic Perspective" (2006) *The Journal of World Intellectual Property* 303.

6 Abdul-Same' Abu al-Khīr, *al-Haq al-Mali li al-Muwalif fi al-Fiqh al-Islami wa al-Qānun al-Masri* (Wahba Library, 1988) 1.

contend this means that IP protection could lead to *maisir* and therefore should not be protected under Islamic law.[7]

There is a legitimate concern that in some cases an IP holder obtains substantial market leverage that is incommensurate with the intrinsic value of his or her labor. One may doubt the fairness of granting expansive exclusive rights to control products that the IP holders managed to obtain through little intellectual input or through substantial assistance and inspiration from existing innovation. Is it possible to allow *ex ante* regulatory intervention to adjust the scope of the property right? Should the law empower courts to restrict market leverage in cases where an IP holder possesses substantial control over an IP product which it created with very little effort? I will leave a detailed discussion of this issue for Chapter 6.

However, I do not believe that objections around disproportionate reward poses an existential threat to justifying IP under Islamic doctrine. The view expressed above, without sufficient analysis, assumes that the norm in the world of IP is to make substantial amounts of revenue from little or no work. This is inaccurate. Those who end up as billionaires from selling IP products are by no means the norm. The majority of creators spend time and effort creating knowledge and cultural products and end up earning incomes within or below the national average in many nations. For instance, the average income of professional artists in Australia is significantly lower than in other areas of activity.[8] Professional authors in the United Kingdom and Germany make around 64 percent and 42 percent of the average national income, respectively.[9] Why deny IP protection for everyone based on the assumption that some will earn easy money? Even those few who end up earning large sums of money from disproportionate work are not necessarily engaging in *mayser* practices within the meaning prohibited by the textual sources. Creators of intellectual products that generate massive amounts of money are exposed to financial obligations in different forms, including registration and renewal fees, income taxes, expenses related to managing the product, and compensation where their creations cause harm to others. On top of that, there could be alternative doctrinal adjustments to address disproportionate rewards that do not necessarily involve rejecting IP rights altogether.

7 Raslan, "Shari'a and the Protection of Intellectual Property," 529.

8 David Throsby and Anita Zednick, "Do You Really Expect to Get Paid?" (2010) 9, www.australiacouncil.gov.au/__data/assets/pdf_file/0007/79108/Do_you_really_expect_to_get_paid.pdf

9 Martin Kretschmer and Philip Hardwick, "Authors' Earnings from Copyright and Noncopyright Sources: A Survey of 25,000 British and German Writers" (July 13, 2007) 23, www.cippm.org.uk/alcs_study.html

In general, opponents of IP failed to establish a convincing case on the existence of a conceptual conflict between Islamic sources and IP. IP is a diverse field with complex concepts and doctrines. Strong exclusive rights that restrict the dissemination of knowledge or contribute to generating disproportionate gains for IP holders should not lead us to think that we should condemn IP as incompatible with Islamic sources. Concerns around the scope of exclusive rights and disproportionate gains could be addressed through renegotiating the relevant IP doctrines – for instance, proposing shorter terms, stronger threshold requirements for originality in copyright, tighter patentability requirements, and redefining the scope of the exclusive rights, to name but a few. I will come back to these issues with more analysis and examples in Chapters 5, 6, and 7. However, these objections, do not seem to provide well-reasoned grounds for rejecting IP protection altogether.

II IP IN ISLAMIC SCHOLARSHIP: THE MAJORITY VIEW

The majority of contemporary Muslim scholars hold the position that Islamic law should protect legal rights over intellectual products. They rely on verses from the Quran and sayings of the Prophet to point out conceptual harmony with existing notions of IP protection. This is an important contribution. However, it falls short of demonstrating the possibility of discerning a fully developed theoretical framework for IP in Islamic legal philosophy.

A *IP as* Mulk

One view holds that the concept of *mulk* (ownership) in Islamic law is not confined to physical property. It also includes intangible assets. Since intellectual products are intangible assets, they must be treated as *mulk* worthy of protection.[10] Fathi al-Durini traced the position on intangible assets in the main schools of the Sunni version of Islamic doctrine (Hanafis, Malikis, Hanbalis, and Shafi'is). His findings indicate that the overwhelming majority of jurists contend that the protection available in the textual sources for physical property also includes intangible assets.[11] For example, Shihab al-Din al-Qarafi (d. 1285 CE) devotes parts of his famous treatise (*al-Furuq*) to addressing the ownership of nonphysical assets under Islamic law.[12] A minority of classical Hanafi scholars reject intangibles as a form of *mulk* as they consider

10 Bakre, *Mulkiyyat al-Ta'if*, 66.

11 Fathi al-Dirini, *Haq al-ibtikar fi al-fiqh al-islami al-muqāran* (al-Risāla Foundation, 1977) 20.

12 Al-Qarafi, *al-Furuq* (3rd ed., Dar Al-Salam Publications, 2010) vol. 3, 1009.

physical possession an essential requirement for granting property rights under Islamic law.[13] But al-Durini objects to this view and argues that "no direct or indirect rejection of protecting intangible assets can be found in the Holy Quran, the Sunnah, nor in any other source of Islamic law."[14]

The view that *mulk* is not confined to physical property does very little to convince us why intangible assets should be compared to physical property in the first place. It starts from a proposition that Islamic law protects *mulk* because it is useful (*bihi manfa'a*). However, no adequate explanation is provided to address two important challenges. First, how is ownership of physical property rights justified under Islamic law? Second, do physical property and IP share similar characteristics that justify extending property rights to intangible items? I argue below that a sound theory on extending legal protection from physical property to intangible items must start by unpacking the justifications provided for physical property under Islamic law and then defining similarities with intangible items and explaining why protection should be extended to those items.

B IP Promotes Wealth

Another view within Islamic studies of IP proposes a consequentialist analysis to justify IP from an Islamic perspective. The Quran instructs Muslims to increase their wealth – 'seek from the bounty of Allah."[15] The Prophet himself used to trade for his family and praised trade that leads to acquiring wealth for the benefit of all members of society. IP should be protected under Islamic law because it promotes innovation. This view assumes that if no protection is provided, people will find no incentive to create useful cultural products such as books, or make new technologies and produce products to make people's lives easier. Accordingly, IP promotes wealth as encouraged by Islamic sources. Therefore, it must be protected under Islamic law.[16]

This view seems to have an intuitive appeal. It is true that one of the main objectives of Islamic doctrine, as discussed in Chapter 2, is to promote wealth. However, this view suffers from weakness on three fronts. First, there is no conclusive evidence to support the assumption that people are better off with IP protection. It is probably true that some data could be found to show that IP can promote innovation in some situations. However, the idea that people will

13 Raslan, "Shari'a and the Protection of Intellectual Property," 517.
14 Al-Dirini, *Haq al-ibtikar*, 42.
15 Quran, trans. Sahih International, 62:10.
16 Amir Khory, "Ancient and Islamic Sources of Intellectual Property Protection in the Middle East: A Focus on Trademarks" (2003) 43 *IDEA: The Journal of Law and Technology* 165.

create intellectual products only if they are promised legal protection does not account for widespread practices where people are intrinsically motivated to write books, participate in open source movements to make software products, or write entries in Wikipedia. Additionally, the consequentialist analysis is not a solid justification for some essential features of the IP system, such as moral rights. Many would argue that moral rights are granted not because of a potential utilitarian benefit but because it is the right thing to do for the authors who have expressed their personalities in a work of art. Finally, this view does not explain how far we can go in protecting IP to promote wealth. IP can have a negative impact on third-party interests safeguarded by the objectives of Islamic law, such as life and intellect. It could affect access to patented pharmaceuticals needed to save human life and educational materials needed to promote intellect. This view does not take these other objectives of Islamic law into account.

C *IP and Productive Labor*

A third view draws a link between an injunction within Islamic law that aims to promote productive labor and IP.[17] The Prophet is reported to have said that "whoever revives a vacant piece of land shall own it."[18] This text is a foundational authority on land ownership in Islamic jurisprudence, known as *ihya al-mawat* (developing or improving vacant land). Under this authority, if a person occupies an unclaimed piece of land for a certain period of time and spends effort and money on developing it, he or she will have the right of ownership over that land. Creators of intellectual products are making similar productive contributions. Accordingly, individuals spending time and effort writing literary works, inventing technology, or creating new drugs deserve to be granted legal rights over their creations.

This view does a good job of justifying ownership rights in products that require hard work, similar to the work needed to develop a dead piece of land into something useful. For instance, it might be relevant to justifying ownership over pharmaceutical products or multivolume literary works created after painstaking research. However, IP protection covers a wider range of intellectual products. For instance, copyright protection includes any subject matter reducible into material form, regardless of the level of labor. This includes letters, email, and amateur videos. How do we go about justifying the

[17] Jamar D. Steven, "The Protection of Intellectual Property under Islamic Law" (1992) 21 *Capital University Law Review* 1085.

[18] Mansur al-Bahūti, *Kashaf al-Qina' 'an matn al-Iqna'* ('ālam al-Kutub, 1997) 398.

ownership of these intellectual products? Additionally, as was the case with the previous utilitarian account of IP, this view does not tell us much on the appropriate scope of IP protection justified under productive labor in Islamic doctrine. Does productive labor qualify for absolute ownership under Islamic law? If it does not, what are the sources and scope of the limits? The following section proposes a more comprehensive theoretical coverage to justify IP protection from an Islamic perspective.

III AN ALTERNATIVE CONCEPTUAL FRAMEWORK

Identifying conceptual similarities between Islamic values derived from textual sources and IP is a good start. More needs to be done. In this chapter, I aim to expand on the existing Islamic literature on IP theory and provide an expanded theoretical coverage that accounts for the complex doctrines and operational features of IP. There is room within Islamic sources and scholarship to introduce general theories of IP. The sources of Islamic law, along with existing Islamic scholarship on physical property, could be canvassed to construct a more comprehensive theoretical framework to justify IP protection and define its limits. In this part, I show that a link can be drawn between Islamic sources and jurisprudence and theories justifying IP protection in comparative legal philosophy. In this context, comparative legal philosophy employs three theories, namely fairness, utilitarianism, and personality to justify IP. Theorists undertook a conceptual analysis arguing that these theories can be extended to justify IP protection in the same way they were used to justify physical property. One of this chapter's fundamental propositions is that, conceptually, it is possible to initiate discussions on broader IP theories of fairness, efficiency, and personality within Islamic doctrine. In other words, an argument can be made that property in general can be seen, from an Islamic perspective, as being fair, efficient, and personally satisfying, and these characteristics apply to intangible assets as well.

I want to be clear that I am not suggesting that justifying IP protection under Islamic doctrine should rely on comparative theories of IP. While there are substantial similarities between Islamic doctrine and comparative accounts on justifying property and ownership, there are points of divergence as well. As I will show later in this chapter, the normative vision of the purpose of property rights in Islamic doctrine offers conceptually different grounds for reorienting property, including IP, so as to take the social good into consideration. These grounds may eventually lead to limiting or modifying the existence or the scope of individual IP rights.

A A Bridge to the West: *Justifying IP in Comparative and Islamic Scholarship*

I shall start here with a different approach to justifying IP under Islamic law. I will not follow existing scholarship in justifying IP protection through searching for one conceptual framework to justify every aspect of the IP system. Instead, I hope to show that it is better to use the three theories together as a unified comprehensive framework to explain why the law should provide coverage for the disparate features, doctrines, and institutional practices in the IP system. My argument is that it is possible to rely on Islamic sources and scholarship to construct a more comprehensive theoretical framework for IP that, to a large extent, fits with modern theories justifying IP. I see no problem in using a Western context to explain an Eastern concept.

1 Locke, Islamic Doctrine, and IP

One of the popular justifications for IP comes from John Locke's proposition that a person who labors upon common, unowned resources should have a natural right of property in the resultant fruits of her or his labor. Since the creation of intellectual products requires labor, the law should also provide legal rights for the exploitation of these products. Failing to do so unfairly violates a natural right to property. I argue here that this exact same argument finds strong support in Islamic doctrine.

In the fifth chapter of the second of his *Two Treatises of Government*,[19] Locke attempts to establish the case that fairness of private property rights stems from natural law. He maintains that "God gave the world to men in common,"[20] and that the resources of nature are available for all people.[21] He goes on to explain that each individual owns "the labor of his body and the work of his hands ... Whatsoever then he removes out of the state that nature hath provided, and left it in, he hath mixed his labor with, and joined to it something that is his own, and thereby makes it his property."[22] Thus, "no man but he can have a right to what that is once joined to, at least where there is enough, and as good, left in common for others."[23] Labor that leads to appropriating resources held in common is a legitimate means of obtaining

19 John Locke, *The Second Treatise of Civil Government* (1690), www.constitution.org/jl/2ndtreat.htm

20 Ibid., sec. 34.

21 Ibid., sec. 27.

22 Ibid.

23 Ibid., secs. 27, 44.

property rights and excluding others, by the force of the law, from interfering with the owner's exploitation of the resultant subject matter. The most prominent example in Locke's treatise is the private ownership of land (sections 32, 37 and 43). An individual who tills, plants, improves, and cultivates a piece of land,[24] has "added something to [it] more than nature . . . and so [it] became his private right."[25] "Thus, labor ... [gives] a right of property, whenever anyone was pleased to employ it upon what was common."[26]

The theological premise upon which Locke's work is based (section 34) is emphasized throughout the Quran. For instance, "it is He (God) who created for you (humankind) all of that which is on the earth."[27] The same basic argument as that on which Lockean theory justifying property rights is based is used to establish the fairness of private property under Islamic law. Muslim scholars define the resources held in common as *mubah*.[28] From an Islamic perspective, *mubah* includes vacant land (*al-ard al-jarda*), marine life (*al-hayat al-bahriyya*), animals (*hayawanat*), plants (*nabatat*), and mines (*ma'adin*).[29] Generally, appropriation from *mubah* is a means to ownership (*mulkiyyah*) for the appropriator.[30] This takes place through labor that leads to possession of some of the resources that are held in common (*ihraz al-mubah*).[31]

Another striking similarity with Locke's treatise is the frequent use of the example of land in Islamic jurisprudence to justify granting title over resources held in common (*ihraz al-mubah*). As we have seen above, this is known as *ihya al-mawat* (reviving vacant land), and relies on a *hadith* of the Prophet which implies that whoever labors on an unclaimed piece of vacant land will have the right to own that land.[32]

Ali al-Khafif and Muhammad Abu Zahra explored the meaning of *ihya al-mawat* in the literature of the four dominant schools of Islamic law, namely Hanafis, Malikis, Shafi'is, and Hanbalis.[33] Both scholars argue persuasively that the term *ihya*, used frequently in Islamic law, resembles the concept of

24 Ibid., sec. 32.
25 Ibid., sec. 28.
26 Ibid., sec. 45.
27 Quran, trans. Sahih International, 2:29 and 45:13.
28 See, for instance, Muhammad, *al-Mulkiyyah wa Nazareyat al-'aqd fi al-Shari'a al-Islamiyya* (Dār al-Fikr al-Arabi, 1977) 55.
29 Mustafa al-Zarqa, *al-Madkhal al-Fiqhi al-A'am* (Dār al-Qalam, 1998) 336; Muhammed M. Shalabi, *al-Fiqh al-Islami: Tarīkhuhu wa Madārisahu wa Nazareyatahu: al-Mulkiyyah wa al-'aqd* (Al-Dār al-Jami'iyya, 1985) 381.
30 Muhammed R. Said, *al-Mal, Mulkkiyyatuh, Istithmaruh wa Infāquh* (Dār al-Wafa, 2002) 60.
31 Shalabi, *al-Fiqh al-Islami*, 381.
32 Atef A. S.Ali, *Ihya' al-Aradhi al-Mawat fi al-Islam* (The League of the Islamic World, 1996) 58.
33 Ali al-Khafif, *al-Mulkiyyah fi al-Shari'a al-Islamiyya* (Dār al-Fikr al-Arabi, 1996) 249.

labor in Locke's treatise. Ali al-Khafif contends that ownership of vacant land cannot be recognized without productive labor that adds something to the land and makes it more beneficial than it was in its original or natural condition.[34] Abu Zahra also gives examples of the kind of labor that qualifies for ownership of the vacant land. His examples are identical to the forms of labor needed to grant property rights under Locke's section 32, namely, tilling, improving, and cultivating.[35]

The concept of *ihraz al-mubah* was used as a basis for an Islamic labor theory well before Locke. Two examples help support this claim. Abu-Bakr ibn Abi al-Duniyya (d. 894 CE), in his book *Islah al-Mal* (Maintenance of Wealth), relies on several texts from Islamic sources to establish the claim that collecting, sorting, organizing, reshaping, and creating *mubah* justifies the acquisition of private property rights under Islamic law.[36] Abdul Rahman ibn Khaldun (d. 1406 CE), a prominent Muslim sociologist, developed, in his highly acclaimed book *al-Muqaddimah* (The Prolegomena), an advanced theory of labor that shares the same logic as that of Locke. In the fifth chapter of the first volume of *al-Muqaddimah*, Ibn Khaldun refers to several verses from the Quran which show that God has given the world with all its natural resources for the benefit of humankind.[37] Those capable of labor have an equal opportunity to appropriate those resources, and once an individual exerts his or her labor on a certain object, it becomes his or her own property and thus "cannot be taken without remuneration."[38] Accordingly, exerting labor to develop resources held in common (*mubah*) is a means of ownership (*ihraz*) worthy of protection and third-party exclusion according to both Islamic and Western legal scholarship.

Labor theory, as discussed above, is widely used to justify property rights in intellectual products. Here, I argue that insofar as the ownership of intangible products can be justified by reference to Locke, it can also be justified in relation to the sources of Islamic law. I will rely on leading Western scholarship to make my case. Justin Hughes and Robert Merges establish strong conceptual links between Locke's accounts on justifying physical property rights and the normative foundations of IP.

34 Ibid., 249.

35 Abu Zahra, *al-Mulkeyyah wa Nazareyat al-'aqd fi al-Shari'a al-Islamiyya* (Dār al-Fikr al-Arabi, 1977) 125.

36 Abu-Bakr Ibn Abi al-Duniyya, *Islah al-Mal*, ed., Mustafa M. Alghatat (Al-wafa Publications, 1990) 84.

37 Ibn Khaldun, *al-Muqaddimah* (Bayt al-Ulūm wa al-Funūn wa al-Adab, 2005) vol. 2, 259.

38 Ibid., 259.

Hughes argues that private ownership of ideas can be justified following Locke's approach through three propositions. First, the state of nature, or what Locke calls the "common," can be imagined as the realm of free ideas. Second, transforming ideas into intellectual products generally requires labor by the individual. Third, ideas can be made property and, yet, there must be "enough, and as good, left in common for others," as Locke's proviso of non-waste suggests.[39] Similarly, Merges asserts that Locke's theory "applies . . . well . . . to intellectual property" because the "stock of public domain information from which individual creators draw fits closely with Locke's conception of a vast realm of common resources." Accordingly, "the claiming of intellectual property rights out of the public domain follows the same logic as the emergence of property rights from the state of nature."[40] Merges goes on to make an even bolder claim, arguing that:

> [N]ontrivial creations presumably requiring significant effort are often said to be at the heart of IP law. Although labor is relevant in establishing some real property rights, it is a much larger, and much more prominent, part of the IP landscape. So Locke is more pertinent to IP.[41]

Mubah and commons are identical concepts. Both represent a realm of free resources available for appropriation through labor. *Mubah* can also be thought of as the free stock of public domain information from which individuals can appropriate ideas through their intellect and transform them into intellectual products in the form of artistic and innovative creations. The appropriation of ideas and their transformation into a new form is tantamount to *ihraz al-mubah* (appropriating unowned land or other free natural resources). In other words, since *mubah* and the public domain of information are identical, the acquisition of intellectual property rights from the public domain is equivalent to claiming property rights from *mubah*.

2 Efficiency-Based Justifications of IP

The second and perhaps the most widely used of the three theories relies on the popular utilitarian analysis of property rights. At the core of the utilitarian analysis is a proposition that lawmakers must design a public system of rules that maximizes net social welfare. In justifying property rights, this means that

39 Justin Hughes, "The Philosophy of Intellectual Property" (1988) 77 *Georgetown Law Journal* 287.

40 Robert P. Merges, *Justifying Intellectual Property* (Harvard University Press, 2011) 32–33.

41 Ibid., 33. William Fisher, "Theories of Intellectual Property," in *New Essays in the Legal and Political Theory of Property* (Cambridge University Press, 2001).

those who make socially valuable transformations to resources held in common must be granted private property rights to encourage everyone else to work, thereby maximizing aggregate public welfare. The proposition goes on to suggest that if the law does not provide legal protection for this productive labor, individuals will be deterred from making useful contributions and thereby leave society worse off. Lawmakers need to avoid this economically inefficient result by allocating to productive laborers private property rights in the fruits of their labor. Although the utilitarian analysis is largely associated with Bentham's ideal of "the greatest good for the greatest number," Albert Brogan maintains that it was Locke who formulated the basic thesis of early eighteenth-century utilitarianism in his labor theory.[42] Here, there is shift of focus in the analysis. Instead of justifying property on the basis of the intrinsic value of the natural right to property as a fair reward for labor, the utilitarian analysis employs an instrumental vision arguing that property rights should be protected to induce more people to work.

The same underlying logic could also apply to IP as a utilitarian bargain. The public system of rules must promote the creation of intellectual products to maximize wealth. The law must provide exclusive rights to individuals who transform the raw ideas held in common into socially valuable intellectual products. This is said to incentivize more people to allocate more of their time, energy, and resources to produce socially valuable knowledge and cultural products. William Landes and Richard Posner's economic analysis of copyright law is an ideal example of existing Western literature that views IP as a utilitarian bargain. Landes and Posner argue that the failure to protect the cost of labor (e.g., the work done in writing and publishing) will pose a danger that writers will be disincentivized from making socially beneficial contributions to overall social welfare.[43] The US Constitution adopted a utilitarian approach to IP, stating that the purpose of making patent and copyright laws is "to promote the progress of science and useful arts."[44]

Partial support for the utilitarian account of IP – albeit with many reservations – can be drawn from Islamic doctrine. I mentioned in Chapter 2 that, according to *maqasid al-sharia*, the promotion of wealth is a recurrent theme throughout the textual sources of Islamic doctrine. As such, the promotion of wealth has been proclaimed, since al-Ghazali, as a fundamental objective of

42 Albert Brogan, "John Locke and Utilitarianism" (1959) 69(2) *Ethics* 79.

43 William M. Landes and Richard A. Posner "An Economic Analysis of Copyright Law" (1989) 18 *The Journal of Legal Studies* 325, 326.

44 Article I, section 8, clause 8 of the US Constitution.

Islamic lawmaking. One possible manifestation of this objective can be found in the broad outlines of the utilitarian account on lawmaking mentioned earlier: enhancing economic efficiency. In other words, as is the case with the normative vision of utilitarianism, Islamic doctrine also aims to enhance economic efficiency. However, I need to be cautious here in drawing such a link between *maqasid* and utilitarianism. I hope that I have already made the case in Chapter 2 that Islamic doctrine predominantly promotes deontological views on the social good. I mentioned that economic efficiency is not excluded from the doctrine's views on social good. However, in the general hierarchy of the social good, efficiency-based considerations are to be classified as a second order principle. This means that it is possible to pursue law reform to create wealth, but this must take place within the confines of other important deontological objectives within the Islamic framework on human flourishing. This entails prioritizing other objectives such as promoting life, intellect, and freedoms, to name but a few. I will analyze this further below.

Accordingly, under Islamic doctrine, lawmakers can rely on the proposition that the law should provide property rights to incentivize people to develop natural resources into useable products if it is proven that this will to promote wealth. Ibn Khaldun was among the first Muslim sociologists to expound an economic efficiency perspective highlighting an instrumental value for labor in creating wealth. He argues that human labor is a fundamental requirement for wealth accumulation. He goes on to explain that "profits and gains, in their entirety or in the majority of cases, are value realized from human labor." Ibn Khaldun notes that the "welfare and prosperity of a society are dependent on the magnitude of labor." This means that societies in which the fruits of human labor are protected have a greater potential to flourish in comparison with those that are reluctant to provide such protection.[45]

An argument can be made under Islamic doctrine to provide initial support for efficiency-based justifications for IP. Insofar as granting exclusive rights to sell and make copies of intellectual products is proven to incentivize wealth creation, those rights must be protected under Islamic law. Protection will be reduced only when the exclusive rights undermine other objectives of Islamic lawmaking, such as life or intellect. In line with the utilitarian stance, the late, renowned Muslim scholar Wahba al-Zuhili issued a *fatwa* sanctioning copyright under Islamic law, based on the proposition that it brings about an overall public interest for society.[46]

45 Ibn Khaldun, *al-Muqaddimah*, 260–62

46 Wahba al-Zuhili, *Haq al-Ta'alīf wa al-Nashr wa al-Tawzi'* (al-Risalah Foundation, 1977) 188.

3 Personality, *Fitrah*, and IP

Finally, property rights in comparative philosophy are also justified with reference to Kant. According to Kant, every individual, by virtue of his or her humanity, has a natural desire to control external objects. Although Islamic textual sources and scholarship do not share Kant's sophisticated analysis of property as an extension of the individual's will and a means to autonomous life, they both agree on a fundamental proposition. As is the case in the Kantian justification of property, the Quran and the Sunnah recognize the human need to control external objects as *fitrah*, a fundamental natural disposition compatible with natural reason. Kant expounds his theory of property rights in a work entitled *Metaphysics of Morals*. In this work, Kant imagines a state of affairs where individuals act in accordance with natural reason. A fundamental part of the natural reason of each individual is an impulse to appropriate external objects as his or her own, excluding all others from interfering with such appropriation.[47] This natural desire to control external objects is best satisfied by the state's protection of certain property rights.

Both the Quran and the Sunnah describe the desire to appropriate and control wealth as a natural disposition (*fitrah*). In the context of highlighting the negative nature of greed as undesirable social behavior, the Quran states: "And you (humans) love wealth with immense love."[48] In the textual recorded traditions of the Prophet, it is reported that he confirmed this meaning. "If the son of Adam were to possess two valleys of riches, he would long for the third one."[49] Exegetists of the Quran, both classical and contemporary, interpret the verse in the context of acknowledging the human impulse towards ownership and the need to regulate this impulse to avoid greed and accept the broader social function of property.[50]

A widely held proposition in Islamic jurisprudence is that Islamic law is compatible with *fitrah* and that its values and teachings, collectively, do not aim to undermine natural dispositions but rather to promote and regulate them.[51] Accordingly, proclaiming a particular practice as *fitrah* must have a normative implication. Since the desire to control wealth is *fitrah*, Islamic

47 Immanuel Kant, *Groundwork for the Metaphysic of Morals* (Cambridge University Press, 2012).

48 Quran, trans. Sahih International, 89:20.

49 Translation of Sahih Muslim, Book 5, No. 2282, www.iium.edu.my/deed/hadith/muslim/005_smt.html

50 Al-Hussien ibn Masoud al-Baghawi, *Tafsir al-Baghawi* (Dar Taiyyba, n.d.) vol. 8, 509; Muhammed al-Shanqiti, *Adwa' al-Bayan fi Idah al-Quran bi al-Quran* (Dar al-Fikre, 1995) vol. 9; Sayyid Qutb, *Fi Zilal al-Quran* (Dar al-Shuruq, 2003) vol. 6, 3957.

51 Ibn Ashur, *Maqasid*, 81 et seq.

law must protect this *fitrah*. This protection is best achieved through a set of property rights in external objects attached to individuals and acquired without violation of Islamic law.

Islamic literature justifying IP does not attempt to show that the relationship between IP rights and *fitrah* is analogous to that between physical property rights and *fitrah*. Thus, it might be useful to rely on comparative scholarship to make the case that, insofar as physical property is compatible with *fitrah*/natural disposition, ownership of intellectual products is also a natural human disposition and therefore justified under Islamic law.

Modern comparative scholarship has sought to inject the underlying themes of personality theory to make the case that, as with physical property, the need to control intellectual products through IP rights is "crucial to the satisfaction of some fundamental human needs"[52] or fulfills "human instinct," which is bound up with the existence of an individual's will.[53] Moreover, the personality theory is even more pertinent to IP than it is to physical property. Since ideas and expressions, the subject of IP law, embody an individual's personality, the desire to control the manifestations of those ideas and expressions is even stronger compared to external physical objects. In other words, the natural disposition to control one's own ideas and expressions is more apparent compared to a piece of land or fish caught in the wild.[54] Justin Hughes suggests that personality theory could play a very important role in explaining some doctrines and practices in IP laws. These include (a) legal protection for highly expressive intellectual products such as poems, novels, and paintings; (b) legal protection for a set of moral rights enabling authors to be acknowledged as the creators of their works and to have the right to control the publication and integrity of their works. The human instinct to control wealth, recognized under textual authorities, could form a basis for integrating personality-based justifications into the positivist right to ownership under Islamic law. I see no reason not to approve the broad outlines of the argument that even the ownership of intellectual products through IP rights is compatible with *fitrah*.

VI FOUNDATIONAL PLURALISM

The persuasive powers of each theory are limited in explaining the complex forms and doctrinal details of the IP system. A better approach to justifying IP

52 Fisher, "Theories of Intellectual Property," 5.

53 Merges, *Justifying Intellectual Property*, 72.

54 Compare Hughes, "The Philosophy of Intellectual Property," 333 et seq.; Merges, *Justifying Intellectual Property*, 68 et seq.

is to think of the system as a diverse field with multifaceted aspects, doctrines, practices, values, and institutions. The next step is to find which of the three theories above best responds to a particular theoretical problem. In other words, we need to shift from one theory to another whenever we find that one of the three abovementioned theories falls short of providing a persuasive justification for a particular aspect of the IP system. Below are a few examples.

Labor theory seems to offer a strong theoretical grounding for intellectual products that require hard work, including many forms of literary works such as novels, technological products such as inventions, or business reputation acquired through producing high quality products over a period of time. However, the theory offers inadequate justification for ownership over intellectual products whose production requires little or no labor, including different forms of copyright subject matter such as photos, emails, letters, and amateur videos. Here, we can rely on the personality theory to justify ownership of these intellectual products, based on the assumption that these products represent an expression of personality. Similarly, when utilitarian justifications fail to account for important features of the IP system such as moral rights, the personality theory could be used to explain why those rights should exist.

As a second example, when we try to justify IP rights in products which do not adequately reflect personality, such as microchips, software programs, pharmaceuticals, and other technological products, we can turn to labor or utilitarian justification to compensate for the weaknesses of personality justification. For instance, we might rely on empirical research to support the proposition that the protection of pharmaceutical inventions through patent laws stimulates innovation in the pharmaceutical industry.[55] Therefore, patent protection can be justified under a utilitarian analysis as means of promoting net social utility.

As a final example, the labor and personality-based justifications do not seem to capture a significant feature of most forms of IP, that is, the limited duration of the protection. An argument suggesting that ownership of a certain intellectual product is fair or personally satisfying does not offer much guidance on whether the resultant property rights should be perpetual, as is the case with physical property. To overcome this doctrinal difficulty, we can rely

[55] See, for instance, William Fisher, "Intellectual Property and Innovation: Theoretical, Empirical, and Historical Perspectives," paper prepared for the Programme Seminar on Intellectual Property and Innovation in the Knowledge-Based Economy (2002); John Kay, "The Economics of Intellectual Property Rights" (1993) 13 *International Review of Law & Economics* 337, 344–46.

on the utilitarian theory to make the case that limited protection for patent, copyright, and some other forms of IP promotes access to knowledge and culture, enriches the public domain, and allows people to build upon intellectual products whose protection has expired. In this way, a limited period of protection might be conducive to more innovation and enhanced overall social utility.[56]

IP theories need to be brought together to form multidimensional theoretical frameworks justifying each component of the system. I believe that this is the best way to provide more comprehensive and coherent coverage for the system and remedy the shortcomings associated with the attempts to force disparate rules and doctrines into a unidimensional theoretical framework.

V LIMITS ON INDIVIDUAL IP RIGHTS

Even if we were convinced that property rights in intellectual products are fair under labor theory, useful under the efficiency-based analysis, or personally satisfying under personality theory, we still need to define the limits of ownership. How far can an IP rights holder control his or her intellectual product? Existing scholarship on IP and Islamic doctrine does not take up this task. I believe the theoretical framework explored so far provides a benchmark for exploring the limits of IP rights under Islamic doctrine.

In Western legal philosophy, Robert Merges relied on Locke and Kant to discuss possible limits on the appropriation and exercise of IP rights when they impact third parties' interests. He argues that Locke's charity proviso and Kant's universal principle of right (UPR) are designed in recognition of the potential conflicts between the exclusionary nature of property rights and the public interest. Both Locke's proviso and Kant's UPR suggest that property rights must be restricted when granting or exercising them would inflict harm on other individuals. Merges then moves on to apply Locke and Kant to the world of IP, where he suggests that UPR and charity proviso can be used as a basis to impose limitations on IP rights, particularly when they affect human survival, as is the case with patents for AIDS drugs or patents on food products in poor developing countries.[57]

Similarly, justifying IP rights under Islamic doctrine as fair, useful, or personally satisfying does not lead by any means to absolute ownership.

56 Rufus Pollock, "Forever Minus a Day? Some Theory and Empirics of Optimal Copyright," paper presented to the Annual Congress of SERCI, Berlin, 2007, 16 (suggesting that a limited copyright term is important to stimulate the creation of more knowledge and cultural products).

57 Merges, *Justifying Intellectual Property*, 64, 87

The very legitimacy of the IP grant could be brought into question when the exercise of IP rights impinges on third parties' interests as laid out in *maqasid*. In order to outline the scope of the IP grant under *maqasid*, I need to draw from the materials introduced in Chapter 2 to show how *maqasid* could form a starting point to inform an Islamic theory of IP.

As explained in Chapter 2, *maqasid*, as a manifestation of the social good in Islamic doctrine, is centered on the promotion of human flourishing. This is reflected in the plural values embodied in *maqasid* since its systemization in the eleventh century CE. These plural values suggest that the public system of rules must be arranged to prioritize the protection of life, intellect, justice, and freedom, among other things. Under *maqasid*, actions are judged as legitimate only if they are in harmony with the Islamic conception of flourishing. Ibn Abd al-Salam (d. 1262 CE), in *al-Qawa'id*, and al-Shatibi (d. 1388 CE), in *al-Muwafaqat*, indicate that the entire point of Islamic lawmaking is to further the interests of people so that they may flourish. When they exercise their rights – including property rights – they have the liberty to further their own interests in any way they deem appropriate. However, when the existence or operation of such rights interferes with *maqasid al-Sharia*, the rights can be nullified or modified. According to Ibn Abdul al-Salam, the right could interfere with *maqasid* when it results in *mafsada* (harm) to others. In this case, the lawmaker must lean towards preventing harm from being inflicted on others, regardless of the potential loss to the owner.[58] In the realm of property rights, the doctrine of abuse of rights (*su isti'mal al-haqq*) was devised in Islamic scholarship to ensure that the acquisition and exercise of those rights conform to *maqasid* and that property must be structured to promote the plural values embodied in *maqasid*.

The basic rule of the doctrine is that a property right – like any other right within Islamic law – has a social function in addition to its private functions for the proprietor. Its legitimacy, at both the acquisition and exercise stages, is contingent on ensuring that third parties are not harmed as a result of the initial grant or exercise of the property rights. Property rights are considered to cause harm when they violate any of the objectives of Islamic lawmaking explained in Chapter 2, including the promotion of life, wealth, liberties, justice, and cooperation. Fathi al-Durini provides examples where property rights could be restricted or modified when they undermine third parties' interests protected under *maqasid*. For instance, (a) the scope of land ownership will be modified under Islamic law when such ownership causes harm to

[58] Abd al-Salam, Qaw'aid al-Ahkām, vol. 1, 83 Al-Shatibi, *al-Muwafaqat fi Usūl al-Shari'a* (Dār ibn Affan, 2003) vol. 2, 331.

third parties, including blocking access or the supply of water; (b) a person can be forced to sell their goods or services to prevent harm associated with a monopoly; and (c) a person might be forced to destroy or rebuild a property on the verge of collapse to avoid injuring others.[59]

The bottom line is that all property rights must conform to *maqasid*. We know from Chapter 2 that *maqasid* was essentially intended to further human flourishing. But the question that we need to answer here is: How can we explain the normative implications of this proposition? What does it mean to say that property must contribute to serving human flourishing under *maqasid*? I believe that the best way to put this proposition in policymaking terms is to think of *maqasid*-based limits on property as sources of legal claims for society, which entitle its representatives to structure and adjust property rights to account for the foundational elements of human flourishing under *maqasid*. The understanding that property rights are fair, useful, or personally satisfying can be retained, provided that the property conforms to *maqasid*. Now, I turn to explain how we can apply *maqasid* to a discussion of the appropriate scope of IP rights.

A *Maqasid and IP Norm Setting*

Maqasid can be very helpful in creating a conceptual edifice to separate individual IP rights and third-party interests in accessing and reusing IP products when doing so is compatible with *maqasid*. In fact, *maqasid* holds greater promise in the field of IP compared to physical property. As stressed throughout this book, *maqasid* aims to reorient law and policymaking to take account of a set of plural values necessary for human flourishing, including the protection of human life, intellect, justice, and freedoms. IP protection enables owners to control access to intellectual products necessary to promote values such as life, the intellect, and liberties. For instance, patents on drugs or food can impact the quality of life, educational materials can impact the nourishment of the intellect, and access to cultural products can impact liberty and self-autonomy. In this part, I shall sketch the main features of an IP system informed by *maqasid*. First, I show that the dual nature of rights under *maqasid* positions third-party interests at the center of the IP structure. Second, I explain how third-party interests are defined under *maqasid*.

59 Fathi al-Durini, *nazariyat al-ta'asuf fi isti 'mal al-hagg* (4th ed., Muassasah al-Risalah, 1988) 37.

B *The Dual Nature of IP Rights under* Maqasid

From the perspective of *maqasid*, individual IP rights have a dual function. The owner of the right can control how to use and exploit the intellectual product, provided that such use and exploitation fit into the plural values at the heart of *maqasid*. The role that *maqasid* is performing here is to make the validity of the granting of IP rights contingent upon third-party interests. *Maqasid*-based constraints are not constructs external to the IP right; they are layered into the individual right itself. Individual IP rights do not hold a position of supremacy, with third-party interests playing a secondary role. On the contrary, the very existence of the right depends on its conformity with *maqasid*. Whether we rely on natural rights analysis, personality theory, or efficiency-based claims to IP rights, the control of the IP right cannot run afoul of essential values protected under *maqasid*. The legitimacy of the private function of individual IP rights is conditional upon satisfying a social function, this is, promoting values protected under *maqasid*.

Viewing IP rights from the perspective of *maqasid* can be a game changer in the global debate over the place of users of intellectual products within the IP system. While IP systems throughout the world recognize users' interests through bundles of permitted uses, the limited way in which these are generally interpreted often makes them necessarily subservient to the interests of IP holders. As William Patry explains, the system assumes a natural state of affairs where the ability to control all unauthorized uses is the norm and the provisions protecting third parties are the exceptions.[60] The existing law gives individual owners exclusive rights as control mechanisms which can be used to prevent users from accessing drugs, food, reading, listening, viewing, and reusing knowledge and culture. In practice, IP law is shaped to empower rights holders to exercise substantial control over vital human needs. International IP instruments such as the Berne Convention,[61] the TRIPS Agreement,[62] and other international treaties entrench an "exceptions paradigm."[63] For instance, according to the "three-step test," any derogation from the exclusive rights is only permissible where it is limited to "certain special cases" that do not "conflict" with rights holders' "normal exploitation" and do not

60 William Patry, "Limitations and Exceptions in the Digital Era" (2011) 7(2) *The Indian Journal of Law and Technology*.

61 Berne Convention for the Protection of Literary and Artistic Works, Article 7.

62 Agreement on Trade-Related Aspects of Intellectual Property Rights, Article 12.

63 Paul Harpur and Nicolas Suzor, "Copyright Protections and Disability Rights: Turning the Page to a New International Paradigm" (2013) 36 *University of New South Wales Law Journal* 745.

"unreasonably prejudice" their "legitimate interests." Put simply, current IP systems are more about rights holders and less about users.

This exception rhetoric has come under substantial criticism in international scholarship. In copyright law, the Max Planck Declaration calls for a stronger recognition of third-party interests, as opposed to those of the owners, when interpreting the three-step test. The declaration notes that "there is no complementary mechanism prohibiting an unduly narrow or restrictive approach."[64] The declaration urges a more expansive reading of the test, which would ensure greater protection for user interests. Crucially, the declaration suggests that international copyright law should be interpreted in a way that "does not require limitations and exceptions to be interpreted narrowly."[65]

The systematic marginalization of users' interests needs to be reconsidered for at least two reasons. First, the modern digital environment has transformed the role of a great number of users of knowledge and culture from mere consumers of intellectual works into creators of these works. Internet technologies and personal computers are widely available to billions of people around the world. They provide great potential for the development of an enabling environment allowing users to reshape knowledge and culture. Users of internet technologies and personal computers have more opportunities to advance their personal interests, learn, express, and expand cultural production. These are not unsubstantiated observations but propositions that enjoy substantial empirical support in studies that examine user activism in innovation and creativity.[66] The exceptions paradigm seems to undervalue the importance of users' creativity. The centrality of the exclusive rights of IP holders means that much user creativity takes place in the periphery of underenforced IP laws, where users are free only to the extent that rights holders choose not to exert their rights.[67]

Second, the predominant owner-centric approach leads to essential issues such as access to medicine being addressed in a dehumanizing way. Treating

64 Christophe Geiger et al., "Declaration: A Balanced Interpretation of the 'Three-Step Test' in Copyright Law" (2010) 1 *Journal of Intellectual Property, Information Technology and E-Commerce Law* 119.

65 Ibid., 119, 120.

66 Niva Koren, "Making Room for Consumers under the DMCA" (2007) 22 *Berkeley Technology Law Journal* 1152; Eric von Hippel, *Democratizing Innovation: The Evolving Phenomenon of User Innovation* (MIT Press, 2005).

67 See John Tehranian, "Infringement Nation: Copyright Reform and the Law/Norm Gap" (2007) *Utah Law Review* 537; Tim Wu, "Tolerated Use" (2007) 31 *Columbia Journal of Law & the Arts* 617.

exclusive rights as the norm and public interests as exceptions enables rights holders to negotiate and litigate lifesaving initiatives when these initiatives involve their patents. In 1998, 39 pharmaceutical companies sued the government of South Africa over the enactment of legislation (the Medicines and Related Substances Control Amendment Act No. 90 of 1997) permitting the import of patented AIDS drugs.[68] Similar action was taken by the United States before the WTO Dispute Settlement Body in 2001 for the purpose of protecting US patent owners' "rights against a Brazilian initiative to permit local Brazilian companies to manufacture generic AIDS drugs at cheaper prices for poor populations."[69] The Doha Declaration recognized the severity of prioritizing exclusive rights over essential human needs and proclaimed that IP rights under "the TRIPS Agreement ... should not prevent member governments from acting to protect public health."[70] This development broadened the compulsory licensing scheme under TRIPS to allow manufacturers in developing nations to produce generic drugs and export them to poor nations in times of health crises. However, this development does not fix the underlying problem within the IP system. The system still treats the exclusive rights as superior. Pharmaceutical companies are still able to invoke their rights to dispute lifesaving initiatives.

The dual nature of IP rights under *maqasid* could provide a much-needed paradigm shift to transform the IP system from an author/inventor-centered system to a dual-objective system. A *maqasid*-based approach would reorient the discussion from the viewpoint of users and consumers of intellectual products. Here, IP would still be a legitimate instrument for protecting the private interests of the rights holder, but it must not override important social functions, such as users' creativity and public health. In other words, under *maqasid* individual IP rights are not superior to society's claims to access. Under the proposed shift, instead of thinking about the boundaries of IP rights as limited exceptions that have to be interpreted narrowly, as suggested by the three-step test, we should think of them as legal rights. They must be positioned at the center of the IP structure. A little over decade ago, the Canadian Supreme Court in *CCH Canadian Ltd. v. Law Society of Upper Canada* – a landmark decision – explicitly recognized the dual objective of copyright

68 Ellen, Hoen et al., "Driving a Decade of Change: HIV/AIDS, Patents and Access to Medicines for All" (2011) 14(1) *Journal of the International AIDS Society* 3.

69 Gavin Yamey, "US Trade Action Threatens Brazilian AIDS Programme" (2001) 322(7283) *British Medical Journal* 38.

70 "The Doha Declaration Explained," www.wto.org/english/tratop_e/dda_e/dohaexplained_e.htm

law.[71] The judgment dealt with what is known in the Canadian Copyright Act as "fair dealing" – a restriction of the owner's right for research purposes. The court stated that fair dealing is "perhaps more properly understood as an integral part of the Copyright Act than simply a defence." It specifically referred to it as "a user's right" which "must not be interpreted restrictively."[72]

C Plural Limitations on IP

Maqasid-based limits do not stop at transforming IP into a dual-objective system. They also provide further guidance on the nature of third parties' interests that could represent boundaries for individual IP rights. Here, I must reiterate the fundamental conclusion drawn in Chapter 2. In both the Quran and the teachings of the Prophet, there is an underlying normative vision that instructs lawmakers to seek to promote human flourishing. Under *maqasid*, human flourishing could be achieved if the public system of rules was designed to promote a threshold of objectives derived from Islamic law's textual sources. These objectives include promoting life, intellect, wealth, justice, freedom, and cooperation. Overall, these objectives promote a deontological approach to policymaking, where laws can seek to achieve economic efficiency only to the extent that they do not undermine people's rights to life, nourishment of the intellect, and liberty.

My argument here is that *maqasid* positions IP within a web of deontological, plural values. Put simply, copyright, patent, and other forms of IP protection must be designed to contribute to promoting life, intellect, wealth, justice, freedom, and cooperation, in addition to securing individual property rights. Existing foundational scholarship on *maqasid* does not provide much guidance on how to discern specific measures to guide law and policymaking in different fields, including IP. This is why I suggested in Chapter 2 that we must rely on the modern normative framework on human flourishing to inform the scope and applications of *maqasid*. Formal human development measures such as the Human Development Report and Human Development Index, along with modern scholarship on human flourishing such as that introduced by Sen and Nussbaum in the central capabilities approach, can be of great assistance in transforming the broad values of *maqasid* into implementable normative standards.

The different forms of IP laws have a direct impact on issues at the center of human development, including access to essential medicine and educational

71 [2004] 1 S.C.R. 339.
72 Ibid., para. 48.

materials, and a wide array of liberties crucial to self-development, including engaging with one's cultural medium through sharing, copying, and recreating knowledge and culture. Under *maqasid*, IP lawmaking must be guided to achieve human development ends. This means that IP law must be structured not only to pursue economic efficiency but, more importantly, to advance human development measures such as those enshrined in the HDI and the capabilities approach, including a healthy life, access to knowledge, social cooperation (*takaful*), and a set of individual social, economic, and political freedoms.

When IP rights intersect with human life, as is the case with patents on drugs or agricultural products needed by poor populations, the individual IP rights must be relaxed or modified to the extent necessary to provide access. The right to access is not an exception to the right to property. The right to access in this case is built into the fabric of the IP right and is a condition for its legitimacy. Under *maqasid*, the right to access is of a deontological nature. It trumps any efficiency claims based on the incentive theory. This means that access will be granted to promote the right to life, regardless of the potential loss to social utility.

Robert Merges argues that Locke's proviso and Kant's UPR "support a relaxing of patent rights over life-saving pharmaceuticals." However, he indicates that Locke and Kant are relevant in setting limits on property rights when those rights impinge on human survival but not necessarily in situations where drugs only extend life or alleviate major symptoms.[73] While *maqasid* certainly bears considerable similarity to Locke's proviso and Kant's UPR in the need to modify property rights in favor of third parties' needs, *maqasid* is different in that it places even more rigorous limits. As explained in Chapter 2, *maqasid* protects three levels of interests. The theory here is that Islamic lawmaking must not only secure necessities (*ḍarūrāt*) related to human survival; the law must also secure needs (*ḥājāt*) and improvements (*taḥsīnāt*) required to alleviate hardship or improve the quality of life. In line with this understanding, *maqasid* instructs lawmakers to consider access to medicine even in situations where the drug only contributes to extending life or treating symptoms, as opposed to survival

Similarly, the promotion of the intellect as a central objective of Islamic lawmaking could play an important role in ensuring that IP is structured to promote human ends as defined by human development measures, including

73 Merges, *Justifying Intellectual Property*, 81 (arguing that Locke's charity proviso does not help in providing limits on IP to improve the quality of life and Kant's UPR is not straightforward on the same issue).

access to knowledge as well as the promotion of the senses, imagination, and thought. I start here from a self-evident proposition. Access to educational material, the dissemination of knowledge, and the freedom to engage with and recreate culture are important to the nourishment of the intellect. Scholars of *maqasid*, both classical and modern, have listed the promotion of the intellect (*aql*) as an undisputed objective of Islamic lawmaking. Accordingly, an IP system crafted in line with *maqasid* must have built-in mechanisms to enable meaningful access to educational materials, knowledge, and a set of capabilities to recreate culture for self-development purposes.

In practice, existing IP laws, both international and domestic, recognize – to different degrees – the need to structure IP rights to promote essential human needs, such as access to life-saving medicine and educational materials. Exceptions and limitations exist to permit the copying of inventions and copyright-protected materials during times of national health emergencies to treat diseases or provide needed educational resources. However, large bodies of IP scholarship suggest that, in practice, these fundamental human needs are obscured by prevailing normative visions of IP centered on economic efficiency. I address these issues in the following chapter, in the light of Islamic doctrine's views on the social good.

4

Social Good in Islamic Doctrine and IP in Practice

In the previous chapter, I explained the theoretical foundations of IP from an Islamic perspective. The mainstream justifications for IP in comparative philosophy are, for the most part, accessible from various angles in Islamic doctrine. However, noticeable differences emerge when considering the nature and scope of limits imposed on IP under *maqasid*. The acceptance of IP – the notion of owning intangible assets – is not to be confused with existing IP policymaking and regulation at international level. *Maqasid*, as introduced in Chapter 2 and applied to limit the scope of IP rights in Chapter 3, will be used here to evaluate the main features of IP in practice. IP in practice refers to the dominant multilateral treaties such as the TRIPS Agreement, bilateral arrangements such as free trade agreements (FTAs), and policymaking in influential developed countries, mainly the United States. These global IP systems have largely been influenced by Western legal traditions. Arguably, other comparative concepts of ownership were not considered. It would be a good addition to the debate over the scope and strength of the global IP policy to evaluate IP in practice in light of *maqasid*.

The nature of the relationship between IP in practice and *maqasid* is open to discussion at a number of levels. However, the essential proposition of this chapter is that IP in practice and *maqasid* largely pull in different directions. Overall, IP norm setting in practice is mainly informed by utilitarian principles and the system is largely built to prioritize economic efficiency. The influential actors in international IP policymaking have been successful in shaping the main features of the global IP regime according to the proposition that strong control rights over knowledge and culture will maximize wealth and net social welfare. This normative vision seems to be in direct conflict with *maqasid*, which prioritizes a deontological normative vision as the first order principle and then supplements it with considerations of economic efficiency.

At a more specific level, several operational features of the IP system in general, and patent and copyright in particular, fail to fully account for some of the plural values of *maqasid*. It is not difficult to point out several features of IP in practice which appear to conflict with fundamental manifestations of the social good under Islamic doctrine. These include the promotion of *nafs* (life), *aql* (intellect), and *mal* (wealth), as measured according to modern human development standards such as access to health care, educational materials, and income.

I GLOBAL IP STANDARD SETTING AND *MAQASID*

The overarching theme of *maqasid*, as stressed throughout Chapter 2, is to prioritize deontological values as first order principles and economic efficiency as a second order principle. Efficiency is an important objective of Islamic lawmaking, but it cannot override plural deontological values. In other words, material gains and losses are acceptable as normative foundations of policymaking but only when they do not run afoul of fundamental human needs. I explained those needs in terms of human development measures including living a healthy life and nourishment of the intellect. Accordingly, an IP system informed by *maqasid* must take into consideration issues that go well beyond providing incentives and rewards to induce creativity, spur innovation, and achieve economic efficiency. Under *maqasid*, the system must be designed to ensure that any institutional arrangements regarding IP contribute to ensuring that human needs and capabilities are properly addressed.

There is enough evidence to support the proposition that much of the IP norm setting process is oriented towards economic growth and income, with minimal attention given to deontological values promoted by *maqasid*. In practice, influential developed countries introduce IP as a tool to spur innovation and increase economic growth. While some developing countries seek to emphasize the need to reorient IP norm setting to take into consideration human development priorities, developed rich countries put pressure on poor developing countries to accept IP provisions designed mainly to secure the economic interests of developed countries' creative industries. It is true that there are situations where developing countries have been successful in ensuring that access to knowledge for human development purposes is taken into account. However, as mentioned in Chapter 3, third-party interests in modern IP policymaking are subservient to the IP holders' exclusive rights.

The TRIPS Agreement is a good example to use when investigating the overall relationship between global IP regimes in practice and *maqasid*. First, it is now the most influential international instrument in the global IP landscape. Second, it covers most forms of IP. Third, most countries around the world are represented in the Agreement, including the majority of Muslim countries – where *maqasid* would matter most. Two issues that influenced the TRIPS Agreement's norm setting support the proposition that the global IP system – contrary to *maqasid* – was built to advance economic efficiency considerations from the very beginning.

First, developed countries sought to bring about a forum shift before negotiating the TRIPS Agreement. They wanted to ensure that IP was placed in a forum where economic efficiency considerations were the most important normative vision guiding the design of the IP world order. Whether they did that in full awareness of theoretical considerations is not at issue here. A great deal of pressure was exerted on developing countries: first to accept the inclusion of IP matters in multilateral trade negotiations, and then to accept a set of rules that are widely believed to be oriented towards private interests. Developed countries, led by the United States, realized that the issue of IP had to be integrated into the realm of international trade where efficient mechanisms for enforcement could be found.[1] Before the TRIPS Agreement, IP was not a trade and commerce issue. IP used to be solely administered by the World Intellectual Property Organization (WIPO). But WIPO was toothless; it lacked mechanisms to secure the economic interests associated with IP rights. Developed countries sought to reorient the discussions on IP and make it a trade issue to secure an efficient outcome for their IP-intensive industries – such as pharmaceutical and entertainment industries – supported by trade sanctions. As a result, the TRIPS Agreement created the World Trade Organization's (WTO) Dispute Settlement Body – an entity responsible for imposing "cross-collateral trade sanctions for non-compliance with the agreed minimum standards of intellectual property protection."[2]

Nobel laureate Joseph Stiglitz notes that a vision to protect the economic interests of developed countries was given priority in designing the TRIPS Agreement – a vision that would make it increasingly difficult to respond to fundamental human needs such as access to essential medicine in poor developing countries. He concludes that "[i]n fact, intellectual property should never have been included in a trade agreement in the first place."[3]

[1] Surendra J. Patel, "Intellectual Property Rights in the Uruguay Round: A Disaster for the South?" (1989) 24(18) *Economic and Political Weekly* 978–93.

[2] J. H. Reichman, "The TRIPS Agreement Comes of Age: Conflict or Cooperation with the Developing Countries?" (2000) 32 *Case Western Reserve Journal of International Law* 443–44.

[3] Joseph E. Stiglitz, "Intellectual-Property Rights and Wrongs," cited in Elizabeth Christopher, *Communication across Cultures* (Palgrave Macmillan, 2012) 357.

Second, the history of the Uruguay Round – leading to the adoption of the TRIPS Agreement – clearly shows that considerations of economic efficiency dominated the negotiations.[4] Developed countries including the United States, Canada, Japan, and those in Europe allowed economic efficiency-based arguments to inform the design and enforcement of the TRIPS Agreement. These countries claimed that IP protection was needed to protect the interests of their big taxpaying industries such as pharmaceuticals, computer software and microelectronics, entertainment, chemicals, and biotechnology, which lost over $50 billion in 1987 from lack of protection.[5] It is noteworthy that during negotiations a coalition was formed between these competing industries in the United States, the European Union, and Japan, which had a shared interest in pressuring the other parties to accept IP provisions that best served their (the coalition's) interests.[6] In this context, Joseph Stiglitz testifies that:

> I served on the Clinton administration's Council of Economic Advisors at the time, and it was clear that there was more interest in pleasing the pharmaceutical and entertainment industries than in ensuring an intellectual-property regime that was good for science, let alone for developing countries.[7]

Developing countries including Argentina, Brazil, Cuba, Egypt, India, Nicaragua, Nigeria, Peru, Tanzania, and Yugoslavia opposed the position taken by the developed countries.[8] These countries aimed to bargain for a norm-setting process guided not only by economic efficiency considerations but, more importantly, by fundamental needs. They wanted an IP system that would assist in achieving their basic development and growth objectives and securing adequate access to the essential medicines critical for treating millions of their citizens with HIV/AIDS and tuberculosis.[9] However, they were not successful.

In *Information Feudalism*, Drahos and Braithwaite point to the pressure exerted on developing countries to ensure that they accept the economic

4 Gana Ruth, "Prospects for Developing Countries under the TRIPS Agreement" (1996) 29(4) *Vanderbilt Journal of Transnational Law* 735, 737.

5 Adronico Aded, "Origins and History of TRIPS Negotiations," in Christophe Bellmann, *Trading in Knowledge: Development Perspectives on TRIPS, Trade, and Sustainability* (International Centre for Trade and Sustainable Development, 2003) 25.

6 Ruth Okidiji, "Public Welfare and the Role of the WTO: Reconsidering the TRIPS Agreement" (2003) 17 *Emory International Law Review* 819, 829, 845.

7 Joseph E. Stiglitz, "Intellectual-Property Rights and Wrongs."

8 Jane A. Bradley, "Intellectual Property Rights, Investment, and Trade in Services in the Uruguay Round: Laying the Foundations" (1987) 23 *Stanford Journal of International Law* 81.

9 Okidiji, "Public Welfare and the Role of the WTO," 821.

efficiency-oriented IP world order. They suggest that the TRIPS Agreement was not designed to secure the public good of every country involved. During the Uruguay Round in 1989, section 301 of the US Trade Act came into effect against the developing countries that would not subscribe to the US legislative agenda on IP. This provision was used as a tool to impose sanctions that include the withdrawal of trade benefits or to impose duties on commodities from foreign countries.[10]

Major developing countries, including Brazil and India, were listed in the so-called Priority Watch List as countries that are most deserving of trade sanctions. Other developing countries such as Argentina and Egypt were also listed in a Watch List as potential recipients of trade sanctions if they did not comply with the US standards on IP protection.[11] The reality was that developing countries had weak bargaining powers. The available options were limited. Either they accepted the IP standards advocated by the United States and other major developed countries, or exposed themselves to a range of trade sanctions that would negatively impact their economies. Herein lies the apparent coercion. The result, according to Ruth Okediji, is "an Agreement that in many respects reflected prevailing U.S. law and policy."[12]

Accordingly, it seems that the phrase in the preamble to the TRIPS Agreement which states that "intellectual property rights are private rights" means that they are so from the developed countries' perspective. Other, local concerning ownership and their roles in advancing society were not considered, including a vision based on *maqasid*.

II IP IN PRACTICE AND *MAQASID'S* PLURAL VALUES

In Chapters 2 and 3, I explained that *maqasid* promotes several values at the center of modern normative frameworks on human flourishing such as the Human Development Index (HDI) and the Human Development Report (HDR). These frameworks are similar to *maqasid* in at least two aspects. First, they place people's interests at the center of their vision of the social order. Under these frameworks, the morally required choices in well-ordered

10 Drahos and Braithwaite, *Information Feudalism*, 88 et seq.

11 Bello H. Judith, "Section 301: The United States' Response to Latin American Trade Barriers Involving Intellectual Property," (1989–1990) 21 *University of Miami Inter-American Law Review* 495, 502 (pointing out that the use of section 301 against Brazil came as a consequence of its refusal to "provide adequate patent protection for pharmaceutical products").

12 Okidiji, "Public Welfare and the Role of the WTO," 825.

societies are not necessarily those which maximize the good consequences for the majority, but rather those which create an equal opportunity for everyone to flourish and secure set intrinsic values. Second, they both focus on plural values to achieve human flourishing. The concept of *maqasid*, HDI, and HDR call for policymaking to arrange the public system of rules so as to achieve several objectives. These include, among other things, promoting *nafs* (life), *'aql* (intellect), and *mal* (wealth).

For instance, if we wanted to translate these objectives of lawmaking into implementable policymaking guidelines, one possible version would run as follows: The objective of preserving human life requires that legislation must not restrict access to essential and lifesaving medicine. Similarly, the objective of nourishing the intellect requires measures to enhance access to educational materials. Finally, the objective of promoting wealth entails the need to promote growth and decent living standards for all members of society.

IP laws bear considerably on important factors needed to achieve human flourishing under *maqasid*'s plural framework. The way in which patent, copyright, and other forms of IP are regulated affects access to healthcare, educational materials, and income. In this section, I aim to examine the relationship between *maqasid*'s plural values and some of the major operational features of the global IP regime. The questions I will attempt to answer here include: Does the patent system promote or impede access to medicine needed to preserve *nafs* (life)? Does copyright law provide sufficient mechanisms to promote *aql* (intellect) through access to educational materials? Finally, what is IP's overall impact in promoting *mal* (wealth), particularly in developing countries?

In order to find answers to these questions, I will have to consult a wide range of scholarship, which examines the relationship between different forms of IP rights and human development measures, including access to medicine, educational materials, and income. As a preliminary finding, this scholarship reinforces the main proposition of this chapter. IP in practice is primarily driven by economic efficiency considerations that benefit developed countries. Much of the qualitative and quantitative research examined here shows that several features of the global IP system are negatively linked – or, at best, neutral – in relation to the main measures of development: public health, access to education, and economic growth, particularly in developing countries. To use *maqasid* language, the economic interests of the developed world seem to be introduced as first order principles in designing IP, while promoting *nafs*, *aql*, and *mal* in developing countries comes second in stark contrast to the *maqasid* normative rhetoric.

A *Patents and Preserving* Nafs *(Right to Life)*

Since the TRIPS Agreement came into effect in 1994, most countries around the world have been required to broaden the scope of patentability to include pharmaceutical products and processes. This development has set up additional roadblocks to access to medicine in developing and least developed countries. The way in which the issue of patents on pharmaceuticals and access to medicine is framed under the global IP regime conflicts with *maqasid*. Under *maqasid*, preserving life – which includes access to medicine – should be at the center of policy and lawmaking. It trumps any calculations based on economic efficiency. There is plenty of evidence to suggest that under the global IP regime access to medicine is a limited exception that must be interpreted in a way that does not affect economic efficiency. Access will only be granted in very limited circumstances, in piecemeal fashion, and after satisfying a set of procedural requirements.

Many developing countries around the world face acute health challenges. Millions of people in poor developing countries are affected by life-threatening, communicable, and non-communicable diseases. If we take the statistics on communicable diseases like HIV/AIDS, malaria, and tuberculosis, the World Health Organization's (WHO) Fact Sheet on Infectious Diseases informs us that a significant number of people in developing countries are infected with dangerous diseases for which pharmaceutical treatments or cures are available. In Africa alone, around 24,200,000 are infected with HIV/AIDS. The number of people who needed antiretrovirals for HIV/AIDs increased from less than 5 percent in 2002 to over 42 percent by the end of 2008. In Africa as well, malaria has infected 174 million people. In 2010, over 270 people per 100,000 were infected with tuberculosis in sub-Saharan African countries. Overall, infectious diseases are one of the largest causes of mortality worldwide, with over 10 million people dying each year, more than 90 percent of whom are in the developing world.[13]

Those infected millions of people (who are still alive) in developing countries will not be productive and, thus, will be considered as inefficient human capital in terms of meeting development needs. The provision of pharmaceutical products for those people would help to alleviate their suffering. Some of these essential products are patented and protected with the threat of sanctions under the TRIPS Agreement.

[13] Kenneth C. Shadlen et al., "Globalization, Intellectual Property Rights, and Pharmaceuticals: Meeting the Challenges to Addressing Health Gaps in the New International Environment," in Kenneth C. Shadlen, *Intellectual Property, Pharmaceuticals and Public Health* (Edward Elgar, 2011) 14.

It is true that the lack of access to patented medicine is not the only factor in the health industry that places the lives of millions of people in different parts of the world in danger. Health care infrastructures and patient behaviors are also important contributing factors to health crises worldwide. However, the introduction of product patent protection under the TRIPS Agreement created legal barriers before developing countries, preventing them from acquiring the necessary knowledge to produce cheap generic alternatives for their suffering populations. Before TRIPS came into force, developing countries with reasonable manufacturing capacity (India, for instance) were able to produce patented drugs to meet their local needs. They were also able to supply least developed countries (LDCs), known generally to lack any manufacturing capacity, with some of the drugs they required at affordable prices.[14]

The TRIPS Agreement was the first international treaty to provide protection (supported by sanctions) for pharmaceutical products.[15] This protection was designed to meet the needs of the pharmaceutical industry in the developed world without "adequately [addressing] the medical access needs of the world's poor."[16] The agreement created strong exclusionary rights enabling the pharmaceutical industry in developed countries to monopolize the supply of patented drugs. Driven by economic efficiency considerations, pharmaceutical companies would normally choose to sell the patented drug at the highest price the market could offer. For instance, when the first patent-protected antiretroviral treatment for HIV was introduced, it was offered at $10,000 per patient per year. Such a price is out of reach for millions in the developing world.[17]

If a developing country wants to produce a patented lifesaving drug, it must wait 20 years.[18] Acting outside the scope of TRIPS could be considered "theft," accompanied by the risk of being brought before the WTO Dispute Settlement Panel for noncompliance with TRIPS, as was the case with South Africa and Brazil.

For developed countries, the TRIPS standards on IP protection in general and on patents for pharmaceuticals in particular were only minimum

14 Bhaven. N. Sampat, "The Accumulation of Capabilities in Indian Pharmaceuticals and Software," in Hiroyuki Odagiri et al., *Intellectual Property Rights, Development and Catch-Up: An International comparative Study* (Oxford University Press, 2010) 368.

15 Article 27, "Patentable Subject Matter."

16 Jamie B. Heren, "TRIPS and Pharmaceutical Patents: The Pharmaceutical Industry vs. The World" (2009–2010) *Intellectual Property Law Bulletin* 43.

17 Germán Velásquez, "The Impact of the Agreement on Trade-Related Aspects of Intellectual Property Rights (TRIPS) over Access to Essential Medicines" (2006) *Centrale Sanitaire Suisse Romande* 15.

18 Peter Drahos, "Four Lessons for Developing Countries from the Trade Negotiations over Access to Medicines" (2007) *Liverpool Law Review* 16.

obligations. They continued to erect more legal barriers preventing access to cheap generic medicines through bilateral agreements with developing countries. Such agreements predominantly took the form of free trade agreements (FTAs) entered into by the European Union and the United States with both developed and developing nations. FTAs include IP provisions that increase the standards of protection offered in the TRIPS Agreement to what is known as "TRIPS Plus. In the area of pharmaceutical patents, two main barriers are normally present. First, developing countries are required to introduce supplementary protection certificates into their patent protection. These certificates provide for an extension of the duration of patent protection for up to five years to compensate patentees for regulatory delays preventing them from immediately exploiting the patent. Second, FTAs oblige developing countries to introduce data exclusivity protection (DEP). DEP forces developing countries to protect, for up to eight years, data submitted for the purpose of obtaining an authorization to put a pharmaceutical product on the market. In 2007, Oxfam conducted an empirical study on the impact of DEP in the US–Jordan FTA on drug prices in Jordan. Oxfam notes that:

> Multinational pharmaceutical companies have prevented generic competition for many medicines by solely enforcing data exclusivity provisions in Jordan's IP law . . . According to Oxfam's analysis of 103 medicines registered and launched since 2001 that currently have no patent protection in Jordan, at least 79 per cent have no competition from a generic equivalent as a consequence of data exclusivity.[19]

The compulsory licensing (CL) scheme under the TRIPS Agreement enables developing countries to relax patent protections to respond to public health crises. Under the CL provisions in the TRIPS Agreement, developing countries can temporarily set aside patent protection and allow local manufacturers to produce, import, and distribute patented products without prior permission from the patent holders. The Doha Declaration (2001) reaffirmed developing countries' ability to use compulsory licenses "to protect public health." The declaration also contributed to the amendment of Article 31(f) of the TRIPS Agreement to allow developing countries with manufacturing capacity to manufacture generic drugs for export to least developed countries (LDCs).[20]

[19] Oxfam, "All Costs, No Benefits: How TRIPS-Plus Intellectual Property Rules in the US-Jordan FTA Affect Access to Medicines" (Oxfam Briefing Paper, March 2007) 7, http://donttradeourlivesaway.files.wordpress.com/2011/01/all-costs-no-benefits.pdf

[20] Jaime B. Herren, "TRIPS and Pharmaceutical Patents: The Pharmaceutical Industry vs. The World" (2010) *Intellectual Property Law Bulletin* 43, 58.

While CL provisions constitute an important first step towards promoting the right to life through providing access to drugs in developing countries, the overall structure of the TRIPS Agreement itself and the attitudes of the pharmaceutical industry in practice make CL provisions of limited utility. CL operates under the "three-step test" (3ST), as laid down in Article 13 of the TRIPS Agreement. Article 13 clearly indicates that the exclusive right to control inventions, including pharmaceutical inventions, is the norm. Any exceptions or limitations, including access to medicine, will only be permissible in "certain special cases" that do not "conflict" with the rights holder's "normal exploitation" and do not "unreasonably prejudice" its "legitimate interests." CL provisions in the TRIPS Agreement reinforce the superiority of the exclusive rights of the patentees by requiring developing countries to satisfy a set of procedural conditions in order to be able to issue compulsory licenses for lifesaving drugs. These procedural conditions include prior negotiations with the patent holder and the payment of adequate remuneration. Furthermore, any decision to grant such a compulsory license is subject to judicial review. Pharmaceutical companies will, in most cases, rely on these provisions to reinforce the rights rhetoric permitted under TRIPS and make the issue of access to essential medicine a difficult task for developing and least developed countries.

The major stakeholders in the pharmaceutical industry are small, homogeneous, well organized, and well financed. As of 2009, 10 firms from developed countries, including the United States, the European Union, and Japan, accounted for 45.1 percent of global pharmaceutical sales. The industry heavily relies on patents to protect its commercial interests in developing countries where, since the 1980s, it has expanded its presence in the production and distribution of pharmaceutical products. For decades, the industry has successfully ensured that patent laws and policies are crafted so as to prioritize its interests. It has the ability to lobby governments and policymakers in developed countries to effectively undermine initiatives facilitating access to medicine that would potentially affect their revenues. For instance, despite the fact that a few countries have amended their patent laws to implement the Article 31(f) waiver allowing generic medicine to be exported to poor countries at low prices, in reality only Canada has used this waiver to date.[21] Pharmaceutical companies put pressure on both developed and developing countries to accept that their monopoly rights in inventions are similar to personal rights of ownership and should receive the same legal protection. The extent to which a particular developing country is reliant on the US market or

[21] Shadlen et al., "Globalization, Intellectual Property Rights," 2, 19.

vulnerable to US trade pressures makes it increasingly difficult to treat access to medicine as a fundamental human right.[22] A dominant feature of US FTAs with developing countries is the inclusion of restrictions on the flexibility to use CL to relax patents on pharmaceuticals.[23]

The CL scheme under the TRIPS Agreement does not adequately capture the fundamental nature of access to medicine as a component of preserving *nafs* (life) under *maqasid*. The existing provisions do not situate access to medicine as a fixed, broad "right to access." Instead, access to medicine is viewed as a limited exception that must be interpreted narrowly on a case-by-case basis.[24] Against this backdrop, the pharmaceutical industry has, over the years, refused to grant access to essential medicines and engaged in heated negotiations and legal battles with several developing countries including South Africa, Thailand, Brazil, Rwanda, India, and Vietnam.[25] Emboldened by the international patent system, pharmaceutical companies normally seek to maximize their profits in developing countries by offering patented essential drugs at prices only the rich can afford. For instance, in South Africa, Flynn, Hollis, and Palmedo statistically documented pharmaceutical firms' tendency to offer essential drugs at prices that "only the top 10% can afford."[26] It is understandable that pharmaceutical firms are rational commercial actors. They seek to maximize their profits and increase economic efficiency for their shareholders. However, we must have a strong system in place to ensure that this does not happen at the expense of the right to a good life.

The way in which preserving *nafs* (life) as a fundamental pillar of *maqasid* is framed takes our normative vision on the access to medicine issue in a different direction. Instead of starting from economic efficiency considerations raised by the pharmaceutical industry, *maqasid* would start from the perspective of people suffering from diseases threatening their quality of life, and in some cases, life itself. The pharmaceutical industry's right to control access will only be valid insofar as it does not undermine access to medicine to save life, even one single life. The Quran, the most important source of

22 Shadlen et al., "Globalization, Intellectual Property Rights," 152

23 B. Mercurio, "TRIPS-Plus Provisions in FTAs: Recent Trends," in L. Bartels and F. Ortino, eds., *Regional Trade Agreements and the WTO Legal System* (Oxford University Press, 2006) 215–38.

24 TRIPS Agreement, Articles 27–34.

25 Jerome H. Reichman, "Compulsory Licensing of Patented Pharmaceutical Inventions: Evaluating the Options" (2009) 37(2) *Journal of Law, Medicine & Ethics* 247–63.

26 S. Flynn, A. Hollis, and M. Palmedo, "An Economic Justification for Open Access to Essential Medicine Patents in Developing Countries" (2009) 37(2) *Journal of Law, Medicine & Ethics* 184–209.

maqasid, unequivocally supports this *maqasid*-based proposition: "whoso saveth the life of one, it shall be as if he had saved the life of all mankind."[27]

B *Copyright and Promoting* al-'Aql *(Intellect)*

Maqasid, through its promotion of the intellect, recognizes access to education as a fundamental human right. In this, *maqasid*, broadly speaking, overlaps with a few international treaties such as the Universal Declaration of Human Rights (Article 26), the International Convention against Discrimination in Education (Article 1) and the International Covenant on Economic, Social, and Cultural Rights (Article 13). As is the case with promoting and protecting *nafs* (life), the promotion of the intellect is a concept of a deontological nature according to *maqasid*. It has intrinsic value and is not subject to economic efficiency calculations. In this part, I examine the extent to which the current international copyright system reflects this *maqasid*-based value through an analysis of its interactions with the right to access educational materials.

Islamic scholarship on *maqasid*, as stressed in Chapter 2, agrees that one of the fundamental objectives of Islamic lawmaking is to protect and promote the human intellect (*al-'Aql*). There is no detailed explanation in the textual sources on the extent of this normative vision of the intellect. However, several textual authorities, both in the Quran and the Sunnah, have regularly been used to argue that the nourishment of the intellect is an overarching Islamic principle that must guide law and policy according to the Islamic vision of a fair society. These textual authorities can be traced back to three different groups. First, both the Quran and the Sunnah prohibit the consumption of intoxicants owing to their capacity to impair the intellect's ability to apply knowledge. Second, they both encourage believers to use their intellect to expand their knowledge about their environment. Finally, an oft-cited textual authority from the Sunnah classifies the virtue of pursuing knowledge as a religious duty. It is reported that the Prophet has said that "seeking knowledge is an obligation upon every Muslim."[28]

My analysis of the interaction between *maqasid* and the international copyright regime starts out from the proposition that the emphasis on promoting the intellect and pursuing knowledge signifies the existence of a right of access to education in Islamic legal philosophy. This proposition is not

[27] Quran, trans. Pickthall, 5:32.

[28] Sunan Ibn Mājah, 220, http://library.islamweb.net/hadith/display_hbook.php?bk_no=173&hid=220&pid=109091

difficult to justify. If Islamic law must promote the intellect according to *maqasid*, it must promote access to education. Access to education is the key to protecting and developing people's intellectual capabilities.

By any standards, education is considered a cornerstone of human development. Its importance is increasing in the age of the information economy, where the driving factor of prosperity and rapid change is knowledge-based innovation. Access to educational materials, including textbooks and journal articles, is a fundamental part of the right to education.[29]

According to UNESCO's 2016 *Global Education Monitoring Report*, textbooks are a scarce commodity in many developing countries around the world. The report examines data from over 30 developing countries located mostly in Africa and South America. The data shows that students at different levels "lack books altogether or are required to share them extensively with others."[30] This suggests that, in developing countries, access to educational materials is the exception, not the norm. The report also indicates that "the cost of textbooks is a key barrier that prevents children from having access to the learning materials they need."[31] So, even if there are textbooks on the shelves, students must pay for them.

To be clear from the start, I am not suggesting that the copyright system is the only construct depriving children in developing countries from accessing educational materials. There are other important factors including the public education infrastructure, funding, corruption, and so forth. However, there is evidence, from both the structure and application of the international copyright system, which shows that the current copyright law is not designed to be part of the solution.

The current international copyright framework, particularly as depicted in the Berne Convention, the TRIPS Agreement, and the WIPO Copyright Treaty (WCT), does not reflect the dual nature of the exclusive rights of *maqasid*, as explained in Chapter 3. These instruments systematically promote the interests of copyright holders. They do not seem to place the interests of children in Africa and other poor developing nations on equal footing by ensuring adequate and effective access to educational materials. Materials are dearly needed to promote intellect, autonomy, and self-development.

Overall, the language and structure of the Berne Convention clearly shows that the system is essentially concerned with securing the private interests of

29 Ruth. L. Okidiji, "The International Copyright System: Limitations, Exceptions and Public Interest Considerations for Developing Countries" (2006) *International Centre for Trade and Sustainable Development (ICTSD)* 32.

30 UNESCO, *Global Education Monitoring Report* (January, 2016) 23.

31 Ibid.

copyright holders and expanding their ability to control knowledge and culture. The convention demonstrates its owner-centric approach from the very beginning when it refers in its preamble to the countries of the Union "being equally animated by the desire to protect, in as effective and uniform a manner as possible, the rights of authors in their literary and artistic works." As for the interests of developing countries, which are in vital need of access to educational materials, they do not seem to have similar importance. Developing countries had to wait until 1971 for limited recognition of their right of access to knowledge, which was placed in an appendix that is widely believed to be inadequate and ineffective, as will be seen below.

Publishers and providers of the most needed educational materials are located in the developed world.[32] They have benefited from the fact that the international copyright system makes the educational materials their property. This enables publishers to control the right of access to educational materials and market them at prices even people in the developed world struggle to afford. This evidently causes problems for developing countries, which generally lack the financial resources to purchase those materials or to obtain licenses to reproduce, translate, or utilize them for their purposes. It is true that the system contains limited mechanisms to obtain access through permissions. However, I will explain below that permissions to access are not guaranteed. They may be refused, involve significant delays, "or even prove impossible."[33]

What if a citizen or provider of educational materials in a developing country tries to act outside the scope of the current international copyright system and copy any of the educational materials needed for a school or university education? If such an action is not sanctioned under one of the limited statutory exceptions permitted under the 3ST, the country in which the "infringement" took place is obliged, under its international commitments, to seize "the infringing copies"[34] or even sanction the doer with "imprisonment and/or monetary fines."[35]

Representatives of copyright holders located in the developed world have not hesitated to rely on the copyright system to prevent people in developing countries from copying the educational materials those people need for their study. For instance, Alan Story reports that the American Association of Publishers (AAP) has advertised its success in "staging armed raids against 'copy shops' in developing countries where textbooks and other materials are reproduced."

32 UNESCO, *Sustainable Book Provision*, www.unesco.org/education/blm/chap1_en.php
33 Sam Ricketson and Jane Ginsburg, *International Copyright and Neighbouring Rights*, 882.
34 Berne Convention, Article 16.
35 TRIPS Agreement, Article 61.

These "raids" have taken place in countries such as India, Malaysia, Pakistan, the Philippines, and Brazil. The AAP gives as an example of their success a case where the owner of a photocopy center was arrested in Mumbai in 2002 and the authorities seized 500 copies of medical books from the establishment.[36] Students in developing countries are unlikely to be able to afford to buy those books at the prices set by publishers in the developed world. It is unlikely that those students will constitute a viable market for those publishers. The copyright system enables copyright holders to control access to knowledge in this instance, without giving due consideration to social utility, let alone the deontological value of the right to access knowledge, as promoted by *maqasid*.

Despite the fact that the current international copyright system tries to recognize the interests of the users of the copyrighted educational materials by granting exceptions to and limitations on the strong exclusive rights of copyright holders (for instance, Article 10 of the Berne Convention),[37] these exceptions and limitations have not provided developing countries with sufficient access to the educational materials they need.

As Ruth Okediji notes, these exceptions and limitations are not "effective and efficient"; they are "broad and vague." Accordingly, when it comes to access to educational material, for instance, the Berne Convention "applies primarily to the use of copyright works by instructors and teachers. Thus, this exception and limitation are of very limited value for supplying the local market with sufficient numbers of affordable copies for students and the general public."[38]

Furthermore, as with the issue of access to medicine explained above, the 3ST interferes here to make access to educational materials even more complicated. It imposes a structural barrier against the introduction of exceptions and limitations for the purpose of education or any other purpose in the copyright users' interests. It simply "sets limits to the limitations on the authors' rights."[39] The following example provides us with an idea of how the 3ST affects any potential access to the needed educational materials. A country that needs to

36 Alan Story et al., *The Copy/South Dossier: Issues in the Economics, Politics, and Ideology of Copyright in the Global South* (The Copy/South Research Group, May 2006) 73.

37 Article 10 refers to "Illustrations for teaching." It allows member states, developing and developed alike, to enact exceptions to permit use of copyrighted material in "publications, broadcasts or sound or visual recordings teaching." However, it uses vague terms such as "the extent justified by the purpose" and "compatible with fair practice." Who determines what would be a justified purpose or fair practice? How will this happen? Article 10 seems to place the burden on those who need access. Developing countries must also adhere to the 3ST, should they decide to rely on Article 10.

38 Ruth Okediji, "International Copyright," 209.

39 Martin Senftleben, *Copyright, Limitations and the Three-Step Test: An Analysis of the Three-Step Test in International and EC Copyright Law* (Kluwer Law International, 2004) 5.

enact an exception that involves restricting copyright has to apply the 3ST to the proposed exception. The 3ST stipulates that any exception may only be invoked in "certain special cases," provided that these cases "do not conflict with a normal exploitation of a work," and it (the exception) should not "unreasonably prejudice the legitimate interests" of the copyright holder. Let us imagine, for instance, that developing country X wants to allow the copying of medical books on the campuses of its universities. Such an exception would certainly draw the attention of the publishing agencies that might assume they have a market share within those campuses. The first line of defense that could be used by those agencies is the 3ST. They could always argue that allowing the mass-copying of their books would conflict with the normal exploitation of their publications as it would deprive them of additional sources of revenue and, as a result, prejudice their legitimate interest in profiting from their work.

Developing countries realized that the international copyright system as it stands could hinder their development plans in relation to education. After gaining their independence in the 1950s and 1960s, major developing countries such as India and Brazil led international efforts to demand a development-oriented international IP system. The 1967 Stockholm Revision Conference was a landmark in the progress of developing countries towards the recognition of their needs in the international copyright system.[40] The result, four years later, was the inclusion of an Appendix in the Paris Act of 1971[41] entitled "Special Provisions Regarding Developing Countries."[42] What are the main components of that Appendix and how has it affected the issue of access to educational materials in developing countries?

The Appendix is considered to be "the dominant and only explicit access regime currently existing in the international copyright relations."[43] It establishes a system of compulsory licenses[44] which allows a developing country, after notifying the Director General of WIPO,[45] to set limitations on the translation[46] and reproduction[47] rights of the copyright holder.

40 Same Ricketson, *The Berne Convention for the Protection of Literary and Artistic Works: 1886–1986* (Kluwer Law International, 1987) 117.

41 Ricketson, *The Berne Convention* 632.

42 Berne Convention, Article 21.

43 Ruth. L. Okidiji, "Sustainable Access to Copyright Digital Information Works in Developing Countries," in Keith E. Maskus and Jerome H. Reichman, *International Public Goods and Transfer of Technology under a Globalized Intellectual Property Regime* (Cambridge University Press, 2005) 147.

44 Appendix, Art. 1.

45 Ibid.

46 Ibid., Article II.

47 Ibid., Article III.

Theoretically, for instance, Article II of the Appendix allows publishers in a developing country to step into the copyright holder's shoes and translate his or her work without asking for permission; provided that (a) three years have elapsed from the first publication and (b) the copyright holder has not translated his or her work into the language in question.[48] The Appendix does not consider situations where speedy access is needed before the three-year period. Accordingly, for literary works used for education, especially those related to technical fields such as computer engineering, the need to wait three years means that some works will be outdated and irrelevant to the ever-developing scientific context.

To make the access problem even more complicated, the Appendix adds a further six-month grace period following the three years.[49] As a result, even if a publisher in a developing country waits for three years and expends effort and money in preparing for the translation, the copyright owner still has the right to translate his or her work. In that case, according to the Appendix, the publisher will not be licensed to translate the work.[50]

It should also be noted that the only channel for resorting to the CL scheme under the Berne Appendix – should the complex legal requirements be met – is the publisher in the developing country that has declared its intent to avail itself of the Appendix. Publishers in the developed world cannot make use of such licenses to supply developing countries with any materials they may need. Publishers in the developing countries are "the [one] (and only) channel for the reprographic copying and the production of materials and their delivery"[51] for developing countries.

Ironically, the compensated (fee-based) compulsory licenses conferred by the Appendix may only be issued for teaching, scholarship, and research purposes. In developed countries such as the United States, Australia, and Canada, uncompensated access for these purposes is freely available, especially if undertaken in a non-profit context under the fair use doctrine. Developed countries have more discretion to set limits on the reproduction rights of the copyright owner, whereas, under the Appendix, developing countries can use such discretion only for certain purposes, despite having greater social, economic, and cultural needs justifying more robust access rights.

48 Ibid., Art II(2)(a).

49 Appendix, Art II(4)(a).

50 Ruth. L. Okidiji, "Sustainable Access to Copyright Digital Information Works in Developing Countries," 164.

51 Story et al., *The Copy/South Dossier*, 140.

In an overall assessment of the Berne Appendix, Ricketson and Ginsburg observe that "it is hard to point to any obvious benefit [that has] flowed directly to developing countries from the adoption of the Appendix."[52] It does not seem to be adequate in providing systematic, expansive, and effective recognition of the right of access to educational materials needed to nourish the intellect, to use the rhetoric of *maqasid*.

The emergence of digital technology has provided an even stronger opportunity to promote access to education and, therefore, nourish the intellect, as required by *maqasid*. Knowledge acquisition is made faster and easier due to features that facilitate the learning process. Technology has made it easy to create educational content, access it, remix it and, most importantly, distribute it.[53] Digital devices, DVDs, and broadband facilities have created conditions in which we are able to learn in our houses, access journal articles in different parts of the world, write, mark, and store our work, or get visual insight into a phenomenon or historical event. Yet, the international copyright system quickly interfered to impose blanket restrictions on this promising opportunity.

On December 20, 1996, WIPO hosted a diplomatic conference which aimed "to respond to challenges that global digital networks pose for intellectual property law."[54] Developed countries, mainly the United States, driven by pressure from its creative industries seeking more financial gains, were successful in introducing provisions that secured increased control for copyright holders and imposed increased liability on copyright users. In this context, Pamela Samuelson reports that:

> Clinton administration officials sought approval in Geneva for international norms that would have (1) granted copyright owners an exclusive right to control virtually all temporary reproductions of protected works in the random access memory of computers; (2) treated digital transmissions of protected works as distributions of copies to the public; (3) curtailed the power of states to adopt exceptions and limitations on the exclusive rights of copyright owners, including fair use and first sale privileges; (4) enabled copyright owners to challenge the manufacture and sale of technologies or services capable of circumventing technological protection for copyright works.[55]

[52] Sam Ricketson and Jane Ginsburg, *International Copyright and Neighbouring Rights*, 957.

[53] William Fisher and William McGeveran, "The Digital Learning Challenge: Obstacles to Educational Uses of Copyright Material in the Digital Age" (2006) *The Berkman Center for Internet & Society* 9.

[54] Pamela Samuelson, "The U.S. Digital Agenda at WIPO"(1996–1997) 37 *Virginia Journal of International Law* 369, 370.

[55] Samuelson, "The U.S. Digital Agenda at WIPO," 370.

On the same day, the WIPO Copyright Treaty (WCT) and WIPO Performances and Phonograms Treaty (WPPT) were adopted. Both included provisions known as technological protection measures (TPMs).[56] TPMs comprise systems incorporated into digital content by various means such as encryption or watermarking to prevent users from accessing or using the content in a manner that is not permitted by the copyright owner.[57] This includes some scientific databases where access is denied to those who are not subscribers and where users are not allowed to copy texts from the content.

WCT and WPPT provide copyright protection "against the circumvention of effective technological measures that are used by copyright holders in connection with the exercise of their rights."[58] As a result, any manipulation made by content users in order to access or use content protected under this provision is deemed illegal and will allow the copyright holder to sue the circumventer or even prosecute him or her under criminal law. In this regard both treaties reflected the US Digital Agenda.[59]

Since the general framework of the treaties "is compatible with the traditional principles of the U.S. copyright law,"[60] the detailed assessment made by William Fisher and William McGeveran on the impact of the principles of US copyright law on digital learning is relevant to the international context. Both Fisher and McGeveran note that the law creates two obstacles that could hinder knowledge acquisition through digital learning. First, there are inefficient provisions relating to educational use. Second, the law extensively adopts "digital rights management: technology to lock up content."[61]

Fisher and McGeveran focus on digital rights management's harmful impact on placing more restrictions on accessing educational content. They point out that TPMs have become a tool to add extra copyright protection in favor of the copyright holders. It allows them to lock up digital content, preventing educators from obtaining access to the materials. Even education providers in wealthy developed countries are not satisfied with TPMs' impact on access to knowledge for educational purposes. For instance, Harvard University declared that copyright holders who use TPMs made the "scholarly communication environment fiscally unsustainable and academically restrictive."[62] TPMs are increasingly

56 WCT, Articles 11–12; WPPT, Articles 18–19.
57 Fisher and McGeveran, "The Digital Learning Challenge," 18.
58 WCT, Article 11.
59 Samuelson, "The U.S Digital Agenda at WIPO," 437.
60 Ibid., 370.
61 Fisher and McGeveran, "The Digital Learning Challenge," 2.
62 Harvard University, *Faculty Advisory Council Memorandum on Journal Pricing* (April 17, 2012), http://isites.harvard.edu/icb/icb.do?keyword=k77982&tabgroupid=icb.tabgroup143448

used by rights holders to set dangerous boundaries such as "no copying allowed for any purpose." Moreover, TPMs make it possible for rights holders "to engage in price discrimination by offering differential access to works at a range of costs."[63]

Through the introduction of prohibitions on circumvention of TPMs applied to copyright materials, the international copyright system added an extra burden to the problem of access to education in developing countries. TPMs are deployed by copyright owners to obstruct access to digital learning by locking volumes of valuable educational materials.[64]

The current global copyright system largely reflects the economic ideology prevalent in policymaking in developed countries. It clearly focuses on expanding copyright-based industries to lock up content to achieve economic gains. It is very difficult to locate provisions that show equal regard for access to education in developing countries as a basic human development requirement. Arguably, this feature is in direct conflict with *maqasid*'s emphasis on the duty to promote the intellect through access to education. *Maqasid* does not deny copyright holders the opportunity to make money from their copyright content. However, this cannot come at the expense of users' rights, particularly in developing countries, to read, learn, and nourish their intellect.

C *IP and Promoting* Mal *(Wealth)*

In this part of the book, I examine the interaction between IP in practice and one of the objectives of lawmaking in Islamic doctrine, namely promoting *mal* (wealth). As stressed in Chapters 2 and 3, the textual sources of Islamic law support law and policymaking that aim to increase a country's wealth. In the context of modern economies, promoting wealth as an objective is expressed in terms of an increase in the gross domestic product (GDP) per capita. Increased wealth, in addition to being an independent objective of Islamic lawmaking, can also be instrumental to achieving other objectives, namely, preserving and promoting *nafs* (life) and *aql* (intellect). In general, societies that have high rates of economic growth are more likely – but not *always* – to offer high levels of living standards in terms of access to health and education.[65]

Islamic visions on lawmaking are more likely to matter in countries with predominantly Muslim populations. Those countries are developing

63 Fisher and McGeveran, "The Digital Learning Challenge," 66.
64 Ibid., 81.
65 Sen, *Development as Freedom*, 1–17.

countries. They could benefit from an IP system that can contribute to promoting their GDP in any form, particularly if a pro-development IP system is socially good from an Islamic perspective. A relevant question here is: To what extent does the current international IP system, particularly as represented in the TRIPS Agreement, contribute to promoting growth in developing countries? Arguably, the extent to which IP promotes the overall growth of all members of the TRIPS Agreement signifies its compatibility with promoting wealth under *maqasid*.

As mentioned earlier, during the international IP norm-setting process, developed countries sought to expand the scope of private rights in knowledge and culture through stronger copyright, patents, and other forms of IP protection. Developed countries have regularly argued that increased IP protection is an essential means of promoting economic growth.[66] Even parts of research on IP and Islamic law have come out in favor of a positive link between IP and economic growth to provide support for IP protection under Islamic sources.[67] However, various empirical studies and qualitative analyses have put this proposition to the test, suggesting that IP in practice could economically benefit large industries, such as pharmaceuticals and entertainment in the developed world, but could harm the economies of developing countries.

Several economists sought to examine the relationship between IP and economic growth over an extended period of time. Scholars including Rivera, Batiz and Romer, and Gould and Gruben (1996),[68] Park and Ginarte (1997), and Patricia Higino (2005) empirically analyzed IP's impact on the economies of both developed and developing counties. Despite the different analytical methods used by these researchers, they largely agreed that strong IP protection might positively affect the growth rates in the developed countries "but not for those of less developed economies."[69]

Almeida and Fernandes conducted a study in 2008, which included 43 developing countries in Africa, Asia, and Latin America and surveyed 17,667

66 National Law Center for Inter-American Free Trade, *Strong Intellectual Property Protection Benefits the Developing Countries*, http://natlaw.com/interam/mx/ip/sp/spmxip11.htm

67 See, for instance, Heba Raslan, "Shari'a and the Protection of Intellectual Property, the Example of Egypt" (2007) *Intellectual Property Law Review* 528; Amir Khory, "Ancient and Islamic Sources of Intellectual Property Protection in the Middle East: A Focus on Trademarks" (2003) 43 *IDEA: The Journal of Law and Technology* 204.

68 David M. Gould and William C. Gruben, "The Role of Intellectual Property Rights in Economic Growth" (1996) *Journal of Development Economics* 324.

69 Park and Juan Ginarte, "Intellectual Property Rights And Economic Growth" (1997) *Contemporary Economic Policy* 60. Similar observations can be found in Carlos M. Correa, *Intellectual Property Rights, the WTO and Developing Countries: The TRIPS Agreement and Policy Option* (Zed Book, 2000) 25.

firms across a wide range of manufacturing industries.[70] They found that the driving factor behind innovation and its accompanying economic growth does not lie in the protection of IP. Rather, growth is fundamentally linked to policies that promote the liberalization of trade regimes, partnerships with foreign firms through joint ventures, and the level of collective absorptive infrastructure of local firms.[71] In a 2012 study, Acemoglu and Akcigit found that the impact of IP on economic growth is state-dependent. States with high technological capacities might experience an increase in "the growth rate of the economy from 1.86% to 2.04%." By contrast, uniform protectionist IP as proposed under the TRIPS Agreement "reduces both welfare and growth"[72] for developing countries.

The available data does not support the existence of any positive correlation between the TRIPS Agreement and increased economic growth. TRIPS could potentially work in more advanced economies where there are higher degrees of macroeconomic stability, market openness, and policies for improving the economy's technological infrastructure and the acquisition of human capital. Accordingly, suggesting that the TRIPS regulation of IP will achieve growth in the absence of these elements lacks evidence. On the contrary, there are indicants demonstrating that the introduction of the TRIPS Agreement may have contributed to erecting more barriers to innovation and economic growth in developing countries. Keith Maskus discusses a few examples of these barriers.

Firstly, IP laws allow rights holders to monopolize the provision of goods. This enables those rights holders to charge substantially higher prices for their products, which put them out of reach for people in developing countries. For instance, under international copyright protection, Microsoft was able to sell its first releases of Microsoft Office products at substantially high prices ranging from $1,000 to $1,500. Additionally, significant increases in the prices of drugs in India (up to 50 percent higher than generic drugs) have been recorded. This in turn hindered access to technological information, making it increasingly difficult for imitative enterprises in developing economies to imitate and reverse engineer products protected by IP.[73]

70 Rita Almeida and Ana Margarida Fernandes, "Openness and Technological Innovations in Developing Countries: Evidence from Firm-Level Surveys" (2008) *The Journal of Development Studies* 707.

71 Almeida and Fernandes, "Openness and Technological Innovations in Developing Countries," 723.

72 Daron Acemoglu and Ufuk Akcigit, "Intellectual Property Rights Policy, Competition, and Innovation" (2012) *Journal of the European Economic Association* 3, 6, 39.

73 K. E. Maskus, "Intellectual Property Rights and Economic Development" (2000) 32 *Case Western Reserve Journal of International Law* 471, 477, 491.

Secondly, according to a World Bank report, implementing the TRIPS Agreement in developing countries comes with high administrative costs. The World Bank report notes that implementing the Agreement requires a set of costly measures including:

> Upgrading offices for registering and examining patents and trademarks, and for accepting deposits of plant materials; training examiners, judges, and lawyers; improving courts to manage intellectual property litigation; and training customs officers and undertaking border and domestic enforcement actions.[74]

These measures could be burdensome for these countries. From an economic perspective, the costs associated with administering an IP system "would divert scarce professional and technical resources ... out of other productive activities,"[75] such as health and education.

Finally, developing countries that have upgraded their laws to levels required by TRIPS will have to pay huge rent transfers to IP owners headquartered in developed countries. Maskus estimates that the United States will gain extra rent inflow of $5.8 billion, and Germany $997 million, while Brazil alone will experience a net outward transfer of around $1.2 billion.[76] Meanwhile, firms in developed countries do not pay any comparable remuneration for exploiting the intellectual heritage of developing countries' communities. James Boyle cynically notes that, while the "dance *lambada* flows out of developing countries unprotected by intellectual property rights ... the movie *Lambada* flows in protected by intellectual property laws, which in turn are backed by the threat of trade sanctions."[77] Such imbalance adds more doubt with regards to any positive correlation between the current international IP system and economic growth.

It is possible to argue that without the sort of protection provided under the TRIPS Agreement, vital industries such as the pharmaceutical, entertainment, and high-tech sectors may become reluctant to invest in creating useful knowledge and cultural products. This is true. It is even possible to find some empirical support suggesting that these industries rely on IP protection and enforcement to strengthen their innovative infrastructure. However, a valid

74 World Bank, *Global Economic Prospects and the Developing Countries* (The World Bank, 2002) 136, http://siteresources.worldbank.org/INTGEP/Resources/335315-1257200370513/gep2002complete.pdf

75 Keith E. Maskus, "Intellectual Property Rights and Economics Development," 494.

76 Ibid., 493.

77 James Boyle, *Shamans, Software, and Spleens: Law and the Construction of the Information* (Harvard University Press, 1996) 125.

counterargument would be that we should not design an IP policy in a developing country based on what is economically efficient for entertainment, pharmaceutical, and high-tech industries in developed countries. In this context, we should be mindful of the plethora of evidence suggesting that many economies around the world experience increased growth without the TRIPS standards of IP protection.

In previous research, I extensively examined a body of historical data supporting the proposition that several economies in now developed countries were able to flourish under pre-TRIPS standards of IP protection. Countries in Europe and Asia that are now developed used to have standards below the current international standards in terms of the duration and scope of IP protection. Decades before the introduction of the TRIPS Agreement, countries including the United States, Germany, the Netherlands, Finland, Japan, and South Korea had IP systems that allowed for a robust public domain ensuring the circulation and diffusion of knowledge. Infant industries and small and medium enterprises flourished within these countries as a result of more permissible IP regimes. A TRIPS-like IP standard could have made this development more difficult with its emphasis on increasing control on disseminating knowledge.[78]

In summary, the available statistical data shows that IP in practice, as manifested in the TRIPS Agreement and more restrictive additions including FTAs may be working to promote income and growth in a few sectors in the developed world. As shown above, this may explain developed countries' claims – during international IP norm setting – that the introduction of more IP rights will increase economic efficiency. However, when it comes to promoting wealth in developing countries, the evidence suggests no positive correlation between IP and growth. On the contrary, the hypothesis that IP can negatively affect prices, resources, and innovation in developing economies seems to be more plausible. Accordingly, IP in practice seems to be in conflict with yet another value promoted by *maqasid*.

The main underlying argument of this chapter sought to propose that *maqasid* advances a different normative vision to the one guiding the design of global IP policymaking. At a general level, the global IP regime is predominantly crafted along utilitarian lines largely oriented towards securing the economic interests of creative industries in the developed world. *Maqasid*, on the other hand, places economic efficiency as a second order principle and

78 Ezieddin Elmahjub, "A Case for Flexible Intellectual Property Protection in Developing Countries: Brief Lessons from History, Psychology and Economics" (2016) 38(1) *The European Intellectual Property Review*, 31–42.

prioritizes the need to promote a set of deontological values. At a specific level, some operational features of the global IP system do not reflect *maqasid*'s emphasis on prioritizing a set of plural values fundamental in guiding the Islamic lawmaking process. These include promoting and preserving the right to life, nourishment of the intellect through education, and economic growth in developing economies. I do not intend to stop at establishing the incompatibility of the current predominant IP system with notions of *maqasid*. In the following chapter, I aim to explore ways in which *maqasid* may contribute to designing an IP system that assists in remedying the negative ramifications of the current global IP regime as identified in this chapter.

5

IP and the Islamic Principles of Justice

In this chapter, I will lay out a more comprehensive vision of IP from an Islamic perspective – a vision that includes, but goes beyond, *maqasid* as explored in Chapter 2. My aim is to introduce IP within an Islamic theory of a fair and well-ordered society. I would argue that a well-ordered society in the Islamic vision is a flourishing society in which its various institutions operate collectively to make everyone better off. Framed this way, an Islamic theory of justice will provide a stronger analytical benchmark compared to *maqasid*. An Islamic theory of justice will not only employ plural deontological values to assess the fairness of a particular institution but will also include notions of justice that are inclusive of considerations of merit and economic efficiency. The overarching aim is to provide a benchmark for designing a fair IP system that recognizes labor and promotes efficiency, but also accommodates concerns relating to basic human needs.

In order to do that, I will need to show that Islamic sources can be canvassed to set the foundation to construct an expansive theory of social justice. A theory that helps with providing principles of fairness to assess IP in social and economic contexts. In other words, I will need evaluative tools to view IP as an institution that could affect the distribution of basic goods including rights, obligations, privileges, burdens, wealth, income, and opportunities to earn, express, and learn. The task of finding such a broad theory of justice in Islamic moral philosophy is challenging. Concepts bearing on the basic structure of a fair society and the distribution of basic goods are normally scattered across a massive body of literature on Islamic jurisprudence, including *usul al-fiqh* (the principles of Islamic jurisprudence) and *maqasid al-sharia* (the objectives of Islamic law).

As far as mainstream Islamic jurisprudence is concerned, to the best of my knowledge, a fully fledged theory of social justice – in a form accessible to comparative moral philosophy – is lacking. With the exception of Sayyid

Qutb – who, in 1949, attempted to formulate a theory of social justice in Islam by assembling dispersed notions of fairness from the Quran, the Sunnah, and other sources of Islamic legal traditions – the systematic treatment of social justice was not a prevalent feature of Islamic jurisprudence.[1] This is not to say that there is no emphasis on justice and the fair distribution of the burdens and benefits of social cooperation in Islamic jurisprudence, but discussions around these issues are not presented in theoretical models accessible from the perspective of comparative moral philosophy. For instance, discussions around abstract concepts of justice are normally included as part of *kalam* literature (Islamic theological philosophy). Mu'tazilites and Ash'arites, the two dominant schools in *kalam* literature, discuss justice as a divine attribute, arguing around reason's capacity to set standards of fairness through identifying what is *hasan* (good) and *qabih* (evil). Their work generally does not directly help in formulating an accessible normative account on how to organize fair society from an Islamic perspective. Yet, we need a starting point.

To begin, I would propose looking at Islamic sources to identify the society that justice is to serve. Then, we need to identify a set of principles of justice to govern social relations, inform the design of public institutions, and coordinate social cooperation. I will argue, on the basis of these principles, that the Islamic vision of justice will operate as an alternative to utilitarian and merit-based accounts on justice, but will not entirely exclude their application in some contexts. The Islamic vision of justice is equipped with special standards of fairness that address the potential concerns of the various members of society. I will show that a broad distribution of basic goods and opportunities is central to Islamic views on justice. Aggregate utility and individual merit by themselves cannot dominate a normative analysis directed at achieving a fair state of affairs.

I THE ORIGINAL POSITION

The Islamic vision of the society for which justice is to be achieved starts with a metaphysical proposition. This proposition suggests that humans exist on the earth as a species through the Pact of *Istikhlaf*. According to the Quran, *Istikhlaf* is the conceptual backbone of human settlement on the earth. Roughly speaking, it represents the Islamic version of the social contract theory. The closest translation of *Istikhlaf* in English is trusteeship or stewardship. The Pact of *Istikhlaf*, concluded between God and humankind, says that humankind will settle and benefit from the earth and will be held accountable

[1] Sayyid Qutb, al-'adalah al-Ijtima'iyya fi al-Islam (13th ed., Dār al-Shuruq, 1993) 92.

before God, who supplies humankind with instructions on how to conduct itself.

The theological premise of *Istikhlaf* runs along the following lines: God created the earth for the settlement of humankind. To this effect, the Quran says: "He (Allah) brought you forth from the earth and settled you therein."[2] Humans are chosen collectively as God's trustees to develop the earth because of their distinctive capacity to act rationally, understand, learn, and comprehend. In the Islamic version of the genesis of humanity, God communicated to the angels His will to send humankind as his *khalifa* (trustees) over the earth: "your Lord said to the angels, 'Verily, I am going to place (mankind) generations after generations on earth.' The angels replied, 'Will You place therein those who will make mischief therein and shed blood?' God responded, 'I know that which you do not know.'" To prove to the angels that humans would have the distinctive capacity to reason, God created Adam and taught Adam all the names (of everything), then He showed them to the angels and said, "Tell Me the names of these if you are truthful." The angels replied, "We have no knowledge except what you have taught us." God said, "O Adam! Inform them of their names." Adam performed the task of understanding and comprehending successfully, proving to the angels that humans are superior with the capacity to reason, making them capable of fulfilling God's purpose of settling on the earth.[3]

The foundational feature of *Istikhlaf* is that it is a collective pact between God and humankind as a species. The stewardship over the earth and its resources is not assigned to individual human beings, be they rulers or prophets. A very common perception in Islamic theology is that no particular individual can claim divine dominion over the earth exclusive of the rest of humanity.[4] There is a recurrent theme running throughout the Quran, which indicates that *Istikhlaf* has an egalitarian pedigree: "O mankind! We created you from a single (pair) of a male and a female."[5] *Istikhlaf* is a collective entrustment of the earth and its resources to humanity. In the language of modern social contract theory, the original position or the original state of nature under *Istikhlaf* is that humans, in general, are free and equal persons with an overarching duty to establish their settlement on the earth based on social cooperation.

2 Quran, trans. Mohsin Khan, 11:61.
3 Ibid., 2:30–2:32.
4 Azizah Y. al-Hibri, "Islamic Constitutionalism and the Concept of Democracy" (1992) 24(1) *Case Western Reserve Journal of International Law* 11.
5 Quran, trans. Yusuf Ali, 49:13.

In his monograph on social justice in Islam, Qutb maintains that egalitarianism in the form of human equality (*al-musa'wat al-insaniyya*) and social cooperation (*al-takaful al-ijtima'i*) are foundational elements of the Islamic vision of social justice. First, Qutb argues that "Islam came to establish the unity of humankind in its origins and future as well as in its rights and obligations before the law and before God."[6] Qutb draws support for his assertion on the egalitarian pedigree of society in Islam from several textual authorities and concludes that since humankind was created from the same elements and reproduced by the same processes, the default position of humankind should be one of equality with no room for any differences based on color, class, or social status.[7] The other foundational element of social justice Qutb puts forward is that the collectivity of equal individuals is bound by a common commitment to social cooperation. Every individual is expected to adhere to social norms dedicated to achieving maximum social fulfillment, rather than act upon self-focused rational analysis. To support this foundational element of social justice, Qutb embarked on an extensive deductive survey of several textual authorities from both the Quran and the Sunnah. He cites a number of verses from the Quran which impose a duty on believers to cooperate with their family members. He also refers to *hadiths* that impose general obligations on believers to pursue social cooperation.[8]

Justice is the purpose of social cooperation between equal individuals under the Pact of *Istikhlaf*. At a general and abstract level, Islamic scriptures introduce the notion of justice as the guiding principle in arranging the conditions of human association on the earth. The Quran is replete with verses highlighting the significance of justice as the supreme normative standard for organizing the basic structure of society. In one verse, the Quran identifies justice as the purpose of the scriptures revealed to humankind since it has been inhabiting the earth. "We have already sent Our messengers with clear evidences and sent down with them the Scripture and the balance that the people may maintain [their affairs] in justice."[9] In another verse, the Quran highlights the supreme intrinsic value of justice as the ultimate measure of the right thing to do. The Quran commands believers to pursue justice even against their inclination to promote rational analysis of self-interest at a personal level or community level. The Quran says, "O you who have believed, be persistently standing firm in justice, witnesses for Allah, even if

6 Qutb, *al-'adalah al-Ijtima'iyya fi al-Islam*, 44.
7 Ibid., 45–46.
8 Ibid., 54–59.
9 Quran, trans. Sahih International, 57:25.

it be against yourselves or parents and relatives. Whether one is rich or poor."[10] While this crude command to pursue justice does not carry with it further guidelines on how to achieve justice in a dynamic society, it situates the notion of justice as the benchmark for guiding the normative analysis towards the creation of well-ordered society. The starting point is that justice is the foundational benchmark for normative analysis under Islamic legal philosophy. It is the value central to regulating all other institutions and pursuits. How does the abstract notion of justice relate to the distribution of the benefits and burdens of social interaction among humankind and how is it reflected in the basic structure of society? Is there further guidance on how to achieve justice?

I would argue that it is possible to start a discussion on the existence of at least three principles of justice that should inform the basic structure of society and coordinate social cooperation from an Islamic perspective. I must admit that these principles are not the product of a specific account on social justice in Islamic jurisprudence. In this chapter, I initiate an preliminary foray into identifying them. To begin with, these principles will not emerge out of deliberation on the original position, as John Rawls would have us to believe when he was about to introduce his principles of justice.[11] Rather, they are formulated on the basis of both textual and non-textual authorities, anchored in Islamic normativity. They are assembled and categorized based on various readings and interpretations of the scriptures as well as reorganizing scattered notions of fairness from Islamic jurisprudence. Having said that, it does not follow that public reason in the public sphere will necessarily reject these principles.

II THREE PRINCIPLES FOR A FAIR SOCIETY

My argument is that there are enough normative signals in Islamic sources to flesh out a basic theory of social justice in terms of the distribution of the advantages and burdens of social cooperation among humankind. My working hypothesis is that an Islamic theory of social justice comprises at least three general principles designed to regulate the assignment of the sources of satisfaction in the basic structure of society. The starting point is that any distribution scheme must recognize (1) equal priority for a set of deontological plural values compatible with the *maqasid* framework on human flourishing in the sense highlighted in Chapter 2, (2) fair equality of opportunities as a matter of natural divine right, and (3) the continual adjustment of

10 Quran, trans. Sahih International, 4:135.

11 John Rawls, *A Theory of Justice* (rev. ed., Harvard University Press, 1999).

inequalities in the distribution of the sources of satisfaction, such as wealth and power, to promote fair equality of opportunities and improve the conditions of other segments of the society, particularly the least well off.

A *Satisfying Essential Plural Needs*

The first principle of a fair society from an Islamic perspective is to guarantee the fulfilment of a set of essential plural needs for each member of the community. These are to be identified in light of *maqasid*, as explored in Chapter 2. Al-Taher Ibn Ashur, in his treatise on *maqasid al-Sharia*, argues that the propositions of equality derived from Islamic scriptures entail a requirement that society must guarantee equal basic protections to each and every one of its members. He states that:

> Under Islamic legislation, equality in society stems from the equality of human beings in their inborn nature and in all related matters, in which variation [between individuals] has no implications for the well-being and virtue of society. Thus, human beings are the same in respect of their humanity: [The Prophet says,]"All of you are children of Adam." They are also equal in their right to live in this world because of their primal nature, and no differences in color, anatomy, race, or place can affect that equality. This basic equality ensures their equality in the fundamentals of Islamic legislation, such as the right to existence, expressed by the terms "protection of life" and "protection of progeny," and to the means of life, expressed by the term "protection of property." They are also equally entitled to the means of living a proper and good life known as the "protection of intellect" and "protection of honor." Above all is the right of belonging to the religious community . . ., expressed by the phrase "protection of religion."[12]

Each person is to have equal access to the means necessary for promoting, inter alia, life, income, and intellect. Access to these means will not depend on merit or the ability to pay or work. Access is guaranteed as a matter of basic human equality. The exact scope of what constitutes a "basic need" is open to debate. For instance, the discussion around expanding *maqasid* to include freedom and basic human rights can be brought under the first principle. Research or *istiqra* from textual sources and Islamic traditions is open to improving our understanding of additional categories of basic needs. Islamic texts could provide a versatile medium in searching for additional basic needs to be protected as objectives of Islamic law. The search for these new basic needs will operate within the same line of thought that informed and shaped

[12] Ibn Ashur, *Maqasid*, 147.

maqasid. If *maqasid* are the necessary "human capabilities" in Islamic traditions, a basic need is going to be whatever is necessary to make these capabilities function.

In classical and modern Islamic jurisprudence on the distribution of wealth, essential plural needs form part of what is known as *had al-kifayah* (self-sufficiency baseline). The dominant accounts in Islamic jurisprudence refer to *had al-kifayah* in the context of identifying personal property as a basic need. In that context, *had al-kifayah* represents a set of essentials needed to preserve and promote one's life and intellect, among other things. For Imam al-Nawawi (d. 1277), *had al-Kifaya* is understood in terms of basic personal property, including food, clothing, a personal dwelling, and all other essentials needed to maintain life, independence, and self-respect.[13] Muhammad Ibn 'Abidin (d. 1836) expanded on this list. In his treatise on Islamic jurisprudence entitled *al-Hashiya*, Ibn 'Abidin maintains that a basic need is whatever sustains the life of a human being. This includes income for personal expenses, a personal dwelling, tools, clothes, a means of transport, and educational materials.[14] However, *had al-kifayah* need not to be confined to the narrow sphere of personal property. It can also be expanded to include basic human rights and the freedom needed for believers so that they can pursue their own conception of good.

B *Fair Equality of Opportunity*

The second principle requires the establishment and promotion of fair equality of opportunity as an overarching design principle throughout the basic structure of society. If everyone is equal under the Pact of *Istikhlaf*, everyone should have fair equality of opportunity to pursue sources of satisfactions that are important to him or her. As a matter of formal and procedural equality, all institutions making up the basic structure of society must recognize the default position of human equality. For instance, if society decides that private ownership of a particular productive resource would leave everyone better off, everyone is to have equal opportunity to work and claim private ownership of that resource. The public system of rules must not enable a few members of society to have access to that resource and then empower them to control who can get access next. In other words, positions that could enhance one's chances to self-development and self-satisfaction must be open to everyone.

13 Yahya Ibn Sharaf al-Nawawī, al-Majmu' (Maktabat al-Irshad, n.d.) vol. 6, 191.

14 Muhammad Ibn'Abidin, *Hashiyat Radd al-Muhtar 'ala al-Dur al-Mukhtar* (Dar al-Fikr, 1992) vol. 2, 262.

Protecting and promoting fair equality of opportunity is intrinsically and instrumentally important for a fair and flourishing society. Fair equality of opportunity is intrinsically important to promoting independence, exercising free choices, and maximizing self-advancement and self-fulfillment. It is also important as a means by which societies can empower individuals to be more productive and improve the conditions of social cooperation, thereby maximizing social welfare.

C Fair Redistribution

The third principle holds that income and wealth inequality can be tolerated, but must be continually adjusted to benefit everyone in society, particularly the least well off, namely, *al-fuqara wa* and *al-masakin* (the poor and the destitute). In support of this principle, the Quran explicitly indicates that wealth and income inequalities are part of the divine scheme under the Pact of *Istikhlaf*: "God has made some of you richer than others."[15] Qutb opines that income and wealth inequalities are natural consequences for differences in natural talents and capabilities. Some people are created strong, naturally disposed to using their intellectual and physical capabilities to increase the production of useful goods for the society. Fair society must reflect principles of merit where entitlements could be based on contributions. Accordingly, Islamic sources recognize that the distribution of wealth could be skewed for those favorably endowed individuals. Qutb also integrates a social utility-based argument for embracing possible inequalities. He suggests that merit-based rewards could even be necessary to benefit talented individuals and to benefit the community at large. He concludes that it is consistent with Islamic sources to allow a talented individual to work and increase production, and thereby serve the cause of social justice. An increased pool of wealth can be redistributed to benefit public interest.[16]

Under this principle, it is possible to imagine economic inequality in the ownership and control of different sources of satisfaction such as land, chattels, and other productive resources, including knowledge. However, I will explain below that the application of this principle is constrained by the priority of the deontological values identified as part of the first principle. Income and wealth inequalities cannot be allowed to undermine *had al-kifayah*. Income inequality is also limited by other constraints, most importantly the Quranic-based prohibition on the excessive accumulation of wealth, and fair equality of

[15] Quran, trans. Muhammad Sarwar, 16:71.
[16] Qutb, *al-'adalah al-Ijtima'iyya fi al-Islam*, 28.

opportunity. Before I explain the relevance of these principles to the Islamic theory of justice, I must stop to recognize the close affinity between this account on social justice and John Rawls's *A Theory of Justice*.

Admittedly, in assembling the three principles of justice from Islamic sources, I was greatly inspired by John Rawls's theory of justice as fairness. In that theory, John Rawls proposes the most influential reflection on social justice in modern comparative Western philosophy. Rawls's theory of social justice stipulates that a fair and well-ordered society is one that satisfies two principles. Under the first principle, each person is to have an equal access to basic liberties. These are constitutional liberties that must be available for all, for which no inequality is permitted. These basic liberties include "the right to vote and to hold public office and freedom of speech and assembly; liberty of conscience and freedom of thought ... the right to hold personal property ... . "[17] The benchmark to determine what is included under "basic liberties" is the necessity of a particular right or liberty to promote autonomous life, a life of free choices, and maximization of self-advancement and self-fullfilment. While Rawls includes personal property as one of the basic liberties, it is noteworthy that he does not consider a general right of private ownership to be among these liberties. In his later book, *Political Liberalism,* Rawls elaborates on the benchmark for considering something as personal property and, as a result, a basic liberty:

> [A]mong the basic liberties of the person is the right to hold and to have the exclusive use of personal property. The role of this liberty is to allow a sufficient material basis for a sense of personal independence and self-respect, both of which are essential for the development and exercise of the moral powers.[18]

Arguably, Rawls's account on personal property as basic liberty broadly fits with *had al-kifayah*. First, both principles aim to create a necessary threshold for an autonomous and dignified life. Second, both principles have a deontological origin: they are considered as a duty within the social structure that does not depend on merit-based considerations, including the ability to pay or labor. Equal access to personal property and *had al-kifayah* are guaranteed by the mere fact of being a member of a particular society.

The second principle in Rawls's conception of a fair society is that social and economic inequalities are only permissible if they (a) can be arranged to benefit everyone, particularly the least advantaged members of society, and (b)

17 Rawls, *A Theory of Justice*, 53.
18 Rawls, *Political Liberalism*, 298.

are attached to offices and positions open to all under conditions of equality of opportunity.[19] Here Rawls, as is the case in Islamic legal philosophy, accepts that inequalities in wealth and income can be part of the basic structure of society provided that they are supplemented with two subprinciples. First, at least part of the unequal wealth and income is to be redistributed to improve the conditions of the least advantaged. Second, the sources that led to the inequality in wealth (e.g., productive resources or careers) must be available to citizens generally and not be concentrated in the hands of few.

III SOCIAL AND ECONOMIC INEQUALITIES AND DISTRIBUTIVE JUSTICE

A fair society must guarantee *had al-kifayah* or a set of basic human needs. Then, it must deploy varying natural endowments and talents to increase production, even if social and economic inequalities are allowed to occur. However, how far can a fair society go in permitting social and economic inequality and yet remain fair? Obviously, this is a matter of value judgment and intuition. According to John Rawls, it is not abnormal to rely on value judgement and intuition to determine what is fair and unfair when debating the optimal structure of a well-ordered society.[20] No matter how we articulate the answer to this question, we can at least agree that a fair society would not permit the sort of inequality that leads to excessive concentration of power, production resources, and wealth in the hands of a few citizens. We would probably agree that the current distribution of the sources of satisfaction, say, in the United States is far from fair. There, the majority of wealth and income is largely skewed in favor of a small group of society. According to the US Congressional Budget Office, as of 2013 76% of all wealth in the United States belonged to the top 10 percent of the population.[21]

If we agree that an unfair state of affairs is one in which a class of individuals has too much control over a society's sources of satisfaction, while the majority have too little, our task of identifying the fair state of affairs becomes relatively easier. A fair society, despite permitting social and economic inequalities, would leave everyone better off. It would create an enabling environment for all citizens to flourish and become fully cooperating members of their communities. This would likely occur in situations where there is widespread

19 Rawls, *A Theory of Justice*, 302.

20 Rawls, "Justice as Fairness," 30.

21 US Congressional Budget Office, *Trends in Family Wealth, 1989 to 2013*, www.cbo.gov/sites/default/files/114th-congress-2015–2016/reports/51846-familywealth.pdf

dissemination of different sources of satisfaction, including wealth, opportunities, and productive resources, particularly knowledge. Can we reconcile two contradictory arrangements: one permitting inequalities, and one benefiting everyone in society?

We need implementable measures to ensure that permitting inequality remains under control. First, these measures must ensure that inequality does not threaten the wide availability of the set of plural basic needs. Second, they must not open the door to a grossly unfair distribution of sources of satisfaction, including wealth. Islamic scriptures offer two measures, which I include as part of my understanding of Islamic philosophy on distributive justice. First, the scriptures contain a negative measure to address substantial inequalities. They condemn the excessive concentration of wealth as morally wrong. Second, they offer positive measures consisting of several institutions designed to increase the distribution of resources outside market systems, which can lead to inequalities in the first place. These measures should be analyzed with an open mind to see if their underlying design principles can be expanded to inform other distributive institutions.

A *Excessive Concentration of Wealth*

The Quran establishes a broad normative principle creating a negatively framed duty prohibiting the concentration of wealth in the hands of only a few members of society. The Quran says, "and those who hoard gold and silver and spend it not in the way of Allah – give them tidings of a painful punishment."[22] The principle of non-concentration (PNC) is widely regarded as a fundamental pillar of Islamic social and economic policy.[23] A fair society, from an Islamic perspective, may tolerate some form of inequality but cannot allow the excessive concentration of wealth and power. PNC – despite not being known by this technical term – has formed part of Islamic social and economic policy since the early days of the establishment of Islam as a social and political order.

In the context of justifying the normative significance of PNC, Qutb traces the formulation and implementation of the principle back to the Quran and the traditions of the Prophet. He refers to the story of *Hijerah* (Migration) of the Prophet and his followers from Mecca to Madinah (the city) in the

[22] Quran, trans. Sahih International, 9:34.

[23] Yūsuf al-Qaradawi, *Dawr al-Qiyam wa al-Akhlaq fi al-Iqtisad al-Islami* (Maktabat Wahba, 1995) 168; Muhammed al-Ghazali, *al-Islam wa al-Manāhij al-Ishtirākiyya* (4th ed., Nahdat Misr, 2005) 95.

Arabian Peninsula. He maintains that PNC formed part of the fabric of the legal system in the newly created Madinah.[24] According to multiple sources of Islamic traditions, the Prophet and his companions had to leave Mecca to avoid persecution and other forms of suffering and oppression. Leaving their wealth and belongings in Mecca, the Muslim migrants (*al-Muhajirin*) suffered poverty and lacked basic resources.[25] After their arrival, the Prophet created the Bond of Brotherhood between the migrants from Mecca and the residents of Madinah (*al-Muhajirin wa-al-Ansar*) to provide shelter and basic needs for *al-Muhajirin*.[26] According to Qutb, with the first flow of wealth into the newly created community of Medina – which came as a result of a peace agreement with *Banu al-Nadir* – the Prophet decided "to restore balance"[27] among the well-off *Ansar* and worse-off *Muhajirin* by distributing wealth predominantly among the worst-off Muslims of Madinah, namely *al-Muhajirin*. The Quran documents this incident and directly embraces PNC:

> And what Allah restored to His Messenger from the people of the towns – it is for Allah and for the Messenger and for [his] near relatives and orphans and the [stranded] traveler – *so that it will not be a perpetual distribution among the rich from among you*[28]

Qutb opines that this decision by the Prophet to redistribute wealth among the poor and its justification in the Quran "clearly establish an Islamic principle prohibiting the concentration of wealth in the hands of a few members."[29] Whenever there is an imbalance, it is necessary to intervene to adjust gross inequalities by assigning portions of the wealth to the worst off so that "[wealth] will not be a perpetual distribution among the rich." Ownership for the worst off is essential to ensure their livelihood, sense of dignity, and autonomy.[30] Yusuf al-Qaradawi also notes that early Muslim rulers, in particular the second Caliph Umar Ibn al-khatab (d. 644 CE), used to redistribute land among poor Muslims whenever there was a situation where some Muslims would keep large unused sections of land in their possession.[31] Building on these traditions, Sohrab Behdad maintains that resources in an Islamic economy are expected to be used to maximize production to the

[24] Qutb, *al-'adalah al-Ijtima'iyya fi al-Islam*, 92–94.
[25] John Esposito, ed., *The Oxford History of Islam* (Oxford University Press, 2000).
[26] Qutb, *al-'adalah al-Ijtima'iyya fi al-Islam*, 92.
[27] Ibid.
[28] Quran, trans. Sahih International, 59:07.
[29] Qutb, *al-'adalah al-Ijtima'iyya fi al-Islam*, 93.
[30] Ibid., 92–93.
[31] Al-Qaradawi, *Dawr al-Qiyam*, 168.

greatest extent their operational capacity will allow. Concentration of wealth may prevent this from occurring. He notes that:

> firms making an economic profit by producing less than the "Islamic optimum output" could be regarded *hoarders*. If hoarding is *unlawful*, then it must be the duty of the state to eliminate it when it does occur. Thus, prohibition of hoarding may justify *appropriation of "unused" private wealth by the state.*[32]

To sum up, in the Islamic theory of social justice, arrangements that lead to differences in income and wealth among different groups in society should not allow excessive concentration of wealth and power. Such concentration, if left unchecked, could potentially impinge on the basic needs of other income groups, particularly the worst off. One possible outcome of concentration is that a few in society are empowered to exercise so much control over vast sources of satisfaction that other segments of the society are excluded from having an equal opportunity to access these sources. Rawls makes a similar point in *Justice as Fairness*, where he asserts that "excessive concentrations of property and wealth"[33] are "likely to undermine fair equality of opportunity." Therefore, "background institutions must work to keep property and wealth evenly enough shared over time to preserve . . . fair equality of opportunity." This has to be done "by laws . . . [that] prevent excessive concentrations of private power."[34] Indeed, Islamic scriptures introduce several "background institutions" to break wealth concentration, to which I now turn.

B *Redistributive Justice*

Islamic scriptures establish measures, or background institutions, to help dismantle concentrations, remedy disparities in the distribution of wealth, and restore fair equality of opportunity. I do not intend to provide a detailed explanation of these institutions in this book. Rather, I will briefly discuss their essential features, but only to the extent necessary to highlight the existence of redistribution mechanisms as part of the Islamic vision of social justice.

Overall, Islamic scriptures sanction two different types of measures to address social and economic inequalities. Some of these measures are preventative, designed to target the causes of concentration of wealth and power. Others are remedial, predominantly aimed at ameliorating the concentration

32 Sohrab Behdad, "Property Rights in Contemporary Islamic Economic Thought: A Critical Perspective" (1989) 47(2) *Review of Social Economy* 194 (emphasis added).

33 John Rawls, "Justice as Fairness," 44.

34 Ibid., 51–53.

of wealth by prescribing extensive instructions for redistributing wealth in order to continually improve the conditions of the least advantaged in society.

Preventative measures are scattered throughout the main sources of Islamic law, namely, the Quran and the Sunnah. Mohammed Abu Zahra sheds light on some of these measures. In his monograph entitled *The Structure of Islamic Society*, he notes that the scriptures display a consistent pattern towards preventing the concentration of wealth. For instance, the institution of *mīrāth* (Inheritance) in the Quran is designed to ensure that the wealth of a deceased person is as widely distributed as possible. The Quran does not allow any single person to possess the wealth of the deceased. It corrected situations in pre-Islamic Arabia where, upon a person's death, his or her wealth could only be assigned to the older son of the deceased or only among his male relatives. The Quran explicitly included the female relatives of the deceased and limited the extent to which a person could circumvent the arrangements prescribed in the Quran. The Quran also provided for the assignment of shares to an additional nine heirs who had not been eligible to inherit in pre-Islamic societies, six of whom were female.[35] In a related context, Abu Zahra offers another example supporting the trend in Islamic scriptures to prevent the concentration of wealth and power by referring to Sunnah-based prohibitions on monopolistic practices. Consistent reports from the Sunnah reveal that the Prophet made various instructions to Muslims to avoid exclusive control, by way of monopoly, over the supply of goods.[36]

As for remedial measures for tackling inequalities, the institution of *zakat* (obligatory alms) provides an illustration. *Zakat*, as extensively regulated under the Quran, the Sunnah, and a large body of Islamic jurisprudence, is basically intended to impose a religious and legal duty on well-off Muslims to continually contribute to improving the conditions of the worst off. Normatively, *Zakat* is of great significance in the Islamic legal and religious landscape as one of the five pillars of Islamic faith. Honoring the duty to redistribute wealth is an inherent component of Islamic social identity. In every lunar year, well-off Muslims holding different kinds of assets such as money, agricultural goods, valuable metals, and livestock are required to make available for redistribution between 2.5 and 20 percent of their holdings.

Zakat transformed the concept of charity into an *obligation* that is endowed with religious sanctity. *Zakat* does not depend on the charity and compassion of the well-off. It is an obligation owed to the least advantaged as matter of social justice in order to improve their conditions and mitigate the impact of social and economic inequalities.

35 Muhammad Abu Zahrah, *Tanzim al-Islam li al-Mujtama* (Dār al-Fikr al-'Arabi, n.d.) 135.

36 Ibid., 193.

It is important to note that *Zakat* is noticeably different from a tax system. It is not supposed to represent a source of income for governments, but a measure to balance inequality and continually improve the situation of least well off.[37] This understanding is explicit in the Quran and the Sunnah. The Quran describes believers as "those within whose wealth is a known right. For the petitioner and the deprived."[38] In the Sunnah, the Prophet is reported to have said that *Zakat* "should be taken from the rich to be redistributed among the poor."[39] Furthermore, the Quran broadly designates categories of disadvantaged persons to whom an obligation to pay *Zakat* is owed. These categories predominantly consist of impoverished individuals who cannot or struggle to meet their basic needs (*al-Fuqarā' wa al-Masākīn*), individuals to be freed from the bondage of slavery (*Fir-Riqāb*), and those who are unable to pay overwhelming debts (*al-Ghārimīn*).[40]

Arguably, *Zakat* further distances the Islamic approach to social justice from utilitarianism. Under *zakat*, fairness is not measured according to the goodness of states of affairs, where some could have less while others prosper. It focuses on the welfare of particular categories of individuals. It signifies that if some end up earning greater wealth and income, the situation of the least advantaged must be continually improved. In other words, *zakat* further reinforces the position taken in this book that the Islamic sources do not support classical, open-ended utilitarianism but rather utility for the least advantaged. Despite the fact that the base for wealth that is subject to *zakat* is vast (i.e., it includes capital and profits), modern trends in Islamic jurisprudence tend to argue that the normative signals underlying the *zakat* duty can be used to enable governments to take more than the maximum limits of *zakat* to reduce the concentration of wealth and social and economic inequalities.[41] Muhammed al-Bahi argues that in the Islamic vision of a fair society, the fair allocation of wealth in the greater public interest is a fundamental aspect of the function of wealth. After all, Muslims are instructed to believe that wealth was entrusted to them under the Pact of *Istikhlaf* to improve the conditions of their settlement. The best way to do that is by sharing this wealth with the rest of *ummah* (society), especially with the destitute.[42]

37 Yusuf al-Qardawi, Fiqh al-Zakat (Muassasah al-Risalah, 1973) 542.

38 Quran, trans. Sahih International, 70:24–70:25.

39 Sahih al-Bukhari, *Kitab al-Zakat* (Dar Ibn Kathir, 1993) 505.

40 Quran, trans. Sahih International, 9:60.

41 Muhammed M. Shalabi, *al-Fiqh al-Islami: Tarīkhuhu wa Madārisahu wa Nazareyatahu: al-Mulkiyyah wa al-'aqd* (Al-Dār al-Jami'iyya, 1985) 295.

42 Ibid., 123.

Finally, the purpose of redistribution has to be interpreted within our understanding of the ideal vision of society as imagined under the Pact of *Istikhlaf*. The vision there is to create a flourishing society where all individual have an equal opportunity to pursue their own ends. Accordingly, redistribution under the Islamic vision of social justice should not be understood as providing principally consumptive life supplies but, instead, opportunity supplies. In other words, the redistribution of wealth to correct inequalities is not primarily designed to provide food and shelter to the poor and disadvantaged – although this must be done. Rather, distribution should be understood as a way to give individuals independence, put them in a better position to make choices, and enable them to author their life plans on an equal footing with other citizens in society.[43]

To sum up, I have argued that the Islamic vision of social justice requires that the basic structure of society should (1) equally satisfy a set of basic needs compatible with *maqasid*, (2) with a strong commitment to fair equality of opportunity, and if (3) permitting inequalities is necessary to increase the production of goods and wealth, then (4) these inequalities should not lead to excessive concentration of power and resources, but (5) should be continually adjusted to improve the level of income of the least well off and support fair equality of opportunity. I now turn to an analysis of IP in light of these considerations.

IV THE DISTRIBUTIONAL STRUCTURE OF IP LAWS

I appreciate that the shift from discussing the Islamic vision on social justice to applying it to IP may seem abrupt if no justification is offered. My justification is simple: An Islamic theory of social justice can act as an alternative, comprehensive framework to guide the normative analysis of IP. Under an Islamic theory of social justice, IP will not only be viewed as a right to reward labor or a tool to maximize social utilities through providing incentives to creators. Notions of efficiency and merit will form part of a much larger analytical scheme. Instead, IP will be critiqued and reimagined from the ground up as one of the legal and social institutions that affects human basic needs, equality of opportunity, the concentration of wealth, and power to control access to opportunities for expression and innovation. In this part, I show why IP needs to be situated within the Islamic vision of social justice. Then, I move on to evaluate IP within the main compartments of the Islamic theory of social justice. First, I show that IP in general is not designed according to the

43 Al-Qardawi, *Fiqh al-Zakat*, 875.

principle of fair equality of opportunity. The system is largely configured to promote the interest of rights holders, particularly in rich, Northern countries. At an international level, few colonial powers determined what should and should not be protected as IP, and local notions of ownership in poor developing countries were not systematically considered. This attitude is still prevalent today. Second, IP, viewed as an institution in the basic structure of society, is largely responsible for enabling a few rights holders to accumulate excessive wealth and the power to control who can remake culture and build upon existing innovation.

A *IP and Social Justice*

At a theoretical level, IP could significantly benefit from a social justice analysis. The dominant utilitarian analysis of IP is problematic for at least two reasons: First, it is largely uncertain. The proposition that more exclusivity to control knowledge and cultural outputs creates more knowledge and cultural outputs is not empirically solid. We do not know if allocating exclusive rights over knowledge and cultural products is always necessary to incentivize production. A large body of research suggests that the arguments around a consistent positive link between a promised monopoly over one's creative outputs and increased social creativity are overblown.[44] Recent empirical examinations for the rationale behind creativity and innovation identified other reasons clustered around intrinsic motivations to justify creative outputs. Many researchers found that people will create out of desire, curiosity, serendipity, inspiration, and so on.[45] If we agree that a flourishing society is one where content is available in abundance, we need to be careful before endorsing arrangements where some individuals are empowered to control chunks of knowledge and culture. Exclusive control does not always lead to increased social utility, but most certainly could lead to the concentration of wealth and the power to control opportunities to learn and express oneself.

Second, the utilitarian analysis of IP is fundamentally indifferent to the fair distribution of basic needs and other sources of satisfaction. Even if we were to agree that the utilitarian analysis of IP is true, we could most certainly still make the case that it can be unfair. Critical examinations of the moral validity

[44] Diane Leenheer Zimmerman, "Copyrights as Incentives: Did We Just Imagine That?" (2011) 12 *Theoretical Inquiries in Law* 29, 42–48; see Keith Aoki, "Distributive and Syncretic Motives in Intellectual Property Law (with Special Reference to Coercion, Agency, and Development)" (2006) 40 *University of California Davis Law Review* 717, 800.

[45] Jeanne C. Fromer, "A Psychology of Intellectual Property" (2010) 104 *Northwestern University Law Review* 1441, 1483.

of utilitarian ethics maintain that utilitarianism is insensitive to fair distribution of the goods to be maximized. Amartya Sen observes that the utilitarian analysis, at its core, suffers from "[d]istributional indifference." If happiness is the state of affairs to be maximized, utilitarianism "tends to ignore inequalities in the distribution of happiness (only the *sum* total matters no matter how unequally-distributed)."[46] Similarly, the dominant utilitarian analysis of IP attaches no intrinsic importance to the distribution of utilities that are supposed to be aggregated by IP laws. The goal is to create the greatest number of knowledge and cultural products to benefit the greatest number of people. This approach is inherently neutral towards distribution considerations. It does not tell us why social and economic benefits from creativity for the greatest number should compensate for the loss for the rest of society. Why should increased control over knowledge and culture and increased income for rights holders justify income inequality and reduced opportunities to access content for the rest of society? How does this approach affect the least well off in society?

This is particularly relevant to understanding the relationship between IP and the first principle of fairness under an Islamic theory of social justice. Under the notion of *had al-kifayah*, everyone must be equally able to enjoy a set of essential goods needed to preserve and promote their life, intellect, and wealth. Arguably, several features of the modern IP system oriented towards increasing economic efficiency do not leave everyone in society better off. We saw in Chapter 4 that IP is one of the important factors impacting people's abilities to access essential goods necessary for basic human life in developing countries. For instance, the patent system posed enormous challenges for several developing countries in relation to access to medicine and food. I explained how the system is predominantly preoccupied with enabling rights holders to leverage their patents in order to extract substantial market revenue, even at the expense of a sustainable supply of lifesaving drugs or drugs necessary for a comfortable life. Similarly, copyright does not provide effective mechanisms to satisfy the need of poor people in developing countries to access state-of-the-art educational materials controlled by publishers in the developed world. The vital need to access educational materials is not effectively treated as such by the international copyright system. The system is designed to enable large copyright holders to treat educational content as personal property, even at the expense of basic access rights for children who cannot afford to pay.

46 Sen, *Development as Freedom*, 62.

B IP, Representation, and Formal Equality

There is also procedural inequality in IP norm setting. The system is largely constructed by those who would benefit the most from exclusive control, namely, well-established rights holders residing in wealthy nations. In general terms, the interests of those who seek to use or reuse the knowledge and culture protected by IP have not been systematically represented in the creation and development of IP, both domestically and internationally.

As a matter of structure and design, it is not difficult to prove that IP was not a reflection of an inclusive political choice. The history of IP norm setting tells us that established rights holders, technological innovators, and distribution industries relied on their wealth, lobbying networks, and sometimes coercion to design IP laws where the ability to control knowledge and culture is the norm rather than the exception.[47] For instance, it is very difficult to point to a meaningful and consistent role played by public interest groups in shaping many of the controversial features of IP, including copyright duration, the scope of protectable subject matter, and the nature and scope of access and reuse interests. Groups that are supposed typically to support more inclusive participation in shaping IP laws and policymaking were noticeably absent from any meaningful role in modern IP norm setting. These include libraries, educational institutions, research institutes, and non-governmental organizations.[48]

The absence of these groups poses a critical question: To what extent does the structure of IP laws reflect fair equality of opportunity and fair distribution of knowledge and culture? A fair society in which citizens are equal must not make it possible for one segment of the society to be in a position to decide the operating norms to their own advantage, particularly if this segment has obvious interests in increased private control over knowledge and culture.

At a global level, IP was largely crafted by colonial powers in the late nineteenth century. This fact provides a very illuminating illustration of how the one-sided design of the IP system led to undermining fair equality of opportunity. The Berne and Paris Conventions were both drafted by few European countries, mainly Switzerland, Spain, Italy, France Portugal, the Netherlands, and Belgium. Other countries, particularly developing countries

47 Sam Ricketson and Jane C Ginsburg, *International Copyright and Neighbouring Rights: The Berne Convention and Beyond* (Oxford University Press, 2005) vol. 2, 881; Adronico Oduogo Adede, "Origins and History of *TRIPS* Negotiations," in Christophe Bellmann, Graham Dutfield, and Ricardo Meléndez-Ortiz, eds., *Trading in Knowledge: Development Perspectives on TRIPS, Trade, and Sustainability* (Earthscan Publications, 2003) 23.

48 Okidiji, "Public Welfare and the Role of the WTO," 858.

or former colonies of the drafters, joined these conventions without having direct input in shaping their main features. Commenting on the lack participation by, and input from, developing countries and former colonies, Okediji notes that:

> In this respect, non-European peoples and their territories were, initially, *mere objects* of inter-European economic rivalry. Nineteenth century international law offered the doctrinal tools of "war" and "treaties" to resolve competition among Europeans for control and ownership over non-European territories and peoples.[49]

The notions of ownership reflected in these conventions were largely a product of one version of Western philosophy on property rights. The normative vision that guided the design of both conventions was that of a sole romantic author or inventor. Someone who invents out of the thin air and should, therefore, have exclusive rights to enjoy the fruits of his or her labor so that others can create more useful intellectual goods. Other traditional or local forms of ownership and authorship were not considered in the early formative phases of the global IP system or subsequent major developments, including the TRIPS Agreement.

The system ended up protecting ideas and expressions that would originate according to the definitions provided in the global IP regimes. So-called traditional knowledge, such as expressions, cultural artifacts, ideas, and know-how developed and sustained generation after generation in indigenous communities, are not protected because they do not meet the patentability or originality requirements as introduced and developed under the international IP instruments. Furthermore, this traditional knowledge is to be placed in the public domain, free for all to reuse. Whatever is to be created under the Western-designed global IP regime is to be afforded protected private property status. On the other hand, what was already made by disadvantaged indigenous communities is to be fair game for appropriation. While Aladdin, from *alf liliah wa liliah* (The Book of One Thousand and One Nights), is unprotected folklore, Walt Disney's appropriation of the story is considered original copyright. Similarly, because the indigenous people's use of the viper venom was considered free knowledge, Bristol-Myers Squibb was allowed to take out a patent on it and benefit commercially from reusing it, without any benefit for the Brazilian tribe that first made use of its virtues.

49 Ruth L. Okediji, "International Relations of Intellectual Property: Narratives of Developing Country Participation in the Global Intellectual Property System" (2003) 7 *Singapore Journal of International and Comparative Law* 315, 324.

It is worthwhile to contextualize this predicament into a social justice framework. It shows that the system does not afford equal opportunities for everyone to benefit from knowledge and culture on an equal footing. The power to control ideas and expressions and the advantages that flow from that are bestowed on those who meet the specific definitions of protectable subject matter under the international IP system – a definition that was essentially a reflection of the views and interests of the dominant international powers that shaped and controlled the development of the international IP system and norms. The irony is that while the international IP system provides strong protection for rich people's knowledge, it does not do the same for poor people's knowledge. The system literally gives the opportunity to rich people to get richer while preventing poor people from earning income from their traditional knowledge.

IP laws allow rights holders to leverage legal protection to earn income from knowledge and cultural products that have market value. A wide array of these products have substantial market value. Considering that IP rights holders act as rational maximizers for their own self-interest, they attempt to extract as much revenue as practically possible. In the process, relying on IP rights to earn income leads to a concentration of substantial wealth in the hands of a few individuals in society. IP laws also enable rights holders to control access to a particular knowledge or cultural product, its different parts, and the way it is supposed to operate. Using IP as a control mechanism in this sense could concentrate excessive powers of control over the development of innovation and creativity, thereby impinging on opportunities to express, learn, and earn from working with knowledge and cultural products. In this part, I examine whether the patterns of earnings from IP can be considered an "excessive concentration of wealth" and thus unfair. Then, I move on to investigate whether IP can create an enabling environment allowing rights holders to exercise excessive powers of control over subsequent engagements with IP-protected content. I ask if control through IP rights can undermine fair equality of opportunity in remaking and developing knowledge and culture and earning income through that.

1 IP and the Concentration of Wealth

It should be clear by now that in the Islamic vision of a fair society, institutions operate not only to maximize aggregate wealth but also to ensure that wealth is widely distributed rather than concentrated. Widely does not necessarily mean equally. It means that the aggregated wealth is not confined to a small segment of the society, but adjusted to everyone's advantage, particularly those who are worst off. Now, let us put IP to the test. IP is one of the institutions within our public system of rules that has distributive effects. We know that it is supposed to increase the wealth of the society. But does it do so fairly? Does it lead to concentrated or distributed wealth and income? Does it help disadvantaged people to flourish?

I do not think so. There are strong reasons to believe that IP contributes to the concentration of wealth in the hands of a relatively small set of large rights holders. Enormous shares of wealth generated from IP-based industries end up with large corporations rather than individual creators of knowledge and cultural products. Although the available data to support this proposition is generally scarce, it is at least sufficient to cast serious doubts on any claims that IP actually serves distributive justice values.

In order to prove this point, I need to take issue with Justin Hughes and Robert Merges. In a coauthored research paper, Hughes and Merges defended copyright's effects on the distribution of income and wealth. They argue that "[c]opyright is, and can be, an important tool to promote a just distribution of income and wealth in society."[50] As support for this assertion, the authors cite data published in the United States by the Bureau of Labor Statistics (BLS), identifying a number of professions that the authors consider to be "copyright-related," which have higher annual revenues than the average annual income. For instance, as of 2014, according to the BLS, the average annual income for computer programmers was $77,550, for "software developers" $97,990,for "writers and authors" $58,850, and for "editors" $54,890. According to the authors, these earnings are well above the average income for all occupations in the United States, which was $35,540 in 2014.[51] Hughes and Merges make the argument that, even when copyright enables income inequalities, this income inequality should be deemed fair because it actually improves the situation of various income groups. In this instance, people relying on their talents are making more money under copyright protection.

The data presented by Hughes and Merges does not provide a solid informational base to support their claim that copyright positively affects the distribution of wealth and income. First of all, the authors failed to establish a persuasive argument to justify the extent to which copyright contributes to improving wages in the categories listed. We do not know that copyright protection was necessary for creative individuals in computer, software, and film industries to secure above-average annual income. Second – most

[50] Justin Hughes and Robert P. Merges, "Copyright and Distributive Justice" (2016) 92 *Notre Dame Law Review* 513, 576.

[51] Ibid., 529.

importantly – even if we were to agree that copyright had a positive impact on their increased income, this income is grossly disproportionate to the income and wealth of corporations and wealthy shareholders in the corresponding copyright-related industries. For instance, Hughes and Merges did not add to their analysis the relative income of major shareholders of corporations in the said industries, particularly in computer, software, and film industries. For example, while computer programmers and software developers made \$77,550 and \$97,990 in 2014 respectively, only one computer and software conglomerate, Bill Gates, made \$9 billion in the same year![52] We cannot see how this increase can be justified as fair for the majority of computer programmers and software developers.

Overall, statistics from the United States on the performance of copyright-related industries, including films, music, and software, show that a few dozen corporations control the bulk of the market and make the highest incomes. For instance, in 2014, the top eight film corporations had more annual income than the next 100 combined.[53] In terms of market share, in 2014, three US companies controlled 65 percent of the music industry market.[54] Globally, the top six US companies accounted for more than 80 percent of global film market in 2015.[55] As for software, three corporations – Microsoft, Apple, and Google – dominate desktop and mobile operating system markets, and these firms are increasingly able to position themselves to extract a substantial portion of the revenue of software developers, entertainment distributors, and information producers who distribute their products on each firm's platform.[56]

Much of the rhetoric involving copyright revolves around providing a reward for individual authors and artists. Yet much of the reward is going to a small set of large copyright holders. The data from the United States that shows authors earning above-average incomes does not match trends in other

[52] This figure represents the difference between Gates's income in 2013 and 2014, as reported by Forbes:
2013 www.forbes.com/sites/luisakroll/2013/09/16/inside-the-2013-forbes-400-facts-and-figures-on-americas-richest/#515a4b4623d8;
2014 www.forbes.com/sites/afontevecchia/2014/09/29/forbes-400-full-list-of-americas-richest-people/#7441cb9442e3

[53] Box Office Mojo, "Studio Market Share," January 1–December 31, 2014.

[54] Statista, "Revenue Market Share of the Largest Music Publishers Worldwide from 2007 to 2016," www.statista.com/statistics/272520/market-share-of-the-largest-music-publishers-worldwide/

[55] Box Office Mojo, "Studio Market Share," January 1–December 31, 2015, www.boxofficemojo.com/studio/?view=company&view2=yearly&yr=2015&p=.htm

[56] Statista, "Statistics and Market Data on Software," www.statista.com/markets/418/topic/484/software/

developed countries. For instance, a survey of 25,000 authors in the United Kingdom and Germany found that professional authors make considerably less than the average national income in both countries.[57] Similarly, in the United Kingdom, nearly 75 percent of artists earn the equivalent of only 37 percent of the median UK salary,[58] while in Australia more that 50 percent of professional artists make less than $10,000 annually from their creative income, which is well below the average national income.[59]

Successful individual authors and artists normally achieve commercial success and a decent income when they assign their copyright to well-established corporate producers and publishers. Copyright is structured to enable easy assignment with very little safety valves to protect individual authors and artists to achieve better distributive shares from their creative outputs.[60] To benefit from copyright protection and secure market control, it is generally irrelevant who the actual creator of the particular cultural product was. What is more important is who holds the copyright in that product, as the rights holder – not the individual creator of the product – will end up enjoying the copyright reward. In this sense, copyright allows the wealth it generates to become concentrated in the hands of a few well-established corporations.

2 IP and the Concentration of Power to Control Expressive and Innovative Opportunities

IP affects not only the distribution of wealth but also the distribution of power to control access to knowledge and culture. The structure of major compartments of the IP system – namely, patent and copyright – enables rights holders to concentrate substantial powers of control over access to opportunities for expression and innovation. Concentration of any sort is not a feature of a fair society. When a few members have so much control over resources and means of production, there is a risk that fair equality of opportunity will be undermined for larger segments of the population.

57 Martin Kretschmer and Philip Hardwick, "Authors' Earnings from Copyright and Noncopyright Sources," 23.

58 "Artists' Low Income and Status Are International Issues," *The Guardian*, www.theguardian.com/culture-professionals-network/2015/jan/12/artists-low-income-international-issues

59 David Throsby and Anita Zednick, "Do You Really Expect to Get Paid?"

60 Jessica Litman, "The Exclusive Right to Read"(1994) 13 *Cardozo Arts & Entertainment Law Journal* 29, 37–39.

IP is one of the institutions in the social structure that can affect equal opportunities to access knowledge and cultural products and participate in reshaping these products in different contexts. It enables rights holders to control access to and reuse of these products. As rational maximizers of their own interests, rights holders will want to retain as much control as possible to prevent others from accessing and using their intellectual "assets." While it is possible to accept some level of control over some knowledge and cultural products, there is a great risk that the expansive empowerment of rights holders will restrict access to and reuse of culture. This form of power concentration can undermine fair access to opportunities to use existing ideas and expressions to challenge existing culture and remake existing knowledge.

IP does not always coordinate simple market relationships between creators and consumers. With the aid of internet platforms and the power of personal computers, a great numbers of users and consumers of knowledge and culture have transformed from passive recipients into active creators. The rapid growth of internet technologies and the wide use of personal computers empower users to recreate existing knowledge and culture in fascinating new ways. This holds great promise for users, enabling them to enhance their own personal advancement, learning, and expression, as well as to contribute to a vibrant culture.

Niva Koren documents how users are now able to drive "both the production and distribution of new [intellectual] content and applications."[61] Since 1988, Eric Von Hippel has challenged the long held assumption that "product innovations are typically developed by product manufacturers."[62] In a more recent work, he suggests that empirical data shows that between 10 and 40 percent of users of knowledge engage in the developing and modifying of products protected by IP laws such as software programs, integrated circuits, sporting equipment, medical devices, and computer systems.[63]

IP is structured to empower rights holders to exercise substantial control over ideas and expressions. Rights holders get automatic copyright protection for their expressions for a very long time. In fact, protection is extended long after they are dead. Patent holders can prevent others from using ideas they develop, without permission. The scope of the exclusive rights to control knowledge and culture can be so wide as to enable rights holders to determine the conditions under which opportunities become available to new makers of

61 Niva Koren, "Making Room for Consumers under the DMCA" (2007) 22 *Berkeley Technology Law Journal* 1152.

62 Eric von Hippel, *Sources of Innovation* (Oxford University Press, 1988) 3.

63 Eric von Hippel, *Democratizing Innovation: The Evolving Phenomenon of User Innovation* (MIT Press, 2005).

products of knowledge and culture. Theoretically, IP laws are supposed to have mechanisms to prevent excessive control over the distribution of knowledge and culture. Each IP regime has internal doctrines that are supposed to "balance" the system and curb the concentration of power over ideas and expressions. For instance, the scope of copyrightable subject matter is limited to original expressions only. Underlying ideas are free for others to appropriate. Similarly, limitations on the scope of exclusive rights enable the public to use existing copyrighted work freely and without permission whenever the subsequent use carries with it some form of social utility, without such use undermining the fair market of the rights holder.

In practice however, these "pro-distribution" features of IP do not seem to work as intended. IP rights in valuable intellectual products normally enable rights holders to leverage their rights to prevent any attempts to challenge their businesses. At least to a certain degree, IP markets exhibit unbalanced structures where rights holders are able to lock access to knowledge and culture. For instance, it is difficult to argue that the copyright system operates to promote fair equality of opportunity. On the contrary, there is good reason to believe that it tolerates the concentration of private power and control over the distribution of information and culture. A close look at copyright markets supports the assumption that there is significant distributional imbalance in the ability to control culture. Copyright rules create states of affairs where power is skewed in favor of a few members of society, allowing them to destabilize opportunities to access knowledge and participate in culture. A standard example of the extent of the concentration in copyright industries is the mass media's dominance in markets of cultural products. At a global level, Eli Noam's study of 30 countries with the most developed economies and which make the biggest contribution to modern culture reveals that, on average, the top four companies control 60.7 percent of the media in each country.

According to Ruth Towse, copyright can at least provide "a partial explanation for the observed concentration of ownership."[64] The theoretical justifications of the system are fundamentally skewed in favor of more protection. Over the years, small and well-organized groups of copyright holders have relied on strong rights and utility-based arguments to expand their control over access to, and wide distribution of, products of knowledge and culture, as well as to limit competition from newcomers. This concentration of power to control access to culture can be used to undermine fair equality of opportunity to participate

[64] Ruth Towse, "Creative Industries," in Ruth Towse, ed., *A Handbook of Cultural Economics* (Edward Elgar, 2011) 125, 127–28.

in cultural production in the digital age, particularly for underresourced segments of the society. Molly Shaffer Van Houweling observes that copyright particularly burdens poorly financed creators, preventing access to content that would actually make positive changes in their lives and creativity at large. She maintains that:

> The new tools of digital distribution give even amateur artists – without much money, without investors, and without plans to use copyright to make a profit from their work – enough communicative potential that they need worry about copyright's costs when they build upon copyrighted works. Their activities are suddenly on copyright's radar screen. What's more, the cultural importance and ubiquity of copyrighted texts, images, and sounds may make multimedia collage and other forms of creativity that incorporate existing copyrighted works even more vital forms of cultural commentary than they have been in the past.[65]

Patricia Aufderheide and Peter Jaszi's study shows how copyright can be used as a mechanism to create roadblocks for creative individuals, preventing them from pursuing opportunities that could enhance their careers and enrich culture. They documented the experiences of librarians, filmmakers, teachers, open content developers and online video makers. The authors found that a "culture of fear and doubt" dominates people in these creative platforms. These individuals understood that copyright grants exclusive rights for rights holders to control every snippet of cultural expression they wanted to use, which included images, phrases of a song, or a few seconds from cartoon film. Licensing arrangements did not work well for them either because getting a license was expensive or because they "sometimes couldn't get anyone at a studio or music company or archives house to answer their e-mails or calls because there was so little money in the licensing deals."[66] There was a risk in pursuing their plans and creating cultural works without permission. For them, there was a visible danger that if they were sued, their assets and families could be destabilized. In this sense, copyright constrained their imagination and interfered with their work plans and creative opportunities.[67]

This "culture of fear" was found in the United States, where there is an open-ended fair use defense. In its quest to achieve social utility by permitting transformative and non-commercial use of copyrighted works, fair use could

65 Molly Shaffer Van Houweling, "Distributive Values in Copyright" (2005) 83 *Texas Law Review* 1535.
66 Patricia Aufderheide and Peter Jaszi, *Reclaiming Fair Use* (University of Chicago Press, 2011) x.
67 Ibid., xi.

possibly protect fair opportunities to participate in culture. But these people seem to believe that fair use is uncertain and litigation is risky and expensive. Before going to court, they cannot be sure that their use is fair under the complex section 107 of the US Copyright Act. Instead of risking upsetting the businesses of resourceful copyright holders, the easier option is to do the work without copyrighted snippets, even if the resulted output is less creative, less fulfilling, and less valuable. This reinforces the proposition that, in practice, copyright does not balance the opportunities to participate in culture. In countries without open-ended fair use, the situation can be even worse.

In a study of 29 Australian authors and artists, Kylie Pappalardo and her coauthors found that the Australian copyright regime could place some people at a great disadvantage. The system prevents creative individuals from creating new cultural products, even in cases where reusing copyrighted work would not undermine the economic or property interests of the rights holders. Interviewees reported that they wanted to use bits and pieces of music or videos in their films, or long quotes in written works, but were unable because permission from copyright holders was required. For instance, the authors of the study report that one composer had to wait for a year for permission to use poetry in their music. Despite the fact that the original poet was deceased, the composer could not get the publisher that controlled the copyright to respond on time. The composer had to change the initial plan and painstakingly work out a new song. Another documentary filmmaker decided to abandon a plan to make a documentary about a small choir in rural Australia because the cost of obtaining a license for snippets of songs performed by the choir was over $10,000. The filmmaker was unable to raise the money needed to obtain the license.[68]

Copyright provides expansive exclusive rights over the entire copyrighted cultural product. It can prevent use or reuse of the product in various creative contexts. In the two examples mentioned above, reusing a snippet of a song in a short documentary or the poem of a deceased poet to perform a song would not necessarily be detrimental to the copyright holders. However, such reuse was important for the filmmaker and the composer. At a personal level, it could have opened opportunities for career development, and it could have enriched the creative process at a societal level. Copyright stifled the creativity that it was supposed to promote.

68 Kylie Pappalardo et al., *Imagination Foregone: A Qualitative Study of the Reuse Practices of Australian Creators* (2017), https://eprints.qut.edu.au/115940/

Similarly, patents can also pose serious barriers to fair equality of opportunity. Several aspects of the patent system encompassing a wide array of knowledge fields can operate to disempower various segments of society from useful engagement with knowledge products. It is widely acknowledged that patents help to concentrate power by leveraging knowledge to extract significant market control. Firms in diverse knowledge fields, including computers, software, communications, pharmaceuticals, and biotechnology use patents – and IP generally – to position themselves so that they can exercise substantial control over the relevant knowledge fields.[69] The spread of patents as dominant modes of governing knowledge and the strong, exclusive control they afford their holders raise transaction costs, limit opportunities to conduct research and development, and divert significant financial resources towards litigation that could have otherwise promoted innovation.[70]

Overall, patents have a major impact on cumulative innovation. Cumulative innovation is an important aspect of modern economies in which new inventions expand, improve, or totally transform existing inventions. New generations of inventions in biotechnology, drugs, computers, medical instruments, and communications technologies build on prior generations of patents. Within and beyond these fields, opportunities for self-development and social utility are endless. Empirical research suggests that exclusive rights under patent regimes can block downstream innovation in several knowledge fields. An empirical study conducted by Alberto Galasso and Mark Schankerman found that the removal of patent protection through the invalidation of patents by the courts led to a 50 percent increase in downstream innovation in computer technologies, electronics, medical devices, and biotechnology. Interestingly, it found that the invalidation of patents owned by established patentees provided more opportunities for small firms to engage in downstream innovation. In other words, patent protection could have reduced opportunities to innovate in important fields by 50 percent, particularly for small firms.[71]

In this context, it should be noted that patents can allow a patentee to enforce its exclusive rights even when the patentee is unable or unwilling to transform the patented idea into useful products. The international

69 Mark Schankermanand Ariel Pakes, "Estimates of the Value of Patent Rights in European Countries during the Post-1950 Period" (1986) 96 *Economic Journal* 1052–76.

70 Mark Hellerand Rebecca Eisenberg, "Can Patents Deter Innovation? The Anticommons in Biomedical Research" (1998) 280 *Science* 698–701; James Bessenand Eric Maskin "Sequential Innovation, Patents, and Imitation" (2009) 40 *The RAND Journal of Economics* 611–35.

71 Alberto Galasso and Mark Schankerman, "Patents and Cumulative Innovation: Causal Evidence from the Courts" (2015) 130(1) *The Quarterly Journal of Economics* 317–69.

patent regime, particularly the TRIPS Agreement, does not contain a general provision explicitly compelling patentees to make use of their patented inventions. This could have serious ramifications for the ability to engage with knowledge in certain fields if the patentee chooses to lock up knowledge through patents in order to extract income. Arguably, this could be unfair for those able and willing to transform the ideas into something useful. It is also bad for social utility as it deprives society of increased productive outputs. In this sense, patents could actually hinder rather than promote innovation.

Although in several jurisdictions patent legislation does require patentees to use their patents in order to be able to continue enjoying patent protection, this is not the case in all jurisdictions.[72] Patentees are free to rely on their exclusive rights to restrict access to knowledge, even where there are opportunities for others to flourish and contribute to social welfare. This could be a source of great concern to small companies and start-ups, reducing opportunities to grow and create career paths in knowledge production sectors. Colleen Chien examined the impact on start-ups in the United States of excessive assertions of patents by patent assertion entities (PAEs or trolls). PAEs rely on patents to engage in rent seeking without intending to transform ideas into usable products. Of the 223 small firms and innovation start-ups canvassed in the survey, 79 (about one-third) reported that they had received letters from PAEs asserting exclusive rights over particular components of their production process. The study reported that PAEs' interference with start-ups had a significant operational impact on those companies that affected their market opportunities to different degrees. The impact materialized as changes in business strategies and products, delays in hiring or meeting operational milestones, reductions in the value of companies, and even business shutdowns.[73]

The realm of knowledge and culture protected by IP could be an enormously versatile ground for endless opportunities to flourish. Copyrighted and patented cultural and knowledge products such as literary works or snippets of inventions could make or break the potential of a person to comment, sing, or invent. We need to ensure fair equality of opportunity in the realm of knowledge and cultural production, as we would for any other office and position, to use Rawls's terminology. IP holders can, and possibly

[72] Marketa Trimble, "Patent Working Requirements: Historical and Comparative Perspectives" (2016) 6 *University of California Irvine Law Review* 483.

[73] Colleen V. Chien, "Startups and Patent Trolls" (2012) *Stanford Technology Law Review* 2–12.

should, have enough powers to recoup investment and generate income. But these powers should not be extensive and concentrated. They should not be so strong as to close off opportunities in the realm of knowledge and cultural production.

V PRIORITIZING FAIRNESS

This preliminary assessment of IP's distributional effects suggests that there are a number of normative deficiencies in IP from a social justice perspective. To make my point that IP is largely not configured in support of a broad distribution of opportunities to express and innovate, my arguments ran like this: It is simply not sufficient to perceive IP as a fair reward for labor or as a utilitarian bargain that allows rights holders to increase and accumulate wealth in the hope that it increases overall public welfare. IP must be situated in a more comprehensive account of social justice. The way to a fair IP system in a well-ordered society does not start by simply granting exclusive rights to incentivize innovation and creativity. IP must contribute to empowering people's capabilities to access knowledge products and participate in the creation (or recreation) of those products.

I started with a somewhat broad analysis of different Islamic sources with a view to formulating a tentative proposal on Islamic principles of justice. These principles require social institutions to respect basic needs and freedoms, create equal opportunities, and provide mechanisms for correcting social and economic inequalities. Applying these principles to IP's distributional structure, I found that, under the dominant forms of the modern IP system, the power to control access and use could largely be skewed in favor of established groups of IP holders, who would most likely end up with substantial wealth and income. The interests of the bulk of creative and innovative individuals, or even entire poor communities, are not adequately served. Many disadvantaged people around the world are left without access to essential goods needed to save their lives, enough food, and better educational opportunities. The IP system can have the effect of marginalizing large groups of people, denying them access to, and reuse of, knowledge and culture and thereby effective participation in society.

A fairness analysis of IP is essential. It should hold IP doctrines accountable to distribution-based considerations. Instead of pursuing the largely unproven assumptions around IP and social utility, IP under a fairness analysis will be mindful of providing the institutional design that takes into account fair distribution of capabilities affected by IP rights. These include the capability to read, hear, borrow, express, reverse engineer, imitate, research, share, imagine, challenge the existing IP-protected culture and knowledge, and so on. Distribution of these capabilities will not depend essentially on the ability to pay. In particular, if the public system of rules allows some to benefit from their creative talents through IP protection, the system must also ensure that private control does not amount to substantial control of knowledge, culture, and wealth. Disadvantaged members of society must be able to access opportunities to express, innovate, and earn.

In Chapter 7, I will discuss various reform proposals that can be found in comparative IP scholarship. These proposals largely reflect the Islamic ideals of social justice introduced in this chapter. They push for an IP system that is ready to (1) curb concentration mechanisms by establishing a legal environment where a wide range of creative works can be legally shared with others, who can then build upon them; (2) offer a wide distribution of opportunities to engage in innovation and creativity by enhancing the functions, capacities, and legal rights of users within the IP system regardless of social utility; and (3) focus on cooperative approaches to knowledge management and production as a method to break the conventional power structure in IP markets and promote distributive justice. However, before I do all this, I need to further expound the Islamic perspective on fairness and IP by introducing additional considerations on governing intangible assets under Islamic doctrine.

6

Islamic Vision of IP and the Distribution of Intangible Resources

In Chapter 5, I sought to locate IP as an institution within the basic structure of society and examine how it affects the distribution of basic goods and opportunities to access and benefit from knowledge and cultural resources. In this chapter, I intend to situate IP within a more specific distributive framework, namely, the Islamic precepts on governing and distributing intangible resources. I intend to do that with a specific purpose in mind, that is, to clear the way for a better understanding of the optimal modalities for assigning rights to access and benefit from intangible resources. For the purpose of this chapter, intangible resources should be understood to include knowledge and culture.

Under the Pact *of Istikhlaf*, by which humankind was given the capacity to settle on the earth, all wealth, tangible or intangible, is presented as part of a trust arrangement. Since God is the creator of the earth and all that it produces, God – in the Quranic narrative – is the ultimate owner of all resources on the earth. Humans, as trustees of God, can earn and obtain substantial exclusive rights to use wealth and resources, but this does not amount to unconstrained private ownership. *Istikhlaf* introduces a two-faceted account on governing wealth relationships in society. The ultimate ownership of wealth rests with God; however, individuals can possess wealth to improve the conditions of their settlement on the earth. In a sense, this idea of two layers of ownership is broadly similar to what we find in the concept of tenure. A proprietor of land can have a very strong exclusive right (e.g., fee simple), but the ultimate ownership of the land rests with the sovereign. For instance, the sovereign can compel the proprietor to act on the land in a certain way (e.g., create a conduit for water or a passageway for transport) or refrain from acting in a certain way (e.g., erecting barriers to obstruct aviation or leaving a residential dwelling vacant for a long time).

The argument I make in this chapter is that, under the Pact of *Istikhlaf*, intangible resources too are ultimately owned by God . God's ownership of resources represents a common ownership dedicated to achieving the public interest. This results in two important implications in relation to locating the ideal modality for distributing the control and enjoyment of intangible resources.

First, in the scheme of God's ownership of intangible wealth, it is possible to govern some forms of knowledge and culture through the granting of private, exclusive IP rights. However, since IP could directly interfere with important resources necessary for human settlement on the earth to flourish – namely, knowledge and cultural resources – societies must strive to ensure that their IP systems are designed to deploy knowledge and cultural resources in such a way as to permit such flourishing. In particular, assigning private rights through IP must not disturb the distribution of basic needs such as health, education, and cultural participation. *Istikhlaf* and its underlying principles on governing resources provide an interesting medium to guide the normative analysis of IP as a private right. They change our perception of self-interest and lend a strong voice in support of the collective common good. In this holistic vision, we start from the most equitable use of knowledge resources to improve the conditions of human settlement under *Istikhlaf*, and then design and adjust IP doctrines accordingly.

Second, God's ownership will not translate into exclusionary control of any sort, whether by the state or by a religious authority. As I explain below, God's ownership of wealth, including intangible resources, will be understood as a form of common ownership dedicated to achieving the social good for the community at large. Since private property regimes, IP included, will interfere with this common ownership, they will not be considered the norm in managing knowledge and cultural resources. A good case must be made for property rights to be granted. There will be no normative priorities assigned to IP rights as a means of governing and distributing rights to access knowledge and culture. Priority will always be assigned to public interest considerations. If keeping knowledge widely disseminated can lead to increased availability of content and promote greater access and social good, private ownership through IP must not be preferred.

I WEALTH UNDER THE PACT OF *ISTIKHLAF*

Istikhlaf not only provides the overarching framework for the Islamic theory of justice. As explored in Chapter 5, it also contains particular signals on governing wealth and resources. The Quran's accounts of the relationship between humans and wealth is a classic expression of *Istikhlaf*'s vision of the basic structure of society. Ultimate ownership of all resources on the earth rests with God, with humans acting as trustees over that wealth. It is stated in the Quran: "Believe in Allah and His Messenger, and spend of that whereof He has made you trustees."[1] Islamic scholarship, including some of classical exegesis of the Quran, indicates that this verse forms the basic conceptual framework for the initial position on resources and the purpose of wealth in society. For instance, al-Zamakhshari (d. 1144 CE), in his interpretation of this verse, argues that the root of ownership of wealth lies with God. Human beings are entrusted to use that wealth to further the common good of all trustees (i.e., human beings). Wealth sharing through spending, using that which God has given to people, is one way to achieve the purpose of wealth.[2] Contemporary Muslim scholar Yūsuf al-Qaradawi views *Istikhlaf* as an overarching conceptual framework of the Islamic economic vision on the governance of wealth. Nothing is outside the scope of the creative power of God. Al-Qaradawi argues that resources found in common, including seeds, land, and water, belong ultimately to the Creator. It is stated in the Quran that:

> And have you seen that [seed] which you sow? Is it you who makes it grow, or are We the grower? If We willed, We could make it [dry] debris, and you would remain in wonder . . . And have you seen the water that you drink? Is it you who brought it down from the clouds, or is it We who bring it down? If We willed, We could make it bitter, so why are you not grateful?[3]

According to al-Qaradawi, our policy choices in terms of governing resources must acknowledge God's ultimate ownership of resources. In order for this to be the case, these resources must be administered according to God's instructions to achieve the purpose of *Istikhlaf* (i.e., human flourishing).[4] The rationale underlying this portrayal of the nature of ownership of resources under *Istikhlaf* is the guiding of public reason towards considering ownership as a social function. Appropriation and possession of resources under *Istikhlaf* are possible, but ownership cannot be absolute. The use and enjoyment of wealth and resources cannot be subject to personal self-interest, but have to take into consideration the root of ownership and the purpose of *Istikhlaf*. *Istikhlaf* is not contrary to notions of private ownership. God's ownership of resources and private property are not mutually exclusive. As I will explain below, there is room under *Istikhlaf* to reinforce arguments presented in

1 Quran, trans. Mohsin Khan, 57:7.
2 Al-Zamakhshari, *al-Kashaf* (Maktabat al-Abikan, 1998) vol. 6, 43.
3 Quran, trans. Sahih International, 56:63–56:70.
4 Al-Qaradawi, *al-Takaful al-Ijtima'i*, 11.

Chapter 3 around the compatibility of notions of private ownership with Islamic legal philosophy. Even under *Istikhlaf*, we can argue that appropriation of resources can be a fair reward for labor, important to satisfy human instinct, or an efficient way to increase wealth.

What should be kept in mind here is that God's ownership of resources is conceptually different from private ownership. It is not possessory or exclusionary, as we imagine private ownership. In fact, Islamic jurisprudence draws a general distinction between God's rights and individuals' rights in terms of their nature (*huquq Allah* and *huquq al-nas*). Whatever is classified as a right of God (e.g., ownership of wealth) is to be widely distributed across society to achieve social good.[5] In other words, God's ultimate ownership of wealth is to be manifested as a form of common ownership of wealth. This conceptual insight into the root of wealth ownership and its purpose can operate to guide the normative analysis around the distributive structure of private ownership in the basic structure of society. Under God's non-exclusionary ownership of resources, the default position is that all humans have equal and free access to, and use of, resources to flourish. Private property could be permitted under these arrangements, provided that its ultimate purpose is human flourishing, which is considered to be the social good that humans should strive to achieve under the Pact of *Istikhlaf*.

Sūrat l-qaṣaṣ (The Stories) provides a general, multitiered approach to understanding the purpose of ownership in Islamic normative thought. In the context of condemning the danger that unconstrained private ownership of wealth will create an environment enabling tyranny and selfishness, the Quran instructs humans to "seek through that wealth which Allah has given you, the home of the Hereafter; and [yet], do not forget your share of the world. And do good as Allah has done good to you. And desire not corruption in the land. Indeed, Allah does not like corrupters."[6] Here, the Quran introduces a few normative insights to balance the dichotomy between God's ownership and human ownership. First, it reinforces *Istikhlaf*'s holistic vision of wealth as being entrusted by God. Second, humans can appropriate parts of God-given resources. Ibn Kathīr (d. 1303 CE), in his exegesis on *sūrat l-qaṣaṣ*, maintains that this appropriation may cover basic goods including food, clothes, houses, and legitimate pleasures.[7] More recent works of exegesis do not define appropriation in terms of specific items but in the context of ensuring that property serves a social function in addition to its private function for the individual

5 Emon, "Natural Law and Natural Rights in Islamic Law," 351.

6 Quran, trans. Sahih International, 28:77.

7 Ibn Kathīr, Tafsīr al-Quran al-'adhīm (Dār Tayba) vol. 6, 253.

appropriator.[8] Third, humans are instructed to do good with their wealth and not to utilize it to cause "corruption in the land." This basically boils down to some of the issues discussed in Chapters 2 and 3 on the Islamic view of human flourishing and the dual nature of property rights in Islamic legal philosophy. Ownership, like any institution of the basic structure of society, has to serve the public good. The public good from an Islamic perspective is not defined in terms of the aggregate sum of individual interests but rather as a fundamental deontological duty to promote plural values, including life, intellect, welfare, and freedom. Undermining this overarching deontological duty and its associated plural values can lead to corruption on the earth, which has to be avoided in any normative environment under *Istikhlaf*'s framework for governing resources.

The bottom line is that private property under *Istikhlaf* is not treated as intrinsically evil. If privatizing some wealth would help to develop and increase the existing common pool of wealth and resources without undermining any of the plural normative values necessary for human flourishing, *Istikhlaf* would accommodate private ownership. Furthermore, Islamic law would provide civil and criminal protection for it. However, it should be noted that ownership is a vital institution in the basic structure of society. It can impact in various ways the conditions under which settlement on the earth can flourish. A particular design of the rules on ownership of wealth will be determinative of the power structure and living conditions in a given society. Consider the potential dangers that ownership of wealth could bring in relation to the concentration of power and control in the hands of a few stakeholders. Think also of the cost that society at large could bear when ownership interferes with resources important to the existence of society itself. For instance, the cost of assigning property rights in a range of resources such as soil, air, and water, and the associated harmful impact on other species, including animals and plants. Accordingly, the operational aspects of *Istikhlaf* balance the initial legitimacy of private property with a set of corrective normative values. These values represent a system of checks and balances to ensure ownership grants do not lead to, at least, two outcomes. First, private ownership must not be used to concentrate power and control within the hands of few members in society. Second, private property must not contribute to depleting natural resources and harming the environment.

One way to ameliorate some of the potential negative consequences of placing wealth under private control is to keep in mind that private property is not the only possible regime for governing resources under *Istikhlaf*. In fact,

8 Sayyid Qutb, *Fi Zilal al-Quran* (Dar al-Shuruq, 2003) vol. 5, 2710.

there is no presupposed priority for private ownership of wealth as against common ownership. The original position is that resources are shared among humans as trustees of God. So, the starting point is that private ownership is the exception, not the norm. Hence, it possible here to imagine an alternative to private ownership for the governance and distribution of resources. Suppose that a group of individuals agree to keep land or water open for common use and enjoyment. In their agreement, those individuals consent to design norms and rules to regulate their cooperation around sharing and using these common resources to obtain continuing joint benefits. If this alternative system can achieve efficient utilization of resources and fairly distributed benefits among collaborators, then this system of governance fits perfectly within *Istikhlaf*'s vision on governing resources. Obviously, common and equal enjoyment of God-given resources is more compatible with *Istikhlaf*, as opposed to exclusive possession and enjoyment.

An even more compelling case for compatibility could be made if it can be proven that commons arrangements can, at least sometimes, be more conducive to human flourishing. Nobel Prize laureate Elinor Ostrom and many others demonstrated that the sharing of resources and collaboration can actually work very well in governing common-pool resources, including land, forest, water, and fisheries. Ostrom, in a series of empirical studies, investigated multiple situations where groups of between 50 and 15,000 people agreed on rules and norms outside private property to govern common-pool resources. She found that in many situations, common governance of a particular resource can actually be fairer and more efficient than private property arrangements.[9]

In the following sections, I will discuss the ideal modality for distributing wealth and resources under *Istikhlaf*. Intangible wealth, such as knowledge and cultural resources, will be included as well. However, let me be clear at the very beginning: ideal does not always mean free and open. I will discuss governing knowledge as private property and then as a common asset. But before that, I must stop to discuss how intangible wealth is to be perceived under *Istikhlaf*.

II *ISTIKHLAF* AND GOVERNING INTANGIBLE WEALTH

Arguably, intangible resources are also part of *Istikhlaf*'s vision on governing wealth. Here as well, the ultimate ownership of intangible wealth rests with

9 Elinor Ostrom, *Governing the Commons: The Evolution of Institutions for Collective Action* (Cambridge University Press, 1990) 2, 14, 15.

God, who entrusts humans with the use of these resources to settle and flourish on the earth. We could think of a diverse range of intangible resources such as cultural products, information, discoveries, inventions, and research data as originally God-given resources.

The proposition that knowledge is also a God-given resource can be supported by a number of textual authorities from the Quran. In particular, those textual authorities address the origins of the intellect and natural talents, and humans' roles in creating knowledge. In the Quranic vision of the origin of the intellect and natural talents, there is no room for individuals to claim that they inherently deserve their natural talents. The Quran clearly states that the intellect and the ability to reason are gifts from God. "It is Allah who brought you out of your mothers knowing nothing, and gave you hearing, sight and intellect, so perhaps you would be thankful."[10] Whatever results from the intellect and natural talent comes under God's ultimate ownership. Furthermore, there is nothing in the textual authorities to suggest that God's ultimate ownership of resources is confined to tangible assets. For instance, throughout the Quran, there are few indications that suggest knowledge is also a gift from God. The Quran describes how God gifted humans with the ability to read and absorb knowledge: "Read! And your Lord is the Most Generous. Who has taught by the pen. He has taught human that which he/she knew not."[11]

The proposition that humans do not own or inherently deserve their intellectual capabilities or natural talents should not be labeled as an unrealistic theological proposition. Modern accounts on the ideal structure of society start from the proposition that natural intellectual capabilities are originally common assets and that society has a claim over the products of these natural capabilities to promote objectives of distributive fairness.[12] John Rawls, in one of his boldest claims, argues that talents and natural abilities are not things we inherently deserve.[13] They are conferred upon us by "accident and good fortune."[14] This arbitrary distribution of intellectual capabilities requires, according to Rawls, that "we . . . adopt a principle which mitigates the arbitrary effects of the natural lottery itself."[15]

10 Quran, trans. Mustafa Khattab, 16:78.

11 Quran, trans. Sahih International, 96:4–96-5, 21:80 and 2:31.

12 Robert Nozick, *Anarchy, State, and Utopia* (Blackwell, 1999) 228; Michael J. Sandel, *Liberalism and Limits of Justice* (Cambridge University Press) 77–82; Samuel Freeman, *Justice and the Social Contract* (Oxford University Press, 2007) 11.

13 Compare Merges, *Justifying Intellectual Property*, 107.

14 Rawls, *A Theory of Justice*, 72–74.

15 Ibid., 117.

Knowledge and cultural resources are essential to human flourishing. In modern knowledge economies, access to and distribution of knowledge and cultural resources are far more important than tangible resources. Clearly, countries with limited natural resources such as Japan, South Korea, and Singapore are achieving better outcomes in terms of human flourishing compared with many countries with an abundance of natural tangible resources. Modern normative theories on human flourishing place significant emphasis on the impact of knowledge on society's potential to establish, promote, and enlarge people's freedoms, choices, and capabilities to achieve progress. Similarly, knowledge also has a direct bearing on promoting *maqasid*, a plural vision on human flourishing that encompasses the ability to promote not only human life but also the intellect and wealth. For instance, life expectancy could be enhanced through improved access to and distribution of knowledge leading to advancements in agriculture, food production, and pharmaceuticals, be it in the form of research, data, or inventions. Knowledge also has a direct bearing on promoting the intellect. It is the subject matter of education. Thus, effective access to knowledge products such as information, data, journal articles, textbooks, and media products could lead to an improved educational experience and flourishing intellect. Knowledge is also vital in driving economic growth through innovation.

Now, how should knowledge be governed for the betterment of human settlement under *Istikhlaf*? The way in which we design our institutional arrangements on governing knowledge will have a direct impact on our society's potential to establish, promote, and enlarge people's freedoms, choices, and capacity to flourish. If we are to form a flourishing society under *Istikhlaf*, one of our main tasks will be to find an appropriate design for distributing the ability to control access to knowledge and culture. We would surely want an institutional design that promotes a set of intrinsic capabilities such as the imagination, senses, and thought, while also enhancing overall socio-economic progress. This includes vibrant culture with limitless choices for self-autonomy and self-development. We would want to make it easy to access new and useful ideas, and to enjoy stimulating cultural artefacts. We would also want innovation infrastructure to promote economic growth and enable healthy and comfortable living. We would want to promote discoveries and inventions to cure diseases, and to facilitate communication to make us happier and more productive. This could be achieved through governing knowledge as private property or seeking alternative modalities for governing and managing knowledge resources.

A Istikhlaf *and Knowledge as Private Property*

It is possible to imagine some form of private ownership of knowledge under *Istikhlaf*. Commentators on Islamic economics argue that in order for settlement on the earth (*'imara*) to work, humans must be empowered to appropriate things from God-given common resources. To maintain and develop the human race, as *Istikhlaf* instructs, fair and useful appropriation should be rewarded and encouraged.[16] Denying private ownership altogether is not part of *Istikhlaf*'s vision of the basic structure of society, for that could undermine the public conception of justice, opportunities for autonomy and self-development, and motivation to develop existing resources. This is true for both natural resources and knowledge resources.

The textual authorities of Islamic law that make up the Pact of *Istikhlaf* support the proposition that private property can be accepted for the purpose of governing knowledge. In Chapter 3, I presented few justifications as to why private ownership of knowledge and cultural products can have its place in Islamic sources. Drawing with a broad brush, I explained how various justifications for real property ownership under Islamic sources intersect with several justifications for private ownership in comparative legal philosophy. Under Islamic doctrines, private property can be justified as intrinsically valuable for individuals, fair reward for labor, or necessary to induce useful labor. I will turn now to contextualize those justifications within *Istikhlaf*'s framework on governing knowledge resources.

One possible justification is that when God entrusted humans with the mission of settling on the earth and developing it, He instilled in them the tendency (*fitrah*) towards possession and autonomy (Quran, 18:46). Some form of private ownership over one's own intellectual products could be essential to satisfy this *fitrah* and permit autonomy. The way to a flourishing society starts from empowering people with freedoms and capabilities to author their lives and control their overall life plans. A well-ordered society is one that is not structured in such a way as to undermine *fitrah* and autonomy. On the contrary, the basic structure of society must recognize *fitrah* and enable autonomy through ownership of the products of creative efforts. Such empowerment can open the door to more art, literature, knowledge, and a vibrant culture and thereby enrich human settlement of the earth.

Additional justification to support the proposition that private ownership can form part of the possible methods for governing knowledge under *Istikhlaf*

[16] Muhammed al-Fangari, *al-Madhab al-Iqtisādi fi al-Islam* (al-Hay'a al-Misriyya li al-Kitab, 2006) 133; Muhammed Beltagi, *al-Mulkiyyah al-Fardiyya fi al-Nizam al-Iqtisādi al-Islami* (Dār al-Salam, 2007) 44.

is found in the concepts of labor and merit. Here, the public domain of ideas and expressions represent knowledge resources under God's ultimate ownership, available as free materials for humans (*mubah*). Those who spend time and effort on appropriation (*ihraz al-mubah*) should be entitled to some form of reward. Arguably, exclusionary control over the products of one's creative efforts is necessary to support a public conception of fairness. After all, fairness, according to the Quran, is regulative of all affairs in the basic structure of society in the Islamic vision. "We have already sent Our messengers with clear evidences and sent down with them the Scripture and the balance that the people may maintain [their affairs] in justice." It is possible to debate the scope of the exclusive rights a person should have as a reward for their creative efforts. For instance, we could argue that private ownership must respect basic human needs of fair equality of opportunity, as discussed in the previous chapter. However, it would be very difficult to argue that a society that rejects any form of private property as reward for labor is a society that "maintains [its affairs] in justice." A society structured under *Istikhlaf* will not deny recognition for those who transform raw knowledge resources into novel and useful applications. If individual A chooses to use her intellect to work hard, sometimes even during weekends, to create software that makes it easier and more fun for children to learn mathematics, then she should be entitled to a *fair* reward for her labor.

Finally, we could offer a consequentialist argument to support private ownership of knowledge under *Istikhlaf*. Recall that in Chapter 2 I referred to a widely accepted proposition in Islamic legal philosophy that the promotion of wealth is one of the underlying objectives of lawmaking in Islam. This can be translated as pursuing policy objectives that increase growth and economic efficiency. Growth and economic efficiency can be considered important tools to enable prosperous human settlement on the earth under *Istikhlaf*. If it is proven that granting private property rights over knowledge can enable prosperous settlement for humankind on the earth, private property rights can be accepted. This acceptance is of course contingent on adhering to the overarching deontological framework of *maqasid*, as discussed in Chapters 2, 3, and 4.

The problem is that there is great uncertainty in the economic analysis of IP over the correlation between the granting of exclusionary private rights in knowledge and cultural products and increased net social welfare. Part of IP scholarship argues that, overall, private ownership of knowledge through patent and copyright grants, creates efficient outcomes for society at large, not only for the rights holders. Robert Merges defended this proposition in relation to some knowledge and cultural products from patent and copyright-based industries. Merges argues that exclusionary rights through patent and copyright regimes benefit society at large, particularly people in lower income brackets. He provides a few examples showing how patent and copyright regimes can contribute to improving the living conditions of millions of low-income individuals. Merges claims that patented technologies improved communications and revolutionized agricultural production. He also defends copyright by claiming that it has enabled millions of people to enjoy a variety of cultural products.[17]

There is no doubt that increased availability of more knowledge and cultural products improves both the conditions of human settlement under *Istikhlaf* and the objective of promoting wealth under *maqasid*. However, Merges's assertions on the positive correlation between patent and copyright regimes and increased social welfare for the non-IP holders lack sufficient empirical support. We do not exactly know how private ownership – as opposed to no ownership – of knowledge through patent contributed to making communications and agriculture better and more accessible. Additionally, we do not know how copyright enabled more cultural goods to be produced and made available to disadvantaged groups in American society.

While it is very difficult to find empirical support for general statements around positive correlations between IP regimes and increased social welfare, patents on pharmaceutical inventions seem to be the exception. There is consistent empirical support for the proposition that the pharmaceutical industry functions better under patents. In other words, the prospect of patent protection empowers pharmaceutical companies to spend hundreds of millions of dollars and employ thousands of scientists to produce drugs that help people live better and longer lives.[18] Arguably, private ownership of knowledge through patents in this case could be conducive to improving the conditions of human settlement on the earth, to use the language of *Istikhlaf*. This could be one clear case under which governing knowledge through private ownership

17 Merges, *Justifying Intellectual Property*, 118–19.

18 Stuart J. H. Graham, Robert P. Merges, Pam Samuelson, and Ted Sichelman, "High Technology Entrepreneurs and the Patent System: Results of the 2008 Berkeley Patent Survey" (2010) 24 *Berkeley Technology Law Journal* 1256; Frank R. Lichtenberg, "The Impact of New Drug Launches on Longevity: Evidence from Longitudinal, Disease-Level Data from 52 Countries, 1982–2001" (2005) 5 *International Journal of Health Care Finance and Economics* 47–73; Wesley M. Cohen, Richard R. Nelson, and John P. Walsh, "Protecting Their Intellectual Assets: Appropriability Conditions and Why U.S. Manufacturing Firms Patent (or Not)," Working Paper 7552, National Bureau of Economic Research, Cambridge MA (revised 2004); Richard C. Levin et al., "Appropriating the Returns from Industrial Research and Development" (1987) 18 *Brookings Papers on Economic Activity* (Special Issue) 783.

under *Istikhlaf* could be acceptable. Of course, the recognition of patents in this context has to conform to a set deontological values, as discussed below.

Patents for pharmaceuticals is only one case. There could be more. The door is thus open to private ownership of knowledge and culture under *Istikhlaf*. God's gift of the intellect and natural creative capabilities must be empowered, so that it can contribute to human flourishing. If private ownership of knowledge is the most efficient method of governing resources in a manner that leaves everyone in society better off, then it should form part of the basic structure of society under *Istikhlaf*. Here, I feel the need to quote Robert Nozik, who makes a relevant point on the possibility of creating a situation where harmony could exist between individuals with natural creative capabilities who might benefit from IP:

> People's talents and abilities are an asset to a free community; others in the community benefit from their presence and are better off because they are there rather than elsewhere or nowhere. . . . Life, over time, is not a constant-sum game, wherein if greater ability or effort leads to some getting more, that means that others must lose. In a free society, people's talents do benefit others, and not only themselves.[19]

B Fair Exercise of Private Control over Intangible Wealth

The arguments surrounding the acceptance of private ownership as a method for governing knowledge resources are strong. However, we need to be mindful of the significant challenges related to the purpose of *Istikhlaf* when designing individual property rights. In order to ensure that individual property grants are consistent with *Istikhlaf*'s purpose and the plural deontological values of *maqasid*, we need to have a benchmark for deciding how far can we go in granting individual property rights in knowledge. Sometimes, it could be more prudent to keep knowledge outside the property system altogether. We also need to think of mechanisms to ensure that the granting of private property rights does not confer on the rights holders excessive powers of control that are disproportionate to their individual contributions and, at the same time, impinge on pressing public interest considerations.

Not all knowledge and cultural products should be the subject of private property rights. Modern IP laws around the world exclude various forms of knowledge and cultural products from their scope. The rationale for this exclusion is to ensure that certain forms of knowledge and culture remain

[19] Nozick, *Anarchy, State, and Utopia*, 228.

widely accessible as raw materials due to their importance as basic tools for innovation and creativity. For instance, copyright law does not provide protection for ideas behind literary and artistic works. Only original expressions can be copyrightable subject matter. J. K. Rowling can only claim copyright protection over Harry Potter in relation to the expressions she made in her novel, including characters, places, and the particular sequence of her narratives. However, anybody is entitled to use the idea of a young boy fighting evil in presenting another creative vision, perhaps even in a different historical and cultural context, such as Africa or China instead of England.

Similarly, patent laws provide protection only for novel and nonobvious knowledge underpinning inventions. Any invention that forms part of the prior art base or known to the experts in the relevant industry will not be patentable. Many patent laws around the world explicitly exclude some forms of knowledge resources from patentability. These include discoveries, products of nature, scientific theories, and mathematical methods, to name but a few. Again, the assumption is that common ownership of these basic knowledge resources is more in the public interest than is private ownership.

However, privatization started to invade some of the basic knowledge resources such as discoveries, information, and abstract knowledge. In Europe, databases are granted *sui generis* protection under the European Directive 96/9 on the protection of databases. In the United States, the boundaries of privatization were stretched to allow the patenting of products of nature and discovered arrangements of data. Before the famous *Myriad* case,[20] in which the US Supreme Court unanimously invalidated patent claims relating to isolated genes, the US patent system granted patents for gene sequencing. This patent protection continued for years, despite reports indicating that private ownership over this kind of knowledge is an undesirable form of governance, not only because it interferes with basic healthcare but also because of its potential impact on scientific research and innovation in the medical sector.[21]

What can we learn from the information provided above? If we are to stay true to *Istikhlaf*'s vision of settlement on the earth, in particular the part under which humankind is instructed to seek means to flourish, we should keep in mind that not every form of knowledge can be available for privatization.

[20] *Association for Molecular Pathology v. Myriad Genetics*, [1] No. 12–398 (569 US, June 13, 2013).

[21] See, for instance, Report of the Secretary's Advisory Committee on Genetics, Health, and Society, *Gene Patents and Licensing Practices and Their Impact on Patient Access to Genetic Tests* (April, 2010), https://osp.od.nih.gov/wp-content/uploads/2013/11/SACGHS_patents_report_2010.pdf

There should be categories of basic knowledge resources protected against any attempt at privatization. The precise boundaries of these "basic knowledge resources" is a matter for public policy. But knowledge vital for social utility and fair equality of opportunity, such as genetic information, should not be privatized. It should be kept as a common asset for everyone.

If we are able to craft a normative basis to protect basic knowledge from private control, we need to think of mechanisms for ensuring that those property rights that escape the "basic knowledge test" are not used to confer excessive social and economic powers on the rights holders. As we noted in Chapter 5, concentration of power of any sort is not a feature of a fair society. Accordingly, once granted, private property rights should also be subject to *Istikhlaf*'s overarching vision on human flourishing. Even legitimate private ownership of knowledge must not obstruct comfortable and flourishing human settlement on the earth.

Here, the Quran provides a statement of general applicability on the need for proportionality between the inputs provided and the outputs claimed: "And that man hath only that for which he maketh effort."[22] While this general statement from the Quran is not particularly concerned with striking a balance between merit and the ability to control wealth, I would argue that it could be looked on as a general moral principle with normative implications. One possible reading of this principle is that if we are to reward humans for their contributions, each one of them must be proportionately rewarded according to the intrinsic value of his or her contributions. Reward must not be extended to include excessive powers to satisfy potential egotistic conceptions of self-interest at the expense of collective human flourishing. In this context, it is not difficult to point to practical manifestations of the principle of proportionality, even in premodern accounts on Islamic legal traditions. For instance, Qutb cites *Kitab al-kharaj* by the Hanafi jurist Abū Yūsuf (d. 798 CE), who reported that the Prophet established limits on the right of ownership that comes as a result of laboring on a vacant piece of land. Under Islamic law, if someone develops a vacant piece of land, they shall own it. However, ownership as reward for labor does not entitle the appropriator to absolute ownership. In particular, labor in itself will not allow a person to keep a piece of land unproductive for three years.[23] Arguably, the intrinsic merit of the act of laboring to develop a vacant piece of land is not proportionate to claims of perpetual ownership in cases where such ownership could hamper social utility.

[22] Quran, trans. Pickthall, 53:39.

[23] Qutb, *al-'adalah al-Ijtima'iyya fi al-Islam*, 94.

Here, the general and abstract principles of justice introduced in Chapter 5 could be applied to provide additional guidance to assist in delineating the intrinsic merit of individual property rights. There, I explained that determining what is fair starts with adhering to principles of justice derived from various Islamic sources. Those same principles can be used to identify the fair limits of the private property rights in knowledge and culture. For instance, under the first principle of justice discussed in Chapter 5, a private property right will be deemed disproportionate to its intrinsic worth when it encroaches on essential human needs such as a healthy life or a flourishing intellect. Similarly, under the second principle, the rights holder would be deemed to have excessive property rights when his or her private control over a particular knowledge or cultural resource can unduly undermine fair equality of opportunity for others to participate in making and remaking knowledge and culture around them. If a conflict with the principles of justice arises, the individual property right will be considered disproportionate. Then society, through the legislature or the judiciary, will be responsible for rearranging the private right to give precedence to promoting life and the intellect.

In a related context, Merges refers to the proportionality principle as a corrective normative mechanism to set the balance right in IP laws. Courts should be empowered to intervene whenever an already granted IP right enables the rights holder to obtain excessive leverage to control the use of the IP right. Merges explains that:

> Our legal system recognizes that there are times when legal entitlements give someone "excessive" or "disproportionate" leverage. By this I mean power beyond what a person rightfully deserves, or beyond what makes sense, given the circumstances . . . To state it simply, an IPR must not confer on its holder leverage or power that is grossly disproportionate to what is deserved in the situation. If an IPR would effectively confer power or control over a much more vast market or set of markets than what is actually deserved, in light of the work covered by the IP right, that right must be limited in some way.[24]

Merges provides empirical observations to show how IP rights holders are exercising their rights to obtain disproportionate rewards for their respective contributions. In the context of patent litigations, he observes that:

> More recently, some patent owners have found a way to leverage the large-scale investments of technology companies in a way that strikes me (and many others) as quite unfair. Patent owners in these cases use a combination of companies' sunk costs and the "automatic injunction" rule to extract

[24] Merges, *Justifying Intellectual Property*, 162.

> unfairly large payments from technology companies. Often, this grows out of a patent on a single component of a complex product. Such a patent can generate excessive leverage if the patent is discovered or asserted after the design for the complex product is fixed – at which point the costs to switch to another design may be very steep.[25]

The need for proportionality is arguably a fair social claim according to both the Islamic vision of social justice and some comparative accounts of social justice. More importantly, the principle of proportionality can be relied upon to expand the debate around certain features of current IP laws. For instance, in relation to the protection term, how long is long enough to provide just reward for the rights holders without creating excessive leverage to control culture? I said above that under *Istikhlaf* we should strive for a vibrant culture. The design of the individual IP right has to be responsive to that.

Now, is it proportionate to allow copyright holders to control a certain literary work for life and for their heirs to control it for 70 years after their death? Copyright terms have a significant bearing on people's ability to participate in shaping and reshaping culture. An example is the case of Margaret Mitchell's novel *Gone with the Wind* and its counternarrative by Alice Randall, *The Wind Done Gone*. Randall attempted to reconstruct the narrative presented in *Gone with the Wind*, which depicts enslavement from the standpoint of masters. In Mitchell's narrative of life in plantation farms, slave owners are portrayed as noble aristocrats while blacks are described as "creatures of small intelligence ... [l]ike monkeys or small children."[26] She defends slavery as good for them! In *The Wind Done Gone*, Randall flips this narrative on its head, giving black characters "some redeeming quality – whether depth, wit, cunning, beauty, strength, or courage – that their *GWTW* analogues lacked."[27]

Five decades after Mitchell's death, her estate sought to prevent the publication of Randall's novel, relying on copyright protection. They were successful at first. The trial judge found *The Wind Done Gone* to be an unauthorized reproduction of *Gone with the Wind*. However, the Eleventh Circuit decided to reverse the decision and hold that Randall's work was fair use, citing parody as justification. Now, the outcome of this particular case is in itself irrelevant. It does not prevent copyright holders from using their private rights to defend their perception of culture. Furthermore, in many jurisdictions outside the United States, where there is no fair use defense,

[25] Ibid., 160.
[26] Margaret Mitchell, *Gone with the Wind* (Taylor Trade Publishing, 2011) 400.
[27] *Suntrust Bank v. Houghton Mifflin Co.*, 268 F.3d 1257, 1259 (11th Cir. 2001).

copyright holders and their heirs are likely to have a stronger case. Cultural studies consider the ability to participate in shaping and reshaping culture as an empowering act. This ability equips otherwise marginalized groups with the capabilities needed to increase their social, economic, and political powers.[28] Commenting on the ability to participate in culture and flourishing, Sunder argues that:

> Reworking the proprietary icons of our age can lead to both political resistance and economic empowerment. Given a popular media that marginalizes various segments of society, the act of reworking popular stories to assert one's own value is empowering: it opens the path to new livelihoods and roles. Self-insertion changes popular meanings, laying the foundation for economic change. Copying can be an act of both homage and subversion.[29]

Private property rights should not be allowed to enable the rights holder to decide how culture should be reconceptualized and rewritten. Such ability would invest the property right with overarching powers to control narrative and disempower members of society from retelling popular culture from their own perspectives. No individual rights holder should have the power to present a particular historical cultural account on how slavery was like for the slaves without being challenged with a counternarrative. Most certainly this property right should not last for the life of the original maker of the expression plus 70 years after their death. I will come back to the fairness of the copyright term in Chapter 7.

Be that as it may, issues around disproportionate contributions and rewards in relation to copyright and its term is just one example. The principle of proportionality can be used to assess the appropriateness of a larger pattern of potential disparities between contributions and rewards across other forms of IP, particularly patents. For instance, in Chapter 3 I indicated that there is an increasing suspicion that some features of the current international patent regimes empower patentees with substantial rights to the detriment of public health considerations. Patentees can rely on patents to control the supply and price of pharmaceutical products, regardless of the contributions they make in terms of investment in research and development. The principle of proportionality should be relied upon to assess whether it is appropriate to allow pharmaceutical companies to have unrestrained control over the price and supply of a particular drug.

28 Cheryl Harris, "A Sociology of Television Fandom," in Cheryl Harris and Alison Alexander, eds., *Theorizing Fandom: Fans, Subculture and Identity* (1998) 41, 42.

29 Madhavi Sunder, *From Goods to a Good Life: Intellectual Property and Global Justice* (Yale University Press, 2012) 125.

For instance, is it fair to allow Gilead Sciences to rely on its patent to set the price of Sovaldi, an effective cure against hepatitis C? As of 2018, Gilead is selling Sovaldi at $84,000 per course of treatment. According to the US Department of Health and Human Services, 3.2 million people in the United States alone are living with chronic hepatitis C.[30] Despite exhaustive research, I was not able to find out how much the company invested in making the drug, to assess whether $84,000 per course of treatment is actually justified. However, according to its website, the company made more than $9 billion in sales of Sovaldi in 2015–2016 alone.[31]

What we do know is that Gilead has made substantial revenue from trading in Sovaldi. We also know that patent law permits that. What we do not know is whether this is fair. Did Gilead do enough to deserve such an enormous ability to control the market and access for 3.2 million people infected with the disease? This certainly is an area where the proportionality principle can be used to correct any potential imbalance between the intrinsic value of the rights holders' contribution and the control claimed.

One might stop and ask here, didn't you just mention that there is empirical evidence to support the pharmaceutical company's claim that patent protection is necessary? This is correct. I am not questioning the legitimacy of the initial patent grant, but how far it can go. The social claim for proportionality is also reinforced by the widely accepted proposition in IP scholarship that nobody creates out of thin air. Suzanne Scotchmer has shown that developing knowledge is an accumulative process. Patentees rely on existing knowledge resources to make their inventions.[32] This is particularly true for pharmaceutical products. Pharmaceutical companies rarely make new molecular entities. For instance, new drugs approved in the United States each year rely on already existing molecular entities. On top of that, substantial parts of the research relied upon to produce new drugs is publicly funded. Conceivably, this makes it even fairer to modify the scope of the patent right, if needed, to take public health considerations into account. Putting public health considerations ahead of any utilitarian claims seems more faithful to Islamic legal philosophy. After all, its overarching aim is to prioritize the deontic claims

30 US Department of Health & Human Services, "Hepatitis C," www.hhs.gov/opa/reproductive-health/sexually-transmitted-infections/hepatitis-c/index.html

31 Gilead Sciences, "Gilead Sciences Announces Fourth Quarter and Full Year 2016 Financial Results," www.gilead.com/news/press-releases/2017/2/gilead-sciences-announces-fourth-quarter-and-full-year-2016-financial-results

32 Suzanne Scotchmer, *Innovation and Incentives* (MIT Press, 2004).

around human life rather than the efficiency-based arguments put forward by IP rights holders.

Applying the proportionality principle to set the right balance in IP regimes implies a value judgment. We need to provide private rights over knowledge and culture when this is fair and useful to spur sustainable innovation and creativity. Sustainable innovation and creativity are essential to economic growth and a vibrant culture. However, we need to keep in mind that Islamic legal philosophy assesses policy choices in terms of flourishing. Flourishing presupposes an overarching deontological framework where options are guided on deontic grounds rather than in terms of utilitarian values. Setting the appropriate design for an individual IP right starts with the dual objectives of rights in Islamic legal philosophy, as explored in Chapter 3. The rights holder will not be considered as the center of the system. Rather, the system will have dual objectives, or two centers, if you like: a fair and proportionate reward for the person who develops knowledge and culture and a curb on the private right when deontic values are at stake. These values include people's capability to access good healthcare, food, and textbooks, and to participate in culture.

It is interesting to note that this conceptualization of IP is not unique to Islamic legal philosophy under *Istikhlaf*. It has a very strong affinity with the growing trend in comparative scholarship on IP and human rights. For instance, Laurence Helfer surveyed major international human rights treaties to examine the ways in which different forms of human rights interact with private property rights in knowledge and culture. The essence of Helfer's argument is that IP must be arranged to serve a bundle of fundamental human rights to health, food, education, and cultural participation. He recommends that nations around the world adopt a human rights framework for IP lawmaking. Under this framework, Helfer suggests that "[w]here intellectual property laws help to achieve human rights outcomes, governments should embrace it. Where it hinders those outcomes, its rules should be modified."[33]

C Istikhlaf *and Knowledge as a Common Resource*

It is possible to govern knowledge resources without IP. Knowledge could be kept accessible to the entire community or segments of the community through adopting cooperative strategies on its use and development.

33 Laurence R. Helfer, "Toward a Human Rights Framework for Intellectual Property" (2007) 40 *University of California Davis Law Review* 971–1020, 1018.

Keeping knowledge accessible fits very well with the original position on governing resources under *Istikhlaf*. I mentioned above that God's ultimate ownership of all resources is not exclusionary in nature and that private ownership has no normative priority in governing resources. Under *Istikhlaf*, all resources are initially common, open for people to share in order to improve the conditions of their settlement on the earth. In addition, keeping knowledge accessible in the commons broadly aligns with textual sources on encouraging knowledge dissemination. Ibn Majah's (d. 887 CE) collection of the Sunnah provides a good illustration. Ibn Majah reports two *hadiths* in which the Prophet, in very general terms, encourages believers to circulate knowledge within their communities. Ibn Majah reported that the Prophet had said:

- The best of charity is when a Muslim man [or woman] gains knowledge, then teaches it to his Muslim brother [or sister].
- The rewards of good deeds that will reach a believer after his death are: Knowledge which he taught and spread . . .[34]

In addition to the religious justifications for the desirability of wide accessibility and dissemination of knowledge, opting for such an approach is also well justified on grounds of economic efficiency. I mentioned above that Elinor Ostrom conducted extensive research explaining how it is possible to solve common-pool resource problems outside the private property systems. Her work challenges Garrett Hardin's famous theory expounded in "The Tragedy of the Commons," which argues that the open use of limited common-pool resources will lead to the degradation of these resources.[35] The main thesis of her work is that the imposition of private ownership is not the only solution to address the dangers associated with overuse and consumption of common resources.[36] She argues that there are many situations where people can commit themselves to cooperative approaches to share and improve common resources. Individuals can create a collective agreement to set the metes and bounds for the use, consumption, and maintenance of a common resource. They could agree on norms and rules to direct and monitor their behaviors in a way that increases the joint returns to them while preserving the common resources. To prove her hypothesis, Ostrom supplemented her argument with

34 Ibn Majah, *Sunan Ibn Majah*, trans. Nasiruddin Al-Khattab (Dārussalam, 2007) 232–33.

35 Garrett Hardin, "The Tragedy of the Commons" (December 13, 1968) 162 (3859) *Science, New Series* 1243–48.

36 Elinor Ostrom, *Governing the Commons: The Evolution of Institutions for Collective Action* (Cambridge University Press, 1990) 2, 14, 15.

several examples from around the world of people collectively governing resources such as water, fisheries, land, and forest.[37]

Keeping resources open for use and development under cooperative approaches is not only compatible with the original position of resources under *Istikhlaf*, it also enjoys direct support from textual authorities. *Takaful* (cooperation) is the central design principle underlying the organization of relations in the Islamic vision of a well-ordered society. The Arabic term *takaful* comes from *tafa'ul*, which literally means interaction. The Quran instructs believers to "cooperate in righteousness."[38] Writing on the scope of *takaful* as a central value in Islamic ethics, Imam Mahmud Shaltut maintains that under the *takaful* paradigm individuals are bound by a collective religious responsibility to cooperate towards achieving increased welfare for the entire social group.[39] Arguably, creating the institutional conditions for people to cooperate in using and developing common resources to achieve joint benefits is a clear application of *takaful* and the Quranic instruction to "cooperate in righteousness."

Governing knowledge resources through cooperation and sharing is now increasingly recognized as a fair and efficient institutional arrangement to promote innovation and creativity. In fact, sharing and cooperation could be particularly relevant to governing knowledge resources. Unlike natural resources, which can be susceptible to the risk of overconsumption and depletion, knowledge resources can be widely shared without being entirely exhausted. There are several case studies showing that a diverse array of knowledge resources, including technological knowledge, scientific data, news reporting, online knowledge pools (e.g., Wikipedia), and software can be shared and at the same time give rise to increased efficiency in use and development.[40] Even when private property rights in knowledge work to provide an incentive to create more knowledge resources, they simultaneously limit their availability.[41] When knowledge resources such as snippets of code, photos, research findings, and cultural narratives are privatized, privatization can impose costs on innovation.

Ostrom sought to stretch her analysis of the arable common to knowledge resources. Together with Charlotte Hess, she argues that privatization of

37 Ibid., 20.

38 Quran, trans. Sahih International, 5:2.

39 Mahmud Shaltut, al-Islam 'aqeda wa Shari'a (Dār al-Shuruq, 2001) 436.

40 Brett M. Frischmann, Michael J. Madison and Katherine J. Strandburg, eds., *Governing Knowledge Commons* (Oxford University Press, 2014) x.

41 Brett M. Frischmann, *Infrastructure: The Social Value of Shared Resources* (Oxford University Press 2012) 261–68.

knowledge is actually less conducive to increased joint benefits for society. Ostrom points out that as overgrazing had been recognized as the tragedy of tangible commons, commodification and enclosure is the tragedy of knowledge commons.[42] She argues that sharing and cooperation between users and developers of knowledge resources could be more efficient. She believes that people can agree on norms and structures of punishments and rewards to guide their cooperation and sharing of knowledge. For instance, in the same paper with Charlotte Hess, she highlights the positive impact of sharing knowledge in the context of scholarly information in universities. Hess and Ostrom conclude that "collective action and new institutional design play as large a part in the shaping of scholarly information as do legal restrictions and market forces."[43]

If we are to deploy knowledge for flourishing under *Istikhlaf*, we must consider that privatization through IP rights is neither the only, nor the best, mechanism for promoting increased knowledge, use, and development. Openness, sharing, and collaboration as modalities for governing and distributing knowledge are, overall, more faithful to the Islamic vision on governing and distributing wealth. Simultaneously, these modalities can also be more conducive to human flourishing. Institutional arrangements which enable wide diffusion of knowledge resources are intrinsically and instrumentally valuable from a human flourishing perspective.

When knowledge is kept open, people will have more access to opportunities to read, listen, view, imagine, experiment, learn, and reshape knowledge and cultural content. These are intrinsically good things. Accessible knowledge resources are also instrumentally useful in enhancing human capabilities to achieve socio-economic development, as I mentioned above. A society that provides individuals with more opportunities and freedoms to engage with knowledge resources is more likely to have intellectually developed citizens and the increased knowledge and cultural production necessary for socio-economic development.[44]

Modern technological tools and internet platforms are expanding the positive potential of cooperative governance of knowledge resources. With the

42 Charlotte Hess and Elinor Ostrom, "A Framework for Analyzing Scholarly Communication as a Commons" (2004), Digital Library of the Commons (United States), http://surface.syr.edu/cgi/viewcontent.cgi?article=1020&context=sul

43 Charlotte Hess and Elinor Ostrom, "Ideas, Artifacts, and Facilities: Information as a Common-Pool Resource" (2003) 66 (1–2) *Law and Contemporary Problems* 113.

44 Julie E. Cohen, "The Place of the User in Copyright Law" (2005) 74 *Fordham Law Review* 347, 370; Joseph P. Liu, "Copyright Law's Theory of the Consumer" (2003) 44 *Boston College Law Review* 397, 407.

rapid growth of internet technologies, along with the availability of personal computers to a greater number of people, participatory platforms have been brought into existence. The main characteristics of these platforms are that people produce creative works for free and have the opportunity to distribute them for free, dispensing with the traditional and expensive intermediaries who used to dominate the public dissemination of knowledge and information.[45]

Movements such as open software and online knowledge platforms have significantly benefited from the Internet and relatively cheap technological tools in organizing themselves. Thousands of people are working through these movements to learn, experiment, and produce more knowledge. In a sense, these movements are empowering people to, in Nussbaum's words, "use [their] senses, to imagine, think, and reason – and to do these things in a 'truly human' way."[46] Furthermore, unlike IP, these movements pose no danger that could undermine any of the objectives of lawmaking in Islam, as I explained in Chapter 3. On the contrary, knowledge that could be used to promote the plural values of Islamic law is accessible and deployable to serve human flourishing. Excessive privatization of the knowledge underlying patent and copyright could encroach on basic needs such as access to food, medicine, and educational materials.

Yochai Benkler observes that the mechanisms of promoting innovation and creativity in cyberspace inform us that property rights are not the only mechanisms that motivate people to innovate and become creative. Assumptions built on incentives depict human beings as selfish creatures. "Yet, all around us, we see people cooperating and working in collaboration, doing the right thing, behaving fairly, acting generously." In order to benefit most from the potentials of cyberspace, we need "to build new models based on fresh assumptions about human behaviour that can help us design better systems"[47] than those we already have.

In conclusion, when we think normatively about the optimal model for assigning rights and obligations in knowledge and culture, it would not be acceptable to exclude private ownership altogether. I do not believe that such a proposition can be sustained under the Pact of *Istikhlaf*. On the contrary, some justifications for private ownership of ideas and expressions are acceptable. However, when deciding on the optimal governing structure for

45 Niva Elkin Koren, "User Generated Platforms," in Rochelle C. Dreyfuss, Harry First and Diane L. Zimmerman, *Working within the Boundaries of Intellectual Property* (Oxford University Press, 2010) 113.

46 Martha Nussbaum, *Creating Capabilities*, 33.

47 Yochai Benkler, "The Unselfish Gene" (August 2011) *Harvard Business Review* 89.

distributing property rights in intangible wealth from an Islamic perspective, priority is given to achieving notions of the social good as understood in the Islamic principles of social justice explored in Chapter 5. All social institutions are to operate with an awareness of the priority of a set of basic plural values necessary to sustain autonomous life, including the promotion of health, intellect, and equal opportunities in the broadest sense conceivable. In this normative environment, we should be open to the possibility that private ownership of knowledge and culture can achieve economic efficiency without necessarily posing an existential threat to the basic plural values or the principle of fair equality of opportunity. In this case, there will be no good normative reason to deny IP rights over knowledge and culture. Nevertheless, once rights have been granted, IP must be subject to a set of internal measures to ensure the continuing supremacy of justice when exercising exclusive rights. One way to do that is to ensure that the IP system does not enable the rights holders to exercise and concentrate substantial powers that do not correspond to their relevant contributions. For instance, we should ask ourselves if it is fair for someone to market their invention at a prohibitively high price, when it was made possible by substantial reliance on publicly funded research or existing prior knowledge, or for them to prevent others from engaging in follow-up innovation based on that invention.

On the other hand, full consideration of the Islamic vision of social justice requires us to stay true to the metaphysical origin of wealth and resources. Under that vision, God's ultimate ownership implies common ownership of wealth and resources. Since the original position is common ownership, we should not jump to the privatization of knowledge and culture. We need to be open to possibilities that leave knowledge and culture in the common sphere. This is particularly vital when there are possibilities that non-exclusionary governance of knowledge and culture could better serve basic plural values and promote fair equality of opportunity. In the following chapter, I explore some applications within and outside the IP system where such possibilities might exist.

7

A Fair IP Landscape

I A RESTATEMENT OF ISLAMIC NORMATIVITY ON IP

The Islamic theory of justice sketched out in Chapters 5 and 6 can be reduced to a set of normative signals to guide IP policymaking towards fairness. First, the Islamic normative vision on IP does not reject the idea of granting exclusive rights in intangible objects to reward creators or increase production and promote economic efficiency. However, fair reward and economic efficiency are not the prime criteria for judging IP as fair. They form important part of a much larger analytical scheme for defining the Islamic theory of social justice. In addition to covering efficiency and merit-based claims, the theory requires IP to be held accountable to broader basic needs and considerations.

Second, at an abstract level, the Islamic normative vision requires IP to be designed with a particular awareness of basic social needs, including the right to life, access to health and education, and equality of opportunity to make, challenge, and reshape knowledge and culture. According to this normative signal, the ability to exclude others from accessing knowledge and culture that underpins an IP right must not transform into an ability to concentrate power or unduly control access, thereby undermining fair equality of opportunity. Whenever an excessive concentration of power is a reality or a possibility, law and policy must give priority to promoting redistribution. This is particularly important in the case of disadvantaged groups who are unable to pay for access to essential goods protected by IP, whether these goods are essential for life, the mind, or effective participation in society.

Third, although the Islamic normative vision is open to the possibility that IP may have a place in a fair society, it does not assign particular priority to IP as a modality for governing knowledge and culture. The original position of knowledge and cultural resources under the Pact of *Istikhlaf* is common ownership dedicated to the enhancement of human flourishing. Private control through IP is not the norm but the exception. IP claimants must make a case to justify that state-sanctioned protection of the right to exclude others is a fair reward for their labor and/or good for society. The fear of a tragedy of the commons – a scenario where common ownership depletes scarce resources – is not part of the Islamic outlook on governing resources. Accordingly, common governance is always a viable possibility in both arable and knowledge realms alike.

In a nutshell, the Islamic normative framework on IP emphasizes the necessity of a fair and efficient IP system, one which reinforces the importance of promoting openness and achieving a fairer distribution and greater dissemination of knowledge and cultural resources. It stresses the need to avoid unfair concentration of knowledge resources and excessive restrictions on their use and reuse. The important question here is: How can these normative signals be mobilized to hold IP rules and doctrines accountable to social justice considerations?

I locate answers to this question in what I call "critical intellectual property studies" (CIPS). The general theme of these studies neatly reflects social justice concerns in the Islamic worldview. CIPS scholarship challenges and overturns established ideas and norms in IP theory and formal institutional frameworks, including the TRIPS Agreement and FTAs. Proponents of CIPS criticize the structure of IP laws and believe that its "logic" grows out of imbalance in power relationships, domestically and internationally. They believe that IP laws generally exist to protect the interests of the parties who influence their making and development. Powerful and resourceful IP-intensive industries use the law to maintain an excessive concentration of knowledge resources and place a wide range of unnecessary restrictions on their use and reuse. Lawrence Lessig, one of the key figures in CIPS, points to the concentration of culture production enabled by the current IP system. He states that, "never in our history have fewer exercised more control over the development of our culture than now. . . . Never has the concentration been as significant as it is now."[1] CIPS have proposed a range of methods to break the conventional power structure in IP markets and promote distributive justice. CIPS scholars share the fundamental objective of creating equilibrium to enable wide access to knowledge and culture without undermining the necessary incentives that would keep vital IP-intensive markets operational. According to Yochai Benkler, another leading figure in CIPS, this "'will lead to substantial redistribution of power and money from the twentieth-century

[1] Lawrence Lessig, "Creative Commons'" (2004) 65(1) *Montana Law Review* 8–9.

producers of information, culture and communications – like Hollywood, the recording industry and the telecommunications giants – to a widely diffuse population around the globe."[2]

CIPS scholars have channeled their efforts towards creating two distinct but significantly overlapping conceptual frameworks to reorient IP laws towards fairness. They have defended the idea of a powerful public domain and users' rights as necessary and reasonable mediums through which to foster fair IP policymaking. The rest of this chapter will search public domain and users' rights discourses to locate a general reform agenda for fair IP in the Islamic worldview.

The public domain movement within CIPS is constantly challenging the increased private control of knowledge and culture. Advocates of the public domain define its content and operational features in a manner that largely reflects social justice considerations in the Islamic vision. Public domain advocates do not reject IP protection over knowledge and culture but ask for evidence justifying the benefit that will result from the grant of an IP right. They emphasize the need to keep knowledge open and free whenever openness and freedom do not pose existential threats to the particular species of knowledge. The public domain is by nature an open environment, where wide ranges of creative works can be legally shared without being concentrated within the hands of a few members of the society. Intellectual goods that are kept freely available in the public domain will not necessarily lose value through free riding and mass reproduction. It is possible to govern these goods through cooperative modalities of management. People will then be able to organize themselves to use, create, and develop knowledge and cultural products without worrying about rewards through IP protection.

Another important medium of analysis in CIPS is the rhetoric that promotes the language of IP balance and users' rights. Again, the discourse that dominates this medium nicely reflects the concerns of the Islamic vision on social justice. The discourse in this medium is critical of IP's owner-centered approach and the way in which users' interests are represented in the system. Here, IP is given a role that goes beyond catering for rights holders. IP protection is not about providing incentives for large corporate producers and distributors, who could end up with massive powers to control knowledge and culture to the exclusion of the rest of society. IP needs to be designed to enhance distributive justice values. To do that, it must position users of

[2] Yochai Benkler "Freedom in the Commons" (2003) 52 *Duke Law Journal* 1249; Yochai Benkler, *The Wealth of Networks How Social Production Transforms Markets and Freedom* (Yale University Press, 2006) 23.

knowledge and cultural products at the forefront of the IP structure, side by side with IP rights holders. Their interests are not mere exceptions that should be interpreted narrowly, but legal rights as a matter of distributive justice. For instance, just as the law protects a bundle of exclusive rights for IP rights holders, so must it also recognize users' needs to have well-defined opportunities to read, borrow, reverse engineer, imitate, share, research, criticize, experience, recreate, and cultivate the knowledge and culture around them. IP in this medium is not seen as a privilege for rights holders but as a social bargain with users.

Ideas championed by CIPS transcend the informal IP landscape to influence discussions in formal international IP forums. For example, the World Intellectual Property Organization (WIPO) issued the Development Agenda in recognition of the rapidly accelerating privatization of knowledge and culture in favor of large private interests in developed countries. The Development Agenda urges international IP actors to consider alternative policies to promote the public domain and the rights of users of IP. These alternative policies are introduced as necessary steps towards fairer IP bargains, with greater potential to reorient IP laws towards serving a wide array of human needs by promoting access to education, access to medicine and overall development.[3]

II RECOGNIZING THE PUBLIC DOMAIN

CIPS introduce the public domain in the context of criticizing the ongoing expansion of IP protection to new subject matter. The public domain discourse is positioned as a countervailing force against commodification of knowledge and culture.[4] CIPS largely question whether it is fair or efficient to make IP protection the norm whenever we have a question on how to govern a new set of knowledge or cultural resources. The idea here is to introduce the public domain as a conceptual framework to ensure that knowledge and culture remain accessible to everyone unless a very good reason is put forward to justify privatization through IP protection. In this sense, the public domain discourse promotes an original position towards knowledge and cultural governance in which everyone is empowered with equal opportunities to engage with knowledge and cultural resources and pursue their desired life plans. Framed this way, the public domain rhetoric

3 "Development Agenda for WIPO" (2007), www.wipo.int/ip-development/en/agenda/
4 Christopher May, "Between Commodification and 'Openness': The Information Society and the Ownership of Knowledge" (2006) *Journal of Information, Law and Technology* 9.

has significant merit from the perspective of the Islamic normative vision on social justice.

CIPS do not have a uniform understanding of what constitutes the public domain. Pamela Samuelson notes that "[at] least thirteen definitions or conceptions of the public domain are evident in [the] literature."[5] Samuelson contends that these definitions "cluster around three main foci: the legal status of information resources, freedoms to use information resources, and the accessibility of information resources."[6]

In 1981, David Lang put forward the idea of a specific theory for the public domain, to resist the increasing privatization of knowledge and culture.[7] Since then, an increasing body of IP scholarship has focused on the need to keep knowledge and cultural resources widely available for people, not only for self-advancement and empowerment but also to promote innovation and creativity. Openness in the public domain means that raw materials to develop new inventions and cultural expressions are widely available. This will likely counterbalance the costs that would be imposed if these materials are locked under IP protection.[8]

The recognition of the public domain in CIPS discourses can be materialized through several measures to keep free zones of knowledge and culture without necessarily undermining the essence of IP protection. These measures can be linked to two clusters of policy and legislative reforms. First, policymaking must actively protect the public domain by preventing the displacement of important materials from the realm of free knowledge and culture. Second, CIPS introduced an extensive reform agenda targeted at expanding the public domain's periphery, both through legislative reform of IP doctrines and through seeking consent from creative persons to release their work into the public domain. I conclude the discussion by showing that knowledge and culture that reside in the public domain will not necessarily end up creating some form of tragedy of the commons, where people would indulge in consumptive use without productive contributions. Though this might happen, people tapping into the public domain are more likely to

5 Pamela Samuelson "Enriching Discourse on Public Domains" (2006) 55(4) *Duke Law Journal* 783–834, 789.

6 Ibid., 816.

7 David Lang "Recognizing the Public Domain." (1981) 44(4) *Law and Contemporary Problems* 147–178.

8 Lawrence Lessig, "Re-Crafting a Public Domain" (2006) 18 *Yale Journal of Law and the Humanities* 56, 56; Edward Samuels, "Public Domain in Copyright Law"(1993) 41 *Journal of the Copyright Society* 137, 138; Edward Lee, "The Public's Domain: The Evolution of Legal Restraints on the Government's Power to Control Public Access through Secrecy or Intellectual Property" (2003) *Hastings Law Journal* 97.

engage in collective action to improve existing knowledge and cultural products or build upon them.

III PROTECTING THE PUBLIC DOMAIN

CIPS defense of the public domain starts by noting that the open zones of knowledge and culture are shrinking and IP protection zones are expanding. We do not know if this expansion is leaving society at large better off. James Boyle describes this expansion of IP protection as a "second enclosure movement."[9] He refers to "the sarcastic ridicule expansions" of IP protection that took place in the 1970s and 1980s and that are still taking place to this very moment.[10] Julie Cohen also notes that IP is expanding "in length, breadth, depth, and strength." She describes such expansion as a "commodification" of culture and knowledge and warns that it has the potential to squeeze creativity to the margins.[11] Lessing is skeptical about the need to privatize knowledge and culture through IP and notes that IP's expansion does not respond to "the logic of incentives, but to the dynamics of political power."[12]

James Boyle's extensive work on the public domain shows that commons of facts and ideas, which were perceived by scholars as unprotectable some decades ago, are being enclosed within circles of copyright, patent, trademarks, and *sui generis* systems. The original principle of balance between knowledge, that should stay in the public domain, free for all to use, and knowledge that could be privatized has been lost in 30 years of exponential expansion of IP.[13]

Such expansion should be worrisome even for those who think that law and policy should primarily be guided by economic efficiency considerations. No reasonable empirical evidence is put forward to justify the economic efficiency of creating a new species of IP or expanding existing systems. Rather, it is essentially belief that is used to justify this policy, without evidence. It therefore constitutes policy without balance. This belief seems to have been

9 James Boyle, "The Second Enclosure Movement and the Construction of the Public Domain" (2003) 66 *Law and Contemporary Problems*, 33 (the first enclosure movement refers to the enclosure of the arable commons that took place in England in the seventeenth century).

10 Ibid., 47.

11 Julie E. Cohen, "Copyright, Commodification, and Culture: Locating the Public Domain in Copyright," in L. Guibault and P. B. Hugenholtz, *The Future of the Public Domain: Identifying the Commons in Information Law* (Kluwer Law International, 2006) 121, 159.

12 Lessig, "Re-Crafting a Public Domain," 65.

13 James Boyle, "A Manifesto on WIPO and the Future of Intellectual Property," (2004) *Duke Law & Technology Review* 1.

built essentially upon overstated incentive rhetoric, which contends that promoting IP automatically promotes innovation, and "the more rights the better." Such rhetoric is not always true and in some cases is "categorically false."[14]

At the very start, I must clarify something. CIPS – like the Islamic normative vision – do not suggest that IP is intrinsically evil and that IP protection should never exist. IP in the CIPS vision does not enjoy normative priority. IP is the exception, not the norm, in governing knowledge and culture. CIPS have supported their propositions on the exponential expansion of IP with extensive lists of examples showing how knowledge and culture are systematically extracted from the public domain without proper justification. I do not intend to recount all these examples, but I will share just enough of them to substantiate the CIPS propositions.

The US IP landscape provides examples illustrating the scope of IP's expansion. Examples from the United States are given not only because the US economy is the strongest and most influential in the world, but because the US models of IP protection have had greater influence on international IP standard setting since the United States joined the Berne Convention in 1988. Edward Samuel documents how the US legislature brought new subject matter from the public domain under copyright protection.[15] In 1790, copyright protection was granted only to maps, charts, and books. Over the years, the list had been extended to contain, inter alia, historical and other prints (1802), musical compositions (1831), dramatic compositions (1856), photographs (1865), paintings, drawings and sculptures (1870), lectures and motion pictures (1909), sound recordings (1971), pantomimes and choreographic works (1976), and computer programs (1980). Samuel comments:

> With each extension of the federal statute into new subject matter, there has been a diminution in works that are treated as part of the public domain, to the point where there are few subject matter categories that are automatically considered as part of the public domain.[16]

Moreover, the list is likely to continue to grow, extending to other areas of IP too. For instance, after the introduction of European Directive 96/9 on the protection of databases,[17] there were attempts in the United States to introduce

14 Ibid., 2.

15 Samuels, "Public Domain in Copyright Law," 163.

16 Ibid., 164.

17 Directive 96/9/EC of the European Parliament and of the Council of 11 March, 1996 on the legal protection of databases, http://eurlex.europa.eu/LexUriServ/LexUriServ.do?uri=CELEX:31996L0009:EN:HTML

IP rights in mere compilations of facts.[18] These attempts have been criticized by a number of IP scholars. Pamela Samuelson argues that a database is a mere compilation of facts, which, according to the Supreme Court, is "not just unprotected by the Copyright Act of 1976, but unprotectable as a matter of constitutional law."[19] This is because databases do not allow their makers to be qualified as "authors," as they lack the creative originality which is deemed a *sine qua non* of any IP protection. James Boyle questions the economic efficiency of introducing a *sui generis* database protection as it will negatively affect "the flow of information to markets, and inhibit research and innovation."[20]

Even more troubling is the Digital Millennium Copyright Act's (DMCA) antidevice provisions. These provisions are known as Digital Rights Management (DRM). They grant copyright holders the right to decide whether content can be copied, and how often. Copyright holders control the content for as long as it may survive. They control the possibility of sharing the content with other users and whether the content can be transformed.[21] Lessig and Cohen argue that the widespread deployment of DRM will effectively remove content from the public domain and deny the public the right to practice free culture. They see this as resulting from the insensitivity of the technical environment in which DRM operates to the legality, or otherwise, of accessing the content.[22] In other words, DMCA's DRM practically "encloses" works from the public domain in the realm of copyright protection, so that if someone tries to circumvent DRM to view content (even lawfully), they might be prosecuted for doing so, and would therefore incur liability like a copyright infringer.[23]

Similarly, CIPS have also noted that IP through patent law has expanded to privatize what used to be "common knowledge."[24] This expansion is largely

18 Boyle, "The Second Enclosure Movement," 39. Boyle refers to the "Collection of Information Antipiracy Act, S. 2291, 105th Cong. (1998); Database Investment and Intellectual Property Antipiracy Act of 1996, H.R. 3531, 104th Cong. (1996)."

19 Samuelson, "Enriching Discourse on Public Domains," 792; Boyle, "A Manifesto on WIPO," 2.

20 James Boyle, "A Politics of Intellectual Property: Environmentalism for the Net" (1997) 47 *Duke Law Journal* 114.

21 Lessig, "Re-Crafting a Public Domain," 62.

22 Cohen, "Locating the Public Domain," 122–23.

23 Lessig, "Re-Crafting a Public Domain," 63.

24 Rebecca S. Eisenberg, "Obvious to Whom? Evaluating Inventions from the Perspective of PHOSTIA" (2004) *Berkeley Technology Law Journal* 889; Graeme Dinwoodie and Rochelle Dreyfuss, "Patenting Science Protecting the Domain of Accessible Knowledge," in L. Guibault and P.B. Hugenholtz, *The Future of the Public Domain: Identifying the Commons in Information Law* (Kluwer Law International, 2006) 10.

attributed to the assumption that patentability requirements, which are supposed to protect a vibrant public domain, are losing their original purpose. A few IP scholars have pointed out that patentability tests are being read not in the light of the historical rationale for patent protection, but rather from the perspective of an unfounded belief in the more protection the better. For instance, Graeme Dinwoodie and Rochelle Dreyfuss, along with other commentators, observe that the standards of "novelty and non-obviousness," which are supposed to prevent patenting when a person with ordinary skills in the art could have arrived at the claimed invention, are declining. They observe, through reading several Federal Circuit decisions, that "examiners realize that putting known information together can be an inventive process."[25]

Dinwoodie and Dreyfuss contend that the erosion of the standard of non-obviousness is contributing to the withdrawal of information that was effectively already in the public domain through granting patent protection to minor innovations and marginal improvements on existing patents, which extends the duration of patents that are about to expire.[26] Moreover, the Federal Circuit attributes a low level of skill to people with ordinary skills, which "creates other problems for the system's effect on progress," as this might lead to patents being granted for innovations with a low level of inventiveness.[27] Dan Burk and Mark Lemley give another example showing that standards of nonobviousness are being narrowly read with respect to biotechnological inventions. They argue that "the Federal Circuit has gone to inordinate lengths to find biotechnological inventions nonobvious, even if the prior art demonstrates a clear plan for producing the invention."[28]

In the same context, Robert Merges argues that patents are now being stretched to new subject matter which was once thought to be "too purely mathematical" or "too abstract," such as software programs and business methods.[29] He argues that if the patent system is to remain faithful to its rationale, it must "protect technology – *actual* machines, devices, and new chemical compositions – rather than pure concepts," as such subject matter would not be protectable.[30] Michael Meurer sheds light on some of the aspects of the social cost associated with patenting business methods:

25 Dinwoodie and Dreyfuss, "Patenting Science," 11.
26 Ibid., 12–18.
27 Ibid., 12.
28 Dan Burk and Mark Lemley, "Policy Levers in Patent Law" (2003) 89 *Virginia Law Review* 1575, 1593.
29 Robert Merges, "As Many as Six Impossible Patents before Breakfast: Property Rights for Business Concepts and Patent System Reform" (1999) 14 *Berkeley Technology Law Journal* 577–89, 578.
30 Ibid., 581.

> [The] social cost of business method patents may be higher than other types of patents because of the problem of patent floods. Business method inventions are likely to cluster around the time that a new market opens. The cluster of inventions gives rise to a flood of patent ... Those costs are attributable to increased licensing and litigation costs, an increased danger of anticompetitive exclusionary use of patents, and a stifling of refinement and application of the patented inventions.[31]

Additionally, patent protection has been stretched to cover methods of medical treatment (MMT). MMT were for a long time held to be unpatentable because of ethical considerations related to the medical profession and technical considerations related to conditions of patentability. The American Medical Association questioned whether MMT meet the requirement that an invention needs to be industrially applicable to be patentable.[32] Despite all that, the US Patent Act has covered MMT with patent protection since the 1950s.[33] However, other major jurisdictions such as Canada and the European Union specifically exclude MMT from the scope of patentability.[34]

The existing trend towards enclosure through IP protection means that policymakers are working against the norms that prevailed from the early days of the IP system until the early 1980s, which "assumed that intellectual creations were not protectable unless (very) good cause was shown. Today, it often seems the opposite. We now ask: 'why not protect a new form of intellectual creation?' We are protecting everything else like it."[35] When faced with the question of protecting or strengthening the protection of new intellectual creations that are similar to business methods or software programs, there is a tendency to forget that these may not be worthy of protection themselves, and to focus on the fact that they are already protected. Then, by analogy, we extend protection to new inventions that are unworthy of protection

As David Lang observed in 1981, trademark laws have followed copyrights and patents and "begun to spill over [their] boundaries and encroach into territories in which trademark protection amounts to trespass."[36] The only

31 Michael J. Meurer, "Business Method Patents and Patent Floods" (2002) 8 *Washington University Journal of Law & Policy* 309, 338.

32 American Medical Association, "Ethical Issues in Patenting Medical Procedures," www.ama-assn.org/resources/doc/code-medical-ethics/9095a.pdf

33 Todd Martin. 'Patentability of Methods of Medical Treatment: A Comparative Study" (2000) *Journal of Patent and Trademark Office Society* 401.

34 See, for instance, Article 52 of the European Patent Convention (1973). For Canada, see *Tennessee Eastman Co. et al. v. Commissioner of Patents* (1972) 62 C.P.R. 117.

35 Merges, "As Many as Six Impossible Patents," 587.

36 Lang, "Recognizing the Public Domain," 158.

rationale underpinning the existence of trademark protection was consumer protection against confusion or deception as to the source of the goods or their sponsorship, endorsement, affiliation, or association.[37] Nowadays, however, courts and legislatures are increasingly treating trademarks as property that should be protected for its own sake.[38]

For instance, antidilution provisions protect trademarks by preventing a minor use of a mark if this might "dilute" or "whittle away" the selling power of the "senior mark,"[39] regardless of the absence of competition between the relevant parties or the absence of consumer confusion as to the source of goods or services. "Dilution is an amorphous concept, and no anti-dilution statute addresses exactly *what* dilution is or *how* it can be proven."[40] It is but another unwarranted expansion of IP laws in which protection is given to the persona (identity, distinctiveness, and uniqueness) of the mark itself, "quite apart from its function of identifying the source [or quality] of goods and services."[41] Mark Lemely refers to the effect of trademark expansion on social and artistic speech, noting that courts in the United States have in certain cases allowed trademark holders to prevent the reproduction of marks in paintings or, in one case, the use of the term "Godzilla" on the cover of a book.[42]

The list of examples goes on and on. As James Boyle puts it, "[t]he difficulty . . . is not in finding an example of intellectual property expansion, but in knowing which one to pick."[43] Common to all these expansions is the fact that the need for protection is always questionable and refutable. In light of this skepticism towards the need for IP protection, what is the right thing to do?

The Islamic vision on social justice would keep knowledge and culture available to everyone unless privatization is proven to be a better option. There are several policy approaches that CIPS proposed, which I think neatly fit into the Islamic normative framework on IP identified in this book. The proposed policy approaches include an antienclosure framework that would ensure knowledge and culture will be kept free for all to use and capitalize on unless

37 Robert N. Klieger, "Trademark Dilution: The Whittling Away of the Rational Basis for Trademark Protection" (1996–1997) 58 *University of Pittsburgh Law Review* 789, 796.

38 Mark Lamely, "The Modern Lanham Act and the Death of Common Sense" (1999) 108(7) *The Yale Law Journal* 1687–1715, 1688.

39 Klieger, "Trademark Dilution," 794.

40 Ibid., 794.

41 Ellen P. Winner, "Right of Identity: Right of Publicity and Protection for a Trademark's Persona" (1981) 71 *Trademark Reporter* 193, 198.

42 Lamely, "The Modern Lanham Act," 1711.

43 Ibid.

a very good reason is put forward to justify IP protection. Here are a few examples:

First, we need to replace the dominant faith-based approach with an evidence-based approach to IP policymaking.[44] If IP protection is to be introduced for a new intellectual creation, it is not enough to justify protection on the basis of an assumption that IP promotes innovation and progress. Instead, "there must be mandatory, independently-produced, impartial, empirically rigorous impact statements"[45] justifying IP protection. Second, we must understand that IP rights might provide incentive, but do not always lead to more and better innovation. Too many rights are likely to slow innovation and creativity as surely as too few.[46] Third, since IP provisions are not alien to constitutions, we could consider providing constitutional protections for the public domain. Public domain resources such as ideas, facts, words, and so on could be covered by a constitutional clause to prevent the legislature and courts from privatizing such resources through the grant of copyright, patent, or trademark protection.[47]

IV EXPANDING THE PUBLIC DOMAIN

CIPS did not stop at proposals to protect the public domain. A great number of scholars associated with the general theme of CIPS also proposed active measures to enrich the public domain with more intellectual raw materials. Some proposals focused on expanding the public domain through an extensive agenda for legal reform. Others focused on investigating the possibility of expanding the public domain by seeking consent from creative persons to release their work into the public domain. In the following paragraphs, I identify these two trends and highlight how they fit into the Islamic narrative on a fair IP system.

A *Expansion through Legal Reform*

CIPS are extremely critical of the various doctrinal aspects of IP law that empower rights holders with an expansive set of exclusive rights enabling them to control access to knowledge and cultural resources. CIPS dismiss the bundle of exclusive rights as unnecessarily broad and propose an extensive agenda for legal reform. This agenda aims to limit the scope and strength of IP rights holders' exclusive rights to what is necessary to provide creators with

44 William Patry, *How to Fix Copyright* (Oxford University Press, 2011) 49.
45 Ibid., 52.
46 Boyle, "A Manifesto on WIPO," 5.
47 Diane L. Zimmerman "Is There a Right to Have Something to Say? One View of the Public Domain" (2004) 73 *Fordham Law Review* 297, 311–12.

rewards and incentives, while injecting more knowledge and culture into the public domain. In what follows, I highlight several features of the CIPS reform agenda to expand the public domain.

1 IP Protection Term

Depending on the relevant jurisdiction, copyright generally lasts for life, plus 50–70 years thereafter. The copyright holder is granted monopoly rights for a certain period in exchange for an eventual release of the subject matter into the public domain. As a policy matter, copyright duration is one of the most controversial aspects of the IP system. CIPS diverge on many issues but agree that the current copyright duration does not make sense in terms of reward and efficiency-based justifications of IP.[48] It can be reduced without negatively affecting creativity in literary and artistic works. Moreover, its reduction would inject a substantial sum of intellectual products into the free zone and result in the expansion of the public domain.

It is interesting to note that even when the copyright term was only 14 years in the early days of copyright development, it was fiercely debated. In 1841, before the British House of Commons, Thomas Babington Macaulay warned that extending copyright terms beyond certain limits could have a harmful effect on the wide availability of knowledge and culture:

> It is good that authors should be remunerated; and the least exceptionable way of remunerating them is by a monopoly. Yet monopoly is an evil. For the sake of the good we must submit to the evil; but the evil ought not to last a day longer than is necessary for the purpose of securing the good.[49]

Modern IP scholarship agrees that the current term is too long, having an adverse effect on our culture on at least two levels: First, it is locking up, without good and empirically grounded reasons, most of the cultural and educational materials produced in the last century, which could have been made available to the public.[50] We do not know if it is good for authors and

48 Lawrence Lessig, *The Future of Ideas: The Fate of the Commons in a Connected World* (Angus & Robertson, 2001); James Boyle, *The Public Domain: Enclosing the Commons of the Mind* (Yale University Press, 2008) 205; Richard A. Epstein "Dubious Constitutionality of the Copyright Term Extension Act" (2002–2003) 36 *Loyola of Los Angeles Law Review* 123, 128; J. H. Reichman, "The Duration of Copyright and the Limits of Cultural Policy" (1996) *Cardozo Arts & Entertainment Law Journal* 625.

49 For the full text of the speech, see Eric Flint, *Prime Palaver #4Macaulay on copyright law*, 2001, para. 4, www.baen.com/library/palaver4.htm

50 Cohen, "Copyright, Commodification, and Culture," 158; Boyle, *The Public Domain*, 205; Boyle, "A Manifesto on WIPO," 5 (Boyle contends that the loss resulting from locking up the

society to place culture, knowledge, and education in a black hole for over 100 years, preventing the public from reading, listening, and watching creative works from which they could benefit, without adequate proof that this is in the authors' interests. Second, a longer term is largely responsible for creating the orphan works dilemma: the longer the term, the more onerous the task of finding out who owns rights in the work. William Patry argues that long copyright terms place unnecessary burdens on the accessibility of old books, films, and music. He explores the scope of the problem through an example from the BBC's film library. Patry reports that the greater part of a million hours of films is unusable, and there is no way to get clearance because we do not know how to find the authors or their heirs.[51]

CIPS also agree that the right thing to do is to dramatically reduce the copyright term. In doing so, adequate consideration needs to be given to providing authors with a term that does not suppress their incentive, while placing works in the public domain when their protection imposes social costs without meaningful social benefits. But how long is long enough?

Lawrence Lessig suggests a shorter copyright term based on the historical attitudes of authors in the United States. He argues that under the 1909 US Copyright Act the copyright term was 28 years, with the option to renew for an additional 28 years. The overwhelming majority of authors did not seek renewal beyond the first term. In a study conducted in 1973, authors of 85 percent of works copyrighted under that law did not renew their copyright. This means that 85 percent of books, movies, and sound recordings entered into the public domain after the 28-year term, free for all to read, view, listen, learn from, and build upon, with no recorded negative effects on the incentives of the American authors. Lessig argues for a short and nonrenewable copyright term of around the 28 years.[52] James Boyle and Net Netanel made similar proposals based on the same analysis.[53] Lessig asserts that "[a] change in the copyright term would have no effect on incentives for authors to produce [more] work." It is difficult to imagine that authors would not write a book or software program if they knew that their work would be protected for less than 50 or 70 years after their death. Consequentially, the

cultural and educational material "exceeds any possible loss from 'piracy'"); Patry, *How to Fix Copyright*, 189 (Patry argues that "the evidence is overwhelming that the current, excessive length of copyright . . . denies access to vast troves of culture and . . . does not incentivize the creation of new [works]").

51 Patry, *How to Fix Copyright*, 190.

52 Lessig, *The Future of Ideas*, 206–7.

53 Boyle, *The Public Domain*, 238; Neil Netanel, *Copyright Paradox* (Oxford University Press, 2008) 199.

benefits to creativity from works falling into the public domain would be considerable.[54]

The patent term is less contested. The global 20-year term required by Article 33 of the TRIPS Agreement seems to be reasonable for both patentees and the public.[55] Nevertheless, patentees can extend the patent protection through a legal maneuver known as "evergreening." Evergreening takes place when patentees seek to patent incremental improvements just before the protection of the underlying invention expires. If a patent on incremental improvements is granted, the entire invention would effectively be protected for an additional term, thereby resulting in the underlying knowledge being withheld from open use.[56] Patent offices and courts have an important role to play in restricting this practice. When a patentee of an existing invention attempts to acquire protection on successive minor improvements, patent offices and courts should reinvigorate the nonobviousness standard to prevent such a maneuver. This will keep the patent term within reasonable limits and allow the release of patented information into the public domain immediately after the original term expires.[57]

2 Reimposing Copyright Formalities

Scholars of copyright critical of its expansion also propose reimposing formalities as a mechanism to expand the public domain. They argue that registration should be essential for copyright protection. It should also be effortless and cost-free. In this way, any subject matter that is of value to the author can be protected. Massive amounts of cultural content could end up in the public domain for others to enjoy and reshape.

Formalities are not alien to copyright systems. In fact, for most of their history, copyright laws imposed formalities "on the existence and exercise of copyright."[58] Internationally, the Berne Convention recognized the right of member states to impose formalities on the grant and the continued enjoyment of copyright before eliminating such recognition in 1908.[59] Failure to comply with copyright's formalities resulted in the forfeiture of copyright. For

54 Lessig, *The Future of Ideas*, 252.

55 Mark. A Lemley, "An Empirical Study of the Twenty-Year Patent Term" (1994) 22(3–4) *AIPLA Quarterly Journal* 369, 371.

56 Dinwoodie and Dreyfuss, "Patenting Science,"12.

57 Rebecca Halford-Harrison, "Evergreening – Extending Patent Life and Curbs on Repackaging" (2006) 3 *Journal of Generic Medicines: The Business Journal for the Generic Medicines Sector* 314, 315.

58 Patry, *How to Fix Copyright*, 203.

59 Ibid., 206–7.

instance, section 411 of the 1976 US Copyright Act made registration of a work with the Copyright Office a prerequisite for infringement actions.[60]

Forfeiture of copyright for noncompliance with formalities injected a great many creative works into public domain,[61] thereby maintaining a better balance between the permission zone and the free zone of our culture.[62] Abolishing formalities for the existence and exercise of copyright has been described by Lessig as "a bizarre shift."[63] The copyright holder is automatically granted exclusive rights – a monopoly right – for decades, without any effort. Any expression fixed in a material form now has copyright protection, whether or not the copyright notice is affixed and whether or not it is possible to identify who the owner is.[64] Even if someone wants to abandon their copyright, they must express their intent somehow.[65]

The rationale for abolishing formalities is attributed to the high cost and burden they impose on authors, particularly when seeking protection in different jurisdictions.[66] However, internet platforms can make the cost and effort of registering copyright marginal. Accordingly, some copyright scholars strongly recommend that formalities be restored to the copyright system, so that copyright protection is confined "to those works where protection is necessary, at least as judged by the copyright owners."[67] Lessig maintains that "if a copyright isn't worth it to an author to renew for a modest fee, then it isn't worth it to society to support – through an array of criminal and civil statutes – the monopoly protected."[68]

Christopher Sprigman suggests structuring "new-style" formalities that would capture as many of the benefits of the former system as possible without running "afoul of the anti-formalities provision of the Berne Convention."[69] The proposed "new-style" formalities system would ask copyright holders to place a notice on published works, register and renew them, and deposit a copy in a government agency or a public library. However, noncompliance with these formalities should not result in the forfeiture of copyright, but

60 Jane C. Ginsburg and John M. Kernochan, "One Hundred and Two Years Later: The U.S. Joins the Berne Convention" (1988–1989) 13 *Columbia-VLA Journal of Law & the Arts* 1, 12.

61 Samuels, "Public Domain in Copyright Law," 158.

62 Christopher Sprigman, "Reform(aliz)ing Copyright" (2004) 57 *Stanford Law Review* 485.

63 Lessig, *The Future of Ideas*, 250.

64 Lawrence Lessig, *Free Culture: How Big Media Uses Technology and the Law to Lock Down Culture and Control Creativity* (Penguin, 2004) 203.

65 Samuels, "Public Domain in Copyright Law," 156.

66 Lessig, "Re-Crafting a Public Domain," 71.

67 Ibid.

68 Lessig, *The Future of Ideas*, 251.

69 Sprigman, "Reform(aliz)ing Copyright," 491.

"*would subject works to a perpetual and irrevocable 'default license,'* with royalties set at a very low level, thus effectively moving works into the public domain."[70] The Berne Convention contains no provisions relating to the grounds on which such a license would be granted.

3 Recrafting Exclusive Rights

IP systems grant rights holders a bundle of exclusive rights to exclude third parties from using an intellectual product without payment or permission. The power to exclude is broad. Rights holders have wide discretion on deciding what others can do with their work. CIPS scholars argue that we need to recalibrate the doctrines of exclusive rights in order to expand the public domain so users can fully exercise central social capabilities such as reading, researching, transforming, and recreating culture and knowledge around them.[71] Historically, exclusive rights were not a bundle. They were limited in scope and number.[72] In the following paragraphs, I rely on critical evaluation of the doctrine of exclusive rights to show that it does not sit comfortably in the IP landscape. Its fairness and logical legitimacy are in question. Several leading scholars contest its foundations and propose legislative reforms to enable more uses of protected works to enter into the public domain. These reforms revolve around three core proposals: a proposal to redefine the scope of exclusivity in copyright and patent; a proposal to reconsider reproduction rights in copyright law; and a third proposal to limit exclusive control over the scope of derivative works.

1 REDEFINING EXCLUSIVITY It is conceivable – and even feasible – to redefine the scope of an IP holder's exclusive rights as a single right for commercial exploitation of the intellectual products. An IP holder in this case will retain the essence of IP protection, that is, they will be able to commercially exploit their work, and at the same time allow other applications of the work to fall into the public domain, free for others to use, reuse, and

[70] Ibid., 491 (emphasis added).

[71] Michael W. Carrol, "One Size Does Not Fit All: A Framework for Tailoring Intellectual Property Rights" (2009) 70(6) *Ohio State Law Journal* 1409.

[72] For instance, in the first US copyright law of 1790, the only exclusive rights of copyright were the rights to print, reprint, publish, or vend the work. Samuels, "Public Domain in Copyright Law," 143. Sam Ricketson points out that the exclusive rights of the copyright holder "have been added to the Berne Convention text in a piecemeal way." Sam Ricketson, *The Berne Convention for the Protection of Literary and artistic Works*: 1886–1986 (Centre for Commercial Law Studies, Queen Marry College/Kluwer, 1987) 367–68.

build upon. This section provides examples from copyright and patent laws to show how this might happen.

Generally, copyright laws grant copyright holders a raft of exclusive rights for reproduction, performance, distribution, making derivative works, and so on. Normally, copyright holders seek financial benefits from their rights. In their quest to commercially exercise their exclusive rights, copyright holders might prevent beneficial public uses of the copyright works that do not negatively affect their legitimate interests.

Jessica Litman (later supported by others)[73] developed, over the last two decades,[74] a bold proposal in which she pointed to some of the negative effects of multiple expansive and overlapping exclusive rights. Litman made specific proposals for reform, the central point of which was to "get rid of our current bundle-of-rights way of thinking about copyright infringement"[75] and instead:

> [recast] copyright as a *single exclusive right* with carefully drawn boundaries. If we chose to define a single core copyright right, the most promising candidate for that right, in my view, would be a right to control *commercial exploitation. Limiting the scope of copyright to commercial exploitation would be simpler than the current array of five, six, seven, or eight distinct but overlapping rights*. Copyright defined as control over commercial exploitation, moreover, would accord with what we know of the public's understanding of what copyright law does, and should, reserve to the author. It would also preserve for readers, listeners, and viewers the liberty to enjoy works in non-exploitative ways without seeking licenses for each.[76]

In support of her proposal, Litman argued that noncommercial uses of copyright materials are rarely followed by litigation. Even if they are, courts tend to interpret the law with sufficient leeway to be able to exempt the users from liability. Consequently, confining copyright to the right of commercial exploitation is merely "the explicit recognition of a limitation that had always been implicit in the law."[77]

[73] Jessica Litman, "Real Copyright Reform" (2010) *Iowa Law Review*, 43; Glynn S. Lunney, Jr., "Fair Use and Market Failure: Sony Revisited" (2002) 82 *Boston University Law Review* 975, 1017–29; William W. Fisher, *Promises to Keep: Technology, Law, and the Future of Entertainment* (Stanford Law Books, 2004); Neil Netanel, "Impose a Noncommercial Use Levy to Allow Free Peer-to-Peer File Sharing" (2003) 17 *Harvard Journal of Law and Technology* 1.

[74] Jessica Litman "Revising Copyright Law for the Information Age" (1996) 75 *Oregon Law Review* 19. Also in Litman, "Real Copyright Reform."

[75] Jessica Litman, *Digital Copyright* (Prometheus Books, 2001) 180 (emphasis added).

[76] Litman, "Real Copyright Reform," 42 (emphasis added).

[77] Ibid., 46.

Additionally, a single commercial exploitation right would enhance what Litman calls "copyright liberties."[78] Reading, listening, viewing, watching, playing, and using copyright works for personal purpose are nonexploitative uses. The proposed reform would exclude these uses from any discussion of infringement. Transforming a book into an e-book, a DVD into an MP3, or modifying software to work in a certain way should always be lawful and should not be the subject of a discussion on exemptions. It is in this way, by allowing reading, viewing, watching, playing, and so on, that copyright law can achieve its core objective of promoting learning and progress.[79] A single commercial exploitation right would have a significant bearing on the scope of distribution rights, reproduction rights, and rights in derivative works, as explained below.

Admittedly, Litman was concerned that her proposal would clash with the types of noncommercial uses that constitute "large-scale interference" with copyright holders' commercial markets, such as uses of "educational materials by educational institutions."[80] A single commercial exploitation right should be redefined to take into account such concern. Net Netanel came up with two proposals that would mitigate this concern.

First, copyright should be recrafted to remove the current barriers that it imposes on digitizing, archiving, and making available millions of out-of-print books, articles, documents, and the unavailable sound records, paintings, and motion pictures that go to make up our heritage. This should take place as part of a specific legislative reform that allows nonprofit libraries and archives to digitize such content and make it available on a noncommercial basis without any need to obtain a copyright license.[81] Second, peer-to-peer (P2P) file sharing's enormous potential in distributing creative works could be called upon to help.[82] Netanel suggested that noncommercial copying in digital format and noncommercial distribution should be privileged uses giving rise to what he terms a "non-commercial use levy"[83] (NUL). The essence of Netanel's proposal is that users will obtain "an unhindered entitlement" to copy and distribute content for non-commercial purposes[84] and copyright holders will have a levy deducted equivalent to a percentage of the gross

78 Jessica Litman, "Lawful Personal Use" (2007) 85 *Texas Law Review* 1879.

79 Jessica Litman, "Readers' Copyright" (2011) 58 *Journal of the Copyright Society of the USA* 325, 350.

80 Litman, *Digital Copyright*, 181.

81 Netanel, *Copyright Paradox*, 211.

82 Netanel, "Impose a Noncommercial Use Levy."

83 Ibid., 37.

84 Ibid., 84.

revenue received from providers of services and devices which have increased in value as a result of P2P file sharing of the copyright works.[85] Netanel provides a detailed blueprint that shows how the NUL would work in terms of who should pay the levy, the basis of payment, and the payable amount.[86]

In relation to patents, Graeme Dinwoodie and Rochelle Dreyfuss, along with other commentators,[87] argue that the patentees' right to exploit their inventions should not interfere with noncommercial uses, especially by researchers in university laboratories and research centers for the "gratification of scientific tastes, or for curiosity, or for amusement."[88] They refer to case law in the United States in which the Federal Circuit has favored the exclusive rights of the patentee over what is known in the United States as "experimental use defense."[89] Research to verify "the adequacy of the specification and the validity of the patent holder's claims about the invention,"[90] and to determine how the invention worked can be especially beneficial.

2 ELIMINATING THE EXCLUSIVE RIGHT TO REPRODUCTION The reproduction right in copyright law can be replaced with the right to distribute copies to the public. In this case, uses which do not count as distribution to the public should be deemed to fall within the public domain. This may seem to be a fundamental shift. However, as discussed below, it will not lead to the undermining of the legitimate interests of copyright holders but will have a positive impact on the public interest.

The reproduction right is the exclusive right of the copyright holders to make copies of the work and to prevent others from replicating it in a substantial manner. The fabric of current copyright doctrine is characterized by that right. Historically, the original Berne Convention of 1886 did not contain an exclusive right of reproduction. It was added as a result of the

85 Netanel, *Copyright Paradox*, 208.
86 Ibid., 208.
87 Michael A. Carrier, "Cabining Intellectual Property through a Property Paradigm" (2004) 54(1) *Duke Law Journal* 120–21; Rebecca S. Eisenberg, "Patents and the Progress of Science: Exclusive Rights and Experimental Use" (1989) 56(3) *The University of Chicago Law Review* 1019.
88 Dinwoodie and Dreyfuss, "Patenting Science," 13.
89 See, for instance, 733 F.2d 858 (Fed. Cir. 1984), superseded on other grounds by 35 US.C. § 271(e) and 216 F.3d 1343 (Fed. Cir. 2000), cited in Carrier, "Cabining Intellectual Property," 120–21.
90 Rebecca S. Eisenberg, "Patents and the Progress of Science," 1078; Katharine, J. Standburg, "The Research Exemption to Patent Infringement: The Delicate Balance between Current and Future Technical Progress," in Peter K. Yu, *Intellectual Property and Information Wealth: Issues and Practices* (Praeger Publisher, 2007) 132.

Stockholm Revision Conference held in Sweden in 1967.[91] Similarly, from 1790 to 1909, US copyright law did not grant authors an exclusive right of reproduction. Accordingly, there is historically nothing odd about having laws to protect authors without an exclusive right to copy.[92] The Internet and its associated digital technologies have radically changed the platform on which we interact with our culture.[93] Copying in the networked world is as common as breathing. The exclusive right to copy "no longer tracks the necessary or productive control that copyright owner needs." [94] On the contrary, its broad reach "simply introduces strategic costs into the creative process that are mostly irrelevant for providing efficient incentive to create."

In the course of interacting with our current cultural goods on digital platforms, web pages are reproduced into temporary caches so internet browsers can display them quickly; programs and e-books are copied into the RAM so they can be viewed; and a whole file system needs to be copied onto backup storage for later retrieval in case of errors, software bugs, or malicious intruders. These are examples which would legislatively fall within the scope of copyright owners' exclusive rights of reproduction and are presumptively a violation of the copyright, despite the fact that none of them constitute a serious threat to the copyright holders' legitimate interests.[95] The right of reproduction is drafted "extraordinarily broadly in the first instance." It must be changed, so that uses which current reproduction rights illogically encompass fall into the public domain.[96]

Ernest Miller and Joan Feigenbaum propose to "[e]liminate the right to control copying as a fundamental aspect of copyright and as an organising principle of intellectual-property law."[97] In support of their argument, they contend that it is the distribution of copies to the public that might economically affect the copyright holder, not the mere act of reproduction. Therefore, it is the right to public distribution that should be the organizing principle for copyright. Accordingly, uses that do not involve public distribution, including all personal uses, should be deemed part of the public domain and not exposed to questions regarding fair or unfair use or to assessment on a case-

91 Sam Ricketson, *The Berne Convention*, 120, 367.

92 Ernie Miller and Joan Feigenbaum, "Taking the 'Copy' out of Copyright," www.cis.upenn.edu/-ds/SPYCE/papers/MF.pdf

93 Lawrence Lessig, "Getting Our Values around Copyright Right" (2010) 45(2) *EDUCAUSE Review* 26, 28.

94 Lessig, "Re-Crafting a Public Domain," 70.

95 Miller and Feigenbaum, "Taking the 'Copy' out of Copyright," 4–5.

96 Cohen, "Copyright, Commodification, and Culture," 160.

97 Miller and Feigenbaum, "Taking the 'Copy' out of Copyright," 5.

by-case basis, in the context of searches for specific exemptions. They should not be actionable at all.[98]

3 DERIVATIVE WORKS An additional example of legislative reform to expand the public domain relates to the scope of derivative works. The right granted to copyright holders to derive works from their original creations should not be formulated in catch-all language. Instead, such a right should be strictly defined, so as to allow follow-on creativity to flourish, particularly in light of the digital and internet revolutions.

Derivative works are subsequent intellectual creations based on the reworking of an original copyright work and/or presentation of that work in a different form. Examples include translation, dramatization, fictionalization, making motion picture versions or sound recordings, abridgment, and so on. The freedom to derive new works from preexisting works is important to creativity and innovation. IP, in particular copyright laws under different banners, can significantly limit this freedom. Arguably, there is a close affinity between the scope allowed for derivative creativity and the principle of fair equality of opportunity when it comes to cultural participation. The more restriction the law imposes, the less opportunities people will have to challenge and reshape their culture. At this juncture one might ask: To what extent should the copyright owner of the underlying work be allowed to control the production of derivative works?

The Berne Convention recognizes the protection of derivative works in Article 12. It gives "[a]uthors of literary or artistic works . . . the exclusive right of authorizing adaptations, arrangements and other alterations of their works." Legislators and courts in the member states may define what constitutes "adaptations, arrangements and other alterations" that fall within the exclusive right of the copyright owner, and the scope thereof. In whatever terms a legislature might decide to formulate rights in derivative works, they should not imitate the "catch-all language"[99] used in the US Copyright Act. There, rights holders are granted control over any works based upon theirs, "such as a translation, musical arrangement . . . or any other form in which a work may be recast, transformed, or adapted."[100]

98 Ibid., 9–10.

99 Christina Bohannan, "Taming the Derivative Works Right: A Modest Proposal for Reducing Overbreadth and Vagueness in Copyright" (2010) 12(4) *Vanderbilt Journal of Entertainment & Technology Law* 669, 678.

100 Jed Rubinfeld, "Freedom of Imagination: Copyright's Constitutionality" (2002) 112 *The Yale Law Journal* 1 (Rubinfeld argues that exclusive rights in derivative works are incompatible with the constitutional freedom of imagination).

Rights in derivative works interfere significantly with the possibility of borrowing from and reworking of preexisting works. Borrowing and reworking have been central processes in creativity throughout history.[101] The digital age has enhanced the potential to build upon preexisting works enormously. Therefore, a sound conception of rights in derivative works should not place roadblocks in the way of creating new works.

Copyright scholars proposed different approaches to ensure that rights in derivative works do not impinge on follow-on creativity. For instance, Christina Bohannan proposes that the doctrine of the idea-expression dichotomy must be strictly applied with respect to rights in derivative works. In asserting rights in derivative works, a copyright holder must prove not only that the new work is based upon theirs, but that it clearly incorporates copyrighted expressions. Without this requirement, there is a risk that protection will be extended to uncopyrightable ideas.[102] Lessig demands that the scope of rights in derivative works be explicitly specified. It may well be useful to accord exclusive rights in works derived from particular types of subject matter in certain cases. Those cases should be specified case by case. Beyond that, others should be allowed to use their imagination to create new works freely.[103] Pamela Samuelson insisted on the need to keep user-generated content (UGC) outside the scope of derivative works. Creative and artistic mashups and remixes, produced for noncommercial purposes "should be treated as non-infringing derivative" unless a meaningful likelihood of market harm is proven by the copyright holder.[104]

B Expansion through Consent

Expanding the public domain does not necessarily require legislative intervention to reform IP laws. This can be very difficult and time consuming. The public domain could be expanded through consent. One way to do that is by promising creative people some form of reward in exchange for releasing their intellectual products into the public domain. Another way is to support civic initiatives aimed at promoting wide access to knowledge and culture, such as the Access to Knowledge (A2K) movement.

101 Jessica Litman, "The Public Domain" (1990) 39 *Emory Law Journal* 965, 967.
102 Bohannan, "Taming the Derivative Works Right," 677–78.
103 Lessig, *Free Culture*, 208.
104 Pamela Samuelson, "The Quest for a Sound Conception of Copyright's Derivative Work Right" (2012) *Georgetown Law Journal* 36.

1 Knowledge for Instant Rewards

Part of IP scholarship entertained the possibility of encouraging individuals to consent to placing their ideas and expressions in the public domain in exchange for instant tax benefits and/or prizes. Lawrence Lessig suggested the construction of a "public conservancy" wherein holders of copyrights would be encouraged to donate their works in return for tax benefits. Once donated, works would be free for all to use without permission.[105]

Joseph Stiglitz and James Love, among others, proposed to establish a system of state-sponsored prizes to supplement the incentives provided by patent protection.[106] In this context, the prize means "a payment funded out of general revenue that is made to a researcher conditional on delivering a specified invention."[107] The use of prize systems to stimulate the creation of new inventions has a long history.[108] In fact, the antipatent movement that was active in Europe during the nineteenth century advocated a prize system as an alternative to patent laws. It is argued that supplementing our current patent systems with lump-sum prizes not only will provide people with an incentive to invest in innovative activity but also "will do away with the problem of patents blocking further technological progress."[109] Knowledge released into the public domain in exchange for a prize will be freely available for others to build upon.

James Love and Tim Hubbard have intensively researched the potential of a state-sponsored prize system to tackle the problem of access to medicine.[110] They contend that designing prize systems to stimulate medical inventions

105 Lessig, *The Future of Ideas*, 255.

106 Joseph Stiglitz, "Scrooge and Intellectual Property Rights: A Medical Prize Fund Could Improve the Financing of Drug Innovations"(2006) 333 *British Medical Journal* 1279; James Love, "Measures to Enhance Access to Medical Technologies, and New Methods of Stimulating Medical R&D" (2007) 40 *University of California Davis Law Review* 679; Ron Marchant, "Managing Prize Systems: Some Thoughts on the Options" (2008) 2 *Knowledge Ecology Studies*; Daniel R. Cahoy, "Breaking Patents" (2010–2011) 32 *Michigan Journal of International Law* 461.

107 Nancy Gallini and Suzanne Scotchmer, "Intellectual Property: When Is It the Best Incentive System?" in Adam B. Jaffe, Josh Lerner, and Scott Stern, *Innovation Policy and the Economy* (MIT Press, 2002) 53.

108 Fisher, *Promises to Keep*, "Chapter 6: An Alternative Compensation System"; Benjamin Krohmal, "Prominent Innovation Prizes and Reward Programs" (KEI Research Note 2007:1).

109 J. H. Chang, "Intellectual Property Rights and Economic Development: Historical Lessons and Emerging Issues" (2001) 2(2) *Journal of Human Development* 298.

110 Tim Hubbard and James Love, "A New Trade Framework for Global Healthcare R&D' (2004) 2(2) *PLOS Biology*; James Love and Tim Hubbard, "Bid Idea: Prizes to Stimulate R&D for New Medicines"(2007) 82 *Chicago-Kent Law Review* 1519.

could be a good alternative to the current patent system in some cases. In particular, it would help to mitigate the problem of drug prices in developing countries.[111] They provided a detailed proposal covering how to design a prize system, how it works, how to finance it, the possible hurdles that may affect it, and how to overcome them.[112] In the same vein, James Boyle has called upon WIPO to consider "alternative and additional methods of encouraging and organizing innovation." He argues that since the current patent system does not function to provide a cure for the diseases of the global poor, WIPO "should become the most prominent global institution in which those alternative methods are proposed and debated."[113]

2 Access to Knowledge (A2K)

Proprietary models for governing knowledge and culture do not enjoy normative priority in the Islamic vision of justice. However, keeping knowledge and culture accessible to everyone does. The values of openness and sharing knowledge and culture propounded by the A2K movement fit very nicely with the Islamic vision on governing intangible resources identified in Chapter 6. The default outlook of the Islamic theory of justice in relation to resource governance is to keep resources widely shared for everyone's benefit. The A2K movement has attracted the attention and support of a great number of civil society organizations and public sector bodies from all over the world. As I show below, a number of CIPS scholars engage with the movement tin resisting IP's expansion into the domain of emerging knowledge and culture.[114] According to Consumers International:

> Access to Knowledge (A2K) is the umbrella term for a movement that aims to create more *equitable* public access to the products of human culture and learning. The ultimate objective of the movement is to create a world in which educational and cultural works are accessible to all, and in which consumers and creators alike participate in a vibrant ecosystem of innovation and creativity.[115]

111 Love and Hubbard, "Bid Idea," 1554.
112 Ibid., 1528–34.
113 Boyle, "A Manifesto on WIPO," 7.
114 Peter Suber, Open Access (MIT, 2012); Gaëlle Krikorian and Amy Kapczynski, *Access to Knowledge in the Age of Intellectual Property* (Zone Books, 2010); Amy Kapczynski, "The Access to Knowledge Mobilization and the New Politics of Intellectual Property" (2008) 117(5) *The Yale Law Journal* 804–85.
115 Consumers International, *Access to Knowledge – A Guide for Everyone*, Consumers International, KL Office, edited by Fredrick Noroha and Jeremy Malcolm, at 2 (emphasis

The A2K movement perceives cultural and knowledge products as public goods; their provision is linked to fundamental human rights such as access to healthcare, education, and equality of opportunity. The digital revolution has enabled the movement to acquire huge support. Technology has reduced the cost of creating and disseminating knowledge and culture. As a result of that, many advocates of more permissible approaches to knowledge governance sought to position A2K in the international landscape of IP policymaking. A2K now has major international reference frameworks, including the Geneva Declaration on the Future of WIPO, signed in 2004, and a draft Treaty on Access to Knowledge, prepared in 2005. Both initiatives introduce A2K as a model of knowledge governance that will alleviate the negative impacts of the existing proprietary models in terms of access to medicines, educational resources, cultural heritage, and the overall barriers to follow-on innovation, which result in concentrated ownership and disparities in wealth.[116] The A2K movement covers any kind of knowledge or cultural content, including, but not limited to, texts and data in whatever form, be it software, audio, video, or multimedia. The A2K movement has gained momentum in regard to digital materials publishable online, particularly public sector information (PSI), research results (publicly funded or otherwise), and the provision of educational resources. These particular aspects of the A2K movement are commonly addressed within an open access (OA) framework.

OA is the subject of various international statements and declarations, such as the Budapest Open Access Initiative, the Bethesda Statement on Open Access Publishing, and the Berlin Declaration on Open Access to Knowledge in the Sciences and Humanities (BBB). The central feature of OA literature is that it is "digital, online, free of charge, and free of most copyright and licensing restrictions."[117] OA literature is collectively defined in BBB as online literature for which the copyright holder has given general consent in advance for users to read, download, copy, distribute, print, search, and to link to and make and distribute derivatives from in any digital medium for any responsible purpose.[118] OA removes price barriers and some permission barriers through open content licenses (OCLs), most notably Creative Commons

added), www.consumersinternational.org/news-and-media/publications/access-to-knowledge–a-guide-for-everyone

116 See the introduction to the Geneva Declaration and the preamble of the A2K draft treaty.

117 Peter Suber, "Open Access Overview: Focusing on Open Access to Peer-Reviewed Research Articles and Their Preprints" (first put online June 21, 2004; last revised October 7, 2012), www.earlham.edu/~peters/fos/overview.htm

118 Peter Suber, "Praising progress, preserving precision," SPARC *Open Access Newsletter*, issue 77 (September 2, 2004), www.earlham.edu/~peters/fos/newsletter/09-02-04.htm#progress

(CC). It should be noted that these OCLs tend to be selective regarding the permission barriers they remove. Some OCLs permit commercial reuses and some do not. Some permit derivative works and some do not.

OA proponents demand access to knowledge resources for which the public has already paid, namely public sector information (PSI) and the results of publicly funded research.[119] PSI includes information and data produced by public sector bodies such as international organizations, government departments and agencies, and other state-owned bodies. Publicly funded knowledge resources include raw data and results from government-funded research.[120] The value of publicly related knowledge resources is increased if the barriers to access and reuse are lifted and when these resources are made available in common digital formats downloadable online. No restrictions should be placed on the availability of these resources other than those necessitated by national security, the protection of confidentiality and privacy, and, in limited circumstances, reasonable IP claims. This approach of managing publicly funded knowledge resources would "enable researchers, empower citizens and convey tremendous scientific, economic, and social benefits."[121] These benefits come in the form of new medicines, useful technologies, and solutions to problems and informed decisions that benefit everyone.

The best possible approach to implementing OA with regard to PSI is through directives from governments to their branches and agencies requiring them to publish their data and information on their websites under open content licenses (OCLs). As for publicly funded raw data and research results, OA could be implemented through contractually stipulating, in the terms and conditions of governmental research contracts, that the beneficiaries should share the results of their work by making them freely available online.[122]

Peter Suber argues that "OA is not limited to publicly funded research ... but it includes privately funded and unfunded research."[123] A great many research results which are not publicly funded go to online journals, some of which do not permit free access to their content unless payment is made.

119 P. Arzberger et al., "Promoting Access to Public Research Data for Scientific, Economic, and Social Development" (2004) 3 *Data Science Journal* 135, 136.

120 J. J. Reichman and Paul Uhlir, "A Contractually Reconstructed Research Commons for Scientific Data in a Highly Protectionist Intellectual Property Environment" (2003) *Law and Contemporary Problems* 318.

121 Arzberger et al., "Promoting Access to Public Research Data," 136.

122 Peter Suber, "Ensuring Open Access for Publicly Funded Research" (2012) *The BMJ* 345, www.bmj.com/content/345/bmj.e5184

123 Suber, *Open Access*, 97.

Suber takes issue with pay-for-access journals, which he calls toll-access journals. These journals are responsible for placing massive amounts of knowledge behind firewalls by restricting authors' ability to make their work available to the public. Suber argues that authors conduct research mainly for impact, not money. Moreover, toll-access journals do not pay authors any money and restrict access to their work. This in turn harms authors by "shrinking their audience, reducing their impact and distorting their professional goals."[124] Authors can benefit from the dissemination revolution enabled by new technologies and make their work accessible to a large audience by (1) keeping the key rights out of the control of toll-access journals, or (2) publishing in OA journals and transferring copyright to them.[125]

Another related strand of the A2K movement is open educational resources (OER). I have argued earlier that the current IP system does not adequately embrace access to educational materials as a basic human need, especially for developing countries. OER, led mainly by the United Nations Educational, Scientific and Cultural Organization (UNESCO) has since 2002 been raising awareness of the importance of providing OA for learning resources and thereby mitigating the negative impacts of the restrictions imposed by the current IP system.[126]

A2K, in all its aspects, does not allow inequality and concentration of knowledge. It puts "rich and poor on an equal footing."[127] The wide dissemination of information and knowledge enabled by A2K mechanisms allows everybody to benefit from knowledge resources and thereby promotes values of distributive justice. Unlike IP, A2K does not negatively interfere with the Islamic principles of justice discussed in Chapter 5. On the contrary, it can promote basic social needs through its permissive approach to accessing material vital for satisfying human needs such as access to medical research and educational material. A2K also upholds the principle of fair equality of opportunity. Everyone is given an opportunity to access and reuse knowledge available in the common pool. Finally, it has positive distributive impacts on the least advantaged in society because access to knowledge and cultural products does not depend on the ability to pay.

124 Ibid., 2.

125 Peter Suber, "Open access and Copyright," SPARC Open Access Newsletter, issue 159 (July 2, 2011), www.earlham.edu/~peters/fos/newsletter/07–02-11.htm#copyright

126 UNESCO, *Forum on the Impact of Open Courseware for Higher Education in Developing Countries: Final Report* (2002), http://unesdoc.unesco.org/images/0012/001285/128515e.pdf

127 Peter Suber, "Open Access Overview."

V COLLECTIVE ACTION AND KNOWLEDGE REPRODUCTION

What will happen to the knowledge and cultural resources that become freely available in the public domain? The good thing is that sharing knowledge and cultural products with others will not lead to their depletion. Unlike physical items, these products can be shared and still benefit everyone in the same way. However, there is concern that the freely available products will be exposed to free riding, and that nothing but lazy consumptive use will come out of the public domain. Not necessarily. Large bodies of research in various fields including economics, sociology and psychology, built on Elinor Ostrom's collective action paradigm, argue that people are able to work under a collective action paradigm to increase and develop common pool resources for their mutual benefit.[128] Groups of individuals can work together through different mediums of intellectual cooperation to create, develop, and share a wide array of knowledge and cultural products.

People in the public domain are not only passive consumers. For decades, Eric von Hippel has challenged the long-held assumption that only manufacturers who operate though market mechanisms would bother to create and develop products.[129] He refers to empirical data showing that, on average, up to 40 percent of users engage in the development and modification of information and physical products in numerous fields of production, such as software programs, integrated circuits, sporting equipment, medical equipment, and computer telephony integration systems.[130] Von Hippel adds that the contributions made by users are growing progressively as a result of ongoing advances in computer and communication technologies.[131]

Von Hippel refers to the practices of free open source software (FOSS), where developers of certain software waive some of their IP rights in the source code so that other users can study or modify it. The result is a "collective or community effort" by a great number of users towards the provision of public goods.[132] The experience of FOSS has ignited the beacon for studies on the efficacy of collective action in providing knowledge resources.[133]

128 Elinor Ostrom, *Governing the Commons: The Evolution of Institutions for Collective Action* (Cambridge University Press, 1990) 2, 14, 15.

129 Eric von Hippel, *Sources of Innovation* (Oxford University Press, 1988) 3.

130 Eric von Hippel, *Democratizing Innovation: The Evolving Phenomenon of User Innovation* (MIT Press, 2005) 2–11.

131 Ibid., 3.

132 Georg von Krogh and Eric von Hippel, "The Promise of Research on Open Source Software" (2006) Management Science 982.

133 Von Hippel, *Democratizing Innovation*, 11.

No one has captured the impact of digital technologies on cooperation and knowledge production better that Yochai Benkler. For two decades, Benkler has documented the substantial developments in computer and communication technologies and predicted their significant impact on facilitating the production and dissemination of knowledge goods.[134] Benkler argues that contemporary connected technologies have made social sharing and exchange "a common modality of producing valuable desiderata at the very core of the most advanced economies – in information, culture, education, computation, and communications sectors." The provision of information, knowledge, and cultural goods can be "based on social relations, rather than through markets or hierarchies."[135] Benkler called this phenomenon "commons-based peer production," that is, a "large-scale cooperative effort in which the thing shared among the participants is their creative effort."[136] The result is information, knowledge, and cultural goods that are "relatively free of the structuring effects of property rights and the distribution of wealth."[137]

In later stages, Benkler conducted intensive interdisciplinary research to look into the internal dynamics of social sharing and exchange systems as a modality for knowledge production. Benkler's central argument appears to be that people are naturally disposed to cooperate and produce information, knowledge, and cultural goods. Their disposition to cooperate and produce would be enhanced if they found an efficient way to communicate, framed by moral and fair rules of engagement not imposed from above.[138]

First, Benkler regards communication as the most important factor in human cooperation. The success of FOSS, Wikipedia, citizen journalism, online games, and other forms of peer production is a direct result of the flourishing of computation technologies and communication platforms.[139] Contemporary communication platforms allow for the wide circulation of

134 Yochai Benkler, "From Consumers to Users: Shifting the Deeper Structures of Regulation toward Sustainable Commons and User Access" (2004) *Federal Communication Law Journal*; Yochai Benkler, "Coase's Penguin, or Linux and The Nature of the Firm" (2002) 112(3) *The Yale Law Journal*.

135 Yochai Benkler, "Sharing Nicely: On Shareable Goods and the Emergence of Sharing as a Modality of Economic Production" (2004) 114 *The Yale Law Journal* 274, 278.

136 Ibid., 334.

137 Ibid., 343 .

138 Yochai Benkler, *The Penguin and the Leviathan: How Cooperation Triumphs over Self-Interest* (Random House, 2011) 2–13.

139 Yochai Benkler, "Designing Cooperative Systems for Knowledge Production: An Initial Synthesis from Experimental Economics," in Mario Biagioli et al, *Making and Unmaking Intellectual Property: Creative Production in Legal and Cultural Perspective* (University of Chicago Press, 2011) 149.

source codes, collaborative forms of authorship, and rapid news reporting from different places.

Second, Benkler makes a very interesting observation about the kinds of rules needed to enable online cooperation. He argues that the success of the different forms of peer production is due, in a large part, to their departure from the traditional and restrictive approaches of IP in favor of a process of norm creation that is responsive to the logic of cooperation.[140] Richard Stallman realized that making source codes free for everyone would bolster cooperative efforts to develop more efficient operating systems for computers.[141] In response, he developed the GNU General Public License (GPL) to ensure that source codes remain free from proprietary claims so that every user can "share and change all versions of a program."[142] The logic of sharing and cooperation in the production of software programs has contributed to a breathtaking variety of such programs, which have become ubiquitous in our lives.

The success of the logic of sharing and cooperation inspired Lawrence Lessig to help start Creative Commons (CC) in 2001, allowing millions of people to escape from the restrictive sphere of copyright law into a realm in which sharing is the norm.[143] The willingness to share is something which the designers of systems built around incentives do not often consider. Jimmy Wales, the founder of Wikipedia, believed that people could work together and give time and effort to a collaborative form of authorship that aims to write the biggest repository of human knowledge the world has ever known. What people needed was "a reign to set their own norms," review them and revise them in whatever way the logic of cooperation dictates.[144]

Social cooperation in any form is fundamental to religious values across the globe. It has an important place in Islamic textual sources as a way of achieving social good for the community. In this sense, cooperation in the knowledge and cultural spheres is intrinsically good from the Islamic perspective. However, as shown in this section of the book, online cooperation could be instrumental in achieving many good results as well. Through cooperation, people can produce information, knowledge, and culture that is not subject to proprietary systems and is perhaps even more stable and effective than under those systems.

140 Benkler, *The Penguin and the Leviathan*, 158.

141 Richard Stallman, "Free Software,"in Mark Perry and Brian Fitzgerald, *Knowledge Policy for the Twenty-First Century: A Legal Perspective* (Irwin Law, 2011) 2, 415.

142 GNU General Public Licenses, version 3, www.gnu.org/licenses/gpl.html

143 http://creativecommons.org/about

144 Benkler, *The Penguin and the Leviathan*, 158–59.

VI USERS' INTELLECTUAL PROPERTY RIGHTS

In their critical assessment of the IP establishment, CIPS scholars did not stop at reimagining the scope of the exclusive rights of IP rights holders vis-à-vis the public domain. They also sought to position users and consumers of knowledge and culture as central actors in the IP bargain. Again, the way in which CIPS scholars framed their discussions on the need to incorporate the position of users into the IP landscape largely overlaps with the Islamic normative vision of a fair IP system

First, overall, CIPS subscribed to the proposition that the predominant utilitarian and merit-based justifications of IP protection reflect an intention to strengthen the position of IP rights holders within the IP structure both in terms of protection and enforcement priorities. IP enabled large corporate producers and distributors to concentrate powers to control access and reuse of knowledge and cultural products. In this normative environment, users' interests are framed as exceptional departures for what should be the standard practices in IP law and enforcement. This attitude normalizes the systematic exclusion of users, who could represent large groups within society. Such an attitude is incompatible with the Islamic normative vision of fair IP identified in Chapter 5. There, I showed that any concentration of power is likely to affect fair equality of opportunity and therefore will be considered unfair.

Second, CIPS sought to introduce a concept of users' rights as part of IP's overall structure. Current IP laws are not designed to treat users as equal parties in the IP bargain. Users are collections of large heterogeneous groups with different purposes and priorities. They also lack appropriate frameworks to help press their agenda and secure its inclusion in the IP bargain. The major features of the current IP system emerged and developed to safeguard rights holders' interests. When large corporate actors started to regularly intervene to shape IP laws, even more systematic marginalization of users took place. CIPS started to assemble the diverse heterogeneous groups of users into more identifiable actors and started also to define their particular interests.[145]

Users, from the CIPS viewpoint, are not mere passive consumers seeking to freely ride on IP holders' legal rights. This incongruous homogenizing vision of heterogeneous groups of users fails to capture their identities and priorities. Users can be groups of cash-strapped individuals who are unable to pay for basic social needs such as access to medicine and educational materials. They

[145] Yochai Benkler, "From Consumers to Users: Shifting the Deeper Structures of Regulation toward Sustainable Commons and User Access" (2004) *Federal Communication Law Journal* 562–79; Joseph P. Liu, "Copyright Law's Theory of the Consumer" (2003) 44 *Boston College Law Review* 397.

can also be capable creators who challenge existing cultural and knowledge concepts and recast them into new forms of innovation and creativity. In this vision, IP is to be seen not as a mechanism to help rights holders accumulate wealth but as a legal construct that impacts individuals' capabilities to exercise their moral powers, self-autonomy, and self-empowerment.[146]

From this angle, CIPS scholarship started to ask what it is that users of culture and knowledge should get from the IP bargain. What do they need, want, or deserve?[147] Is it enough to have a set of specific exceptions and limitations? Would users be better served with an open-ended right to access IP-protected content whenever it is fair to do so? How should that right be framed? Should it focus on correcting market failure in an efficiency-based calculus? Or alternatively, should it aim to correct any distributional imbalance in controlling access to knowledge and culture?

By and large, CIPS addressed these different questions by drawing attention to three general, major considerations. First, CIPS scholars are extremely critical of the way in which IP laws frame "exceptions and limitations" to IP rights holders' exclusive rights.[148] For instance, in copyright law, the dominant model in this regard provides an extensive list of classes of permitted uses where users can freely access intellectual content without needing to seek permission from the rights holder. A typical example of such a list is Article 5 of the European Information Society Directive, which lists 21 "exceptions" to exclusive reproduction rights. These exceptions permit various free uses, including temporary reproduction, private copying, and exceptions for libraries, educational establishments, archives, museums, and for reporting on current events, and limitations for quotation, criticism, review, and so on. They are context-specific and were largely designed to cater to groups of users who needed some relief from copyright law's expansion and were in a position to promote specific public purposes. They were not designed to promote public right of access to content for the purpose of redistributing opportunities to engage with knowledge and cultural resources.[149] We will see below that, in practice, even open-ended, fair use did not escape the distributive dilemma.

Second, the international IP environment is reinforcing the limited nature of these exceptions, making it difficult to rely on them to address broad

146 Nobuko Kawashima, "The Rise of 'User Creativity' – Web 2.0 and a New Challenge for Copyright Law and Cultural Policy" (2010) *International Journal of Cultural Policy* 338.

147 Jessica Litman, "Lawful Personal Use" (2007) 85 *Texas Law Review* 1879.

148 William Patry, "Limitations and Exceptions in the Digital Era" (2011) 7 *The Indian Journal of Law and Technology* 1, 5.

149 Jessica Litman, "Reforming Information Law in Copyright's Image" (1997) 22 *University of Dayton Law Review* 587, 619.

distributional concerns around access to knowledge and culture. IP's global normative environment requires that any exceptions and limitations must be interpreted narrowly and remain subservient to IP rights holders' interests. For instance, the TRIPS three-step test dictates that any derogation from the exclusive rights is only permissible where it is limited to "certain special cases" that do not "conflict with [the rights holder's] normal exploitation" and do not "unreasonably prejudice [their] legitimate interests."[150]

Third, radical advances in modes of creating and distributing content also prompted fierce debates around the fair place of users in the IP landscape.[151] Users are now engaging with culture and knowledge in a radically different way from what was conceivable in the wake of the Industrial Revolution. Modern technology is shifting the locus of creative production. While traditional actors such as libraries, museums, and news corporations are still benefiting from copyright permissions to create and distribute content, technology has empowered other groups with capabilities to engage with knowledge and culture in ways that are not covered by copyright law. School students and unemployed people are producing and distributing a wide variety of creative content with great promise for learned citizenry and social utility. Networked digital platforms have drastically transformed the role of many users from mere consumers to active participants able to report news, mix videos and pictures, and collaborate to produce information goods, such as computer programs, encyclopaedias, or even to develop devices and processes.[152] Those who consume, transform, or have the potential to be authors or innovators must be included and adequately considered in the IP bargain. It is therefore imperative that users' rights to access and interact creatively with cultural and knowledge goods be incorporated into the conceptual framework of IP policy.

In order to meaningfully weave broad distributive concerns into the fabric of the IP landscape, we need to look not only to those responsible for creating content in corporate settings, but also to those who will consume those products and potentially build upon them. We need to concern ourselves with the least advantaged groups in our societies, who were left worse off by the imbalance of the existing IP system, especially those users who are cash-strapped or resource poor.[153]

150 TRIPS Agreement, Article 12.

151 Julie E. Cohen, "The Place of the User in Copyright Law" (2005) *Fordham Law Review* 347, 349.

152 Von Hippel, *Democratizing Innovation*, 1.

153 Compare Keith Aoki, "Distributive and Syncretic Motives in Intellectual Property Law (with Special Reference to Coercion, Agency, and Development)" (2006–2007) 40 *University of California Davis Law Review* 784.

Taking social justice considerations into account requires a reexamination of "the intellectual property bargain from the vantage point of [users]."[154] In what follows I explore broad CIPS proposals discussing how IP might evolve to better empower users. The main point of reference at this stage is the way in which limitations and exceptions are framed in mainstream normative environments. First, we need a fundamental shift in our mindset; instead of thinking about users' entitlements as limited exceptions, we need to think of them as positive legal rights. This simple shift could go a long way to consolidating the position of users as important characters in the IP landscape. Second, instead of having specific statutory exceptions or vague, open-ended fair use provisions that rely on economic analysis to operate, users need to be empowered with rights of access anchored in distributive considerations and designed to give them more opportunities to express, learn, innovate, and earn.

A *Doctrinal Shift: From Exceptions to Rights*

IP needs to increase its distributional impact in a way that reflects the importance of users and meets their needs. Overall, IP systems throughout the world are structured on the basis of an operative assumption that the entitlements of the bulk of creators, investors, and distributors of knowledge and culture are the norm. The law treats users' permissions to reuse IP-protected content as exceptional derogations that need to be interpreted and applied narrowly so that the rights holders can retain a viable "market" for the intellectual content concerned.[155] The conviction underlying this operative assumption is that the economic interests of rights holders are more important in comparison to users' interests. The rights vs. exceptions rhetoric is blind to the possibility that users' interests can be equally important. Access to protected content can be necessary to satisfy basic needs such as medicine and educational material, or to realize the enormous potential of creative production enabled by digital technology and connected platforms. The legal superiority afforded to rights holders normalizes the exclusion of users and allows rights holders to concentrate powers to control access. This is a sign of the distributional imbalance in the system that needs to be fixed.[156]

154 Jessica Litman, "Exclusive Right to Read" (1994–1995) 13 *Cardozo Arts & Entertainment Law Journal* 29, 34.

155 Patry, "Limitations and Exceptions in the Digital Era," 2.

156 Cohen, "The Place of the User in Copyright Law," 373.

A first step that could go a long way to fixing the distributional imbalance of the IP system is to reverse the rights vs. exceptions rhetoric that permeates the system. This requires a doctrinal shift that will transform the IP system from a rights holder-centered system to a dual-objective system that allows for a broad distribution of rights to access content and expressive and innovative opportunities to reshape knowledge and culture.[157] The proposed shift would have the effect of transforming the legal status of permitted uses from mere exceptions that must be interpreted narrowly to protected legal rights.[158]

IP is supposed to reconcile two different sets of interests: those of rights holders and those of users. If we view the creative process as an accumulative social process, then we need to be open to the possibility of shifting the focus towards users. There is no legitimate normative reason to treat users' entitlements as exceptions. One possible way to increase IP's distributional fairness for users is to adjust the baseline rules of the IP system from the vague language of "striking a balance" between creators and the public interest to a language that recognizes users' rights as an integral part of the IP system side by side with the rights of creators. A growing body of copyright literature supports such a shift in light of the increasing judicial recognition of users' entitlements and their role in making cultural goods in the digital environment, as well as modern concepts of distributive justice.[159]

The norm in comparative copyright law is for users' needs to be addressed as exceptions that should be interpreted narrowly. The Canadian Supreme Court decided to adjust this norm. In a series of decisions over the past decade, the CSC has endorsed the need to transform users' entitlements under the Canadian Copyright Act from being limited exceptions to being positive rights at the core of the copyright structure.[160] In the landmark decision of *CCH Canadian Ltd. v. Law Society of Upper Canada*, the Canadian Supreme Court explicitly recognized the concept of users' rights. In considering "fair dealing" in the Canadian Copyright Act, the court stated that it is "perhaps more properly understood as an integral part of the Copyright Act than simply

157 CompareAbraham Drassinower, "Taking User Rights Seriously," in Michael Geist, *In the Public Interest: The Future of Canadian Copyright Law* (Irwin Law, 2005) 467.

158 David Vaver, *Copyright Law* (Irwin Law, 2000) 171.

159 Rebecca Tushnet, "Copy This Essay: How Fair Use Doctrine Harms Free Speech and How Copying Serves It" (2004) 114(3) *Yale Law Journal* 535–90 ; Margaret Chon "Intellectual Property 'from Below' Copyright and Capability for Education" (2007) 40 *University of California Davis Law Review* 105.

160 Michael Geist, "Fairness Found: How Canada Quietly Shifted from Fair Dealing to Fair Use," in Michael Geist, ed., *The Copyright Pentalogy: How the Supreme Court of Canada Shook the Foundations of Canadian Copyright Law* (University of Ottawa Press, 2013) 157, 176.

a defence." The court referred to fair dealing as "a user's right," which "must not be interpreted restrictively."[161] The court quoted Professor David Vaver, who had argued that "[u]ser rights are not just loopholes. Both owner rights and user rights should therefore be given the fair and balanced reading that befits remedial legislation."[162] This means that permitted uses of copyright materials are to be given a broader and more generous reading and are not mere exceptions to exclusive rights. This shift in the Canadian judicial understanding of users' entitlements is not an isolated decision. The Canadian Supreme Court has followed and expanded the users' rights approach in several other copyright cases.[163] Now, fair dealing as a user right "is rooted in and shaped by the purpose of the Copyright Act." From these judgments it is possible to extrapolate that the purpose of the Canadian Copyright Act can be construed as not only to reward and protect rights holders but also to contribute to the empowerment of users by allowing more access to works and a "vibrant public domain."[164]

The doctrinal shift towards users' rights is not a mere rhetorical move. There are good reasons to believe that such shifts could actually empower users with a greater capacity to engage with knowledge and culture while helping to break the power structure that is skewed in favor of rights holders. In this sense, such a shift fits into the narrative of a fair IP landscape in the Islamic vision. Nicolas Suzor and I have examined the potential impact of adopting the language of users' rights on two current issues in Australian copyright policy.[165]

The first issue concerns the ability of third parties to rely on permitted uses to provide services to users. Both in Canada and in Australia, the fair dealing doctrine permits users to engage in a number of permitted uses for specific purposes, including "research and study" and "reporting the news." In *CCH Canadian*, fair dealing was analyzed as a positive legal right. It can be exercised by the user or on the user's behalf. In other words, it is not an exception that needs to be interpreted narrowly. It is a legal right with an objective presence that can be exercised through third parties. In Australia,

161 *CCH Canadian Ltd v. Law Society of Upper Canada* [2004] 1 *SCR* 339, 364 [48].
162 Ibid., 364–5 [48], quoting Vaver, *Copyright Law*, 171.
163 Geist, "Fairness Found," 178–80.
164 Graham Reynolds, "Of Reasonableness, Fairness and the Public Interest: Judicial Review of Copyright Board Decisions in Canada's Copyright Pentalogy," in Michael Geist, ed., *The Copyright Pentalogy: How the Supreme Court of Canada Shook the Foundations of Canadian Copyright Law* (University of Ottawa Press, 2013) 1, 31–35
165 Ezieddin Elmahjub and Nicolas P. Suzor, "Fair Use and Fairness in Copyright: A Distributive Justice Perspective on Users' Rights" (2017) 43(1) *Monash Law Review* 274, 290–95.

where the exceptions rhetoric remains dominant, it was not possible to have a similar vision and treat users' entitlements as positive rights. Australian courts maintained their restrictive approach towards interpreting users' entitlements. In their view, fair dealing permissions are still limited, exceptional derogations from exclusive rights and must be sought by the user without the intervention of third parties, even if such intervention would serve important social functions such as research or study.

The second issue relates to the ability of rights holders to contract out the statutory permissions under copyright law. Copyright owners of intellectual content, such as software and e-books, draft standard contracts which contain provisions that compel their customers to waive some of the rights granted to them under copyright law. The contractual environment in which users come to agree to these terms is marked by significant inequalities in bargaining powers. In many cases, users buy content from established and resourceful copyright holders, who impose take-it-or-leave-it conditions that oblige their customers not to copy content, reshape it, or resell it to third parties. These conditions further undermine the already limited scope of permitted uses for users and further skew powers to the benefit of already powerful copyright holders. If we follow the lead of the proposed doctrinal shift and treat users' entitlements as positive rights that aim to situate users' interests at the center of the IP structure, it would be easier to add an extra layer of protection to these "rights." We can design the law so as to prevent copyright holders from overriding users' rights through private orderings. Rights holders should not be allowed to take advantage of users' needs to access content and restrict their rights to use an intellectual product even after they have paid for it. In this regard, a review of the intellectual property framework in the United Kingdom recommended amending the UK Copyright Act to make it clear that the rights of users should not be superseded by contractual arrangements.[166]

B A Fair Use Right

Recasting the doctrine of exceptions and limitations into a doctrine for users' rights is a good start but would not be enough. Users need a broad fair use right to promote social justice ideals. This right would achieve at least three important functions. First, it would help prevent the concentration of power within the hands of rights holders through excessive reliance on their exclusive

[166] Ian Hargreaves, "Digital Opportunity: A Review of Intellectual Property and Growth" (2011) 51, www.ipo.gov.uk/ipreview-finalreport.pdf

rights. Second, it would empower users with the capacity to satisfy their basic needs, express, innovate, and earn. Finally, it would promote fair equality of opportunity to speak, challenge culture, and earn a living through producing creative works.

CIPS scholars question the sufficiency of limited lists of exceptions to satisfy distributive concerns. We know that the norm in comparative IP laws is to grant users a number of "exceptions" permitting certain uses that do not conflict with the rights holders' opportunities to exploit their intellectual products and that do not unreasonably prejudice their legitimate interests. There is no inherent problem with this so long as the status of the permitted uses is shifted from "exceptions" to rights, as discussed above. It is true that specific permissions can serve distributive purposes in a limited way. For instance, specific permission to freely use copyrighted work for certain educational purposes can enable libraries to satisfy the basic social need to access educational materials. In this sense, the specific statutory permission could satisfy social justice ideals by empowering students with opportunities to learn while preventing rights holders from concentrating power to control access and obstruct this valuable social purpose.

However, specific categories of permitted uses would not serve broad distributive purposes. This is particularly true in the wake of the Internet and digital revolution. As I have repeatedly indicated throughout this chapter, technology has empowered users with limitless capabilities to restructure IP protected content. Their interaction with images, texts, and inventions might fall under IP's radar without being legal under a specific permission. Accordingly, users would be better served by an open-ended fair use right as part of the overall design of copyright law. This right should be crafted so as to empower users to defend their rights to access and participate in the progress of their cultural medium. A right that equips users with flexibility so they can quickly respond to changes brought by modern technologies, without waiting for governments to legislate on permitted innovation, could potentially increase their ability to access and participate in the advancement of their knowledge and cultural medium.[167]

Crafted this way, an open-ended fair use as a public users' right has the potential to distribute powers and opportunities across larger groups within society, enabling them to be active participants in a vibrant process of innovation and creativity. Fair use could be constructed to stand as a counterpart to the bundle of exclusive rights of the rights holders, so that users have

[167] Patry, "Limitations and Exceptions in the Digital Era," 8.

a mechanism to represent their interests, mirroring the exclusive rights of IP rights holders.[168]

The US copyright fair use model captures some of the abovementioned social justice considerations. Section 107 of the US Copyright Act enables judges to permit free use of copyrighted materials to promote public interest considerations and provides illustrative examples of these considerations. They include use for purposes such as criticism, news reporting, teaching, scholarship, or research. Under section 107, these uses will not be considered as infringements if the court is satisfied that the use is fair based on a list of nonexclusive factors that direct judges to consider the purpose of the use, the nature of the copyrighted work, and the potential impact on the work's commercial market.

However, the US fair use model is not an ideal tool for effectively reflecting distributive justice considerations in copyright law. Molly Shaffer Van Houweling notes that the contemporary US fair use analysis is heavily preoccupied with "the correction of market failure to the exclusion of the distributive concerns."[169] Courts in the United States do not approach the fair use defense as a mechanism to enhance the distributive fairness of copyright by ensuring that creators and consumers who are unable to pay for using the work can get access. In a sense, courts engage in consequentialist analysis, stressing the need to ensure that the use does not deprive the copyright holders of potential commercial gain. The focus as such is not on a duty to distribute access to those who need it. Van Houweling observes that:

> In much of contemporary copyright commentary and jurisprudence, fair use steps in only where transaction costs or copyright holder intransigence make a voluntary bargain impossible. Where, by contrast, there is a functioning market for reuse of copyrighted works, courts are less likely to excuse unauthorized reuse and commentators are less likely to complain . . . cases and commentators do not acknowledge the possibility that iterative creativity could be stifled by the mere expense of seeking and paying for permission to incorporate copyrighted expression into a new work. "Get a license or do not sample" is no answer to a would-be creator who does not have the money to participate in the license marketplace.[170]

168 Wendy J. Gordon and Daniel Bahls, "The Public's Right to Fair Use: Amending Section 107 to Avoid the Fared Use Fallacy" (2007) *Utah Law Review* 619, 621; Sun Haochen, "Fair Use as a Collective User Right" (2011) 90(125) *North Carolina Law Review* 129–30 .

169 Van Houweling, "Distributive Values in Copyright," 1565.

170 Ibid.

The primary focus on market forces to decide when a use of copyrighted material is fair reinforces the utilitarian vision of copyright. The underlying assumption in this vision is that the best way to promote social utility is to ensure that rights holders' markets are always protected. While it is difficult to deny that this could be an important factor in many cases, a broader vision of social justice taught us that we need to ensure that our policies are not directed towards unproven assumptions about IP being the only tool to promote economic efficiency. We need also to take into consideration the duty to broadly distribute opportunities to access intellectual content, particularly for those who cannot pay for access or are unable to obtain a license from the rights holders. Such need becomes even more pressing if those who need access are seeking to reuse the intellectual products to empower their human agency or reshape culture in socially valuable forms.

Michael Madison urged policymakers not to only focus on authors, works, and markets, but equally on "how creative things are produced as well in terms of who does the producing." The exclusive rights of copyright holders should not extend to any use of copyright work that society regularly values in itself. The case for fair use should be established so long as the secondary use is "connected to some social structure or social practice." If the secondary use contributes to the production of a socially desirable outcome, it should not be considered as copyright violation.[171] Therefore, fair use should not be structured as being a tolerated departure from the grand conception of exclusive rights, but as a mechanism to achieve distributive justice in terms of reallocating opportunities to produce creative works that are of value to society. For instance, secondary uses which transform copyright materials such as remixes and mashups should be assumed to be fair use unless the copyright holder proves otherwise.

It is possible to imagine a fair use right beyond copyright. Katherine Strandburg and Maureen O'Rourke suggested that introducing a fair use doctrine in patent law is a better alternative to piecemeal solutions through patent exceptions and limitations. Patent law grants users of patented subject matter the right to engage in unauthorized use under various doctrines such as the experimental use defense and the doctrine of patent exhaustion. These doctrines should be replaced with a fair use right, analogous to that of fair use in copyright law.[172]

171 Michael J. Madison, "Rewriting Fair Use and the Future of Copyright Reform" (2005) 23(2) *Cardozo Arts & Entertainment Law Journal* 391–406

172 Maureen A. O'Rourke, *"Toward a Doctrine of Fair Use in Patent Law"* (2000) 100 *Columbia Law Review* 1177, 1181–93; Katherine Strandburg, "Patent Fair Use 2.0" (2011) New York University Law and Economics Working Papers 17–20.

Strandburg argues that existing permitted uses in patent laws are proving inadequate in light of the controversial relationship between the TRIPS Agreement and access to medicine, and the increasing importance of innovation paradigms based on user innovation.[173] Talented users are becoming able to make substantial modifications on patented subject matter. A fair use right, if integrated into patent law, could serve distributive values, including access to essential medicines at low cost for those with very low income. Moreover, it may contribute to the reallocation of more opportunities for talented users to reverse engineer patented technology.[174]

In summary, an optimal IP system from an Islamic perspective does more than maximize protection to provide incentives or rewards for those who invest, create, and distribute knowledge and culture. In the Islamic worldview, innovation and creativity are seen as complex social processes with significant distributional ramifications. Accordingly, the concerns around economic efficiency and reward must not take priority over plural distributional duties, including the satisfaction of basic social needs and wide distribution of opportunities to express, recreate, and earn from knowledge and culture. This vision of the role of IP intersects with various scholarly discourses critical of IP expansion and its focus on reward and efficiency. IP scholars question the fairness of IP systems centered on expanding protection for established rights holders while marginalizing large groups of users and consumers of knowledge and cultural products. These scholars propose policy and legislative measures to design IP systems that disable the power imbalance in IP markets while helping to satisfy basic needs such as access to medicine and educational materials, and equal opportunities to express, innovate, and reshape innovation and creativity. In this chapter, I have argued that the Islamic normative vision of a fair IP system could be implemented by adopting a bundle of policy and legislative reforms to expand the open zones of knowledge and culture. This could take place through engaging with comparative discourses on expanding the public domain and enhancing the positions and capabilities of users in the IP landscape.

173 Katherine J. Strandburg, "Users as Innovators: Implications for Patent Doctrine" (2008) 79 *University of Colorado Law Review* 467.

174 Strandburg, "Patent Fair Use 2.0," 8–29.

Index